W9-COZ-506

MOTIVATION & EMOTION

MOTIVATION & EMOTION

CHARLES N. COFER

The Pennsylvania State University

Scott, Foresman and Company
Glenview, Illinois London

To Mortimer H. Appley, collaborator without peer, whose thinking has informed every one of the following pages.

Library of Congress Catalog Card Number: 71-190720

Printed in the United States of America.
Regional offices of Scott, Foresman are located in Dallas, Oakland, N.J., Palo Alto, and Tucker, Ga.

Foreword

Both the content and the format of the beginning course in psychology vary widely today, not only between institutions and departments but also between instructors within the same department. There is a range of acceptable possibilities for organizing the course and considerable freedom for the instructor to select and emphasize those aspects of modern psychology which he considers most important and useful. One of the major reasons for course differences is the variety of subject matter and topics that are grouped under psychology. It is impossible to give adequate treatment to all the relevant topics within the time limitations typically imposed on the introductory course. To make matters more complicated, the accumulation of knowledge is proceeding at such a rapid pace in the different areas of psychology that it is virtually impossible for anyone to keep pace with new developments in all these fields. Thus, an instructor often rightfully limits his treatment to those topics which he feels competent to present with knowledge and understanding. Finally, the current emphasis, in response largely to student and public demand, on the uses of psychology, on its relevance, must be noted. To be sure, not all instructors are convinced of the appropriateness of teaching the application of psychology in the beginning course, pointing to the potential dangers of a little knowledge and of premature attempts to use information not well-tested or standardized. In contrast, however, many who teach the introductory course give considerable time and attention to the application and the meaning of what is known.

With this variety in content, technique, and orientation among instructors, there is need for a corresponding variety of textual material. The Scott, Foresman Basic Psychological Concepts Series has been prepared in response to that need. Each title within the Series addresses a single topic. While the volumes are relatively brief, each gives a more intensified development of the topic than is available in any omnibus introductory textbook. Each volume has been prepared by an expert, who presents not only full knowledge of the current substantive and methodological state of his field, but who also provides an original and creative treatment of this material. The books are more than the typical cut-and-dried survey of a topic. There is room in each for the kind of original analysis of the problem heretofore unavailable in introductory reading.

Each title in the Series is independent of the others. They all have been written as a whole so as to maximize the coverage of psychology with minimal overlap and redundancy. No single title is a prerequisite to any other in the Series. At the same time, however, the initial volume, an *Introduction to Psychology*, sets the tone for the Series and attempts to explain how various topics are interrelated. In addition, we should note that there is considerable cross-referencing among the volumes and a general attempt at integrating facts and theories that are pertinent to several topics. While the titles are independent and may be used alone, they are also part of a larger, coordinated, comprehensive survey and interpretation of psychology.

The purpose of the Series is to provide both flexibility and expertise for the instructor and the student in the beginning course. The Series is adaptable to a variety of educational goals. The teacher can select and construct a set of reading units, with the content, emphasis, and sequence he desires and that will fit the general purpose and orientation of this course. He may, for example, base his course on several selected topics, each of which is developed in a separate volume. Alternatively, he might use only a single volume to fill a void or to further develop a topic of special importance. Volumes from the Series may be used in conjunction with most general textbooks or with the initial core book in the Series. It is furthermore conceivable that one or another of the volumes would be useful in advanced courses, as preliminary reading for the student ill-prepared to contend with a topic on that level or as a supplement developing the background in a related topic. Because of the distinguished authorship of this Series, the teacher can feel confident in his selection without fear of uneven quality, superficiality, or duplication. This Series has a variety of uses at different educational levels, depending upon the needs of the student, the purpose of the course, and the creativity and imagination of the instructor.

The present volume, *Motivation and Emotion* by Charles N. Cofer, deals with an area that is central to the understanding of human and animal behavior, and which has seen drastic changes in the past few decades. Almost every field in psychology, and in the behavioral sciences generally, makes motivational assumptions—and asks motivational questions—about stimuli that the organism prefers or seeks to encounter, conditions that he will work to achieve or try to avoid, and situations that increase, lessen, or maintain ongoing effort. Recent research requires, as Professor Cofer clearly demonstrates, that we alter our traditional conception of motivation. The time-hallowed drive theories, which envision behavior as being automatically impelled by internal excitation, must be revised in important respects. Moreover, as Cofer also shows, greater attention should be given to the role of innate mechanisms in behavior. In another departure from the views of earlier years, he places less emphasis on learning-theory considerations than has been customary with experimental psychologists. These changes have profound implications for our understanding of the sources of behavior.

We believe that readers will find this book contemporary, fascinating, and challenging. They may have to revise some of their notions about motivation and emotion and give careful thought to new ideas—but this is what education is all about.

Lyle E. Bourne, Jr., Series Editor, University of Colorado
Leonard Berkowitz, Series Editor, University of Wisconsin

Preface

This book is an introduction to the area of inquiry called motivation and emotion. In it, I have attempted to present the major facts and theories pertinent to the title in an understandable and coherent way. It is not a tome, as was the prior book on this topic, *Motivation: Theory and Research*, by Appley and myself, and it is not entirely a long abstract of that book. I have attempted some updating, so that certain sections of the present book are more current than the earlier one, and I think there are also some changes, albeit somewhat subtle, in the ways I now conceive motivation and certain of its subtopics. One certain change in my own attitudes is that I see more clearly than I did earlier the importance of innate mechanisms in behavior. Another and parallel change is to see less merit than was the case ten years ago in a heavy emphasis on learning theory; the present book devotes only a few pages to Hull, Spence, Guthrie, Tolman, Skinner, and others. The drive theory of their day seems so thoroughly outmoded as not to deserve much space in a short volume like this one. For much the same reasons, I have given less attention to psychoanalysis than Appley and I accorded it.

I have received a good deal of guidance in preparing the manuscript from a number of secondary sources, and I have identified many of these for the reader's benefit in the list of suggested readings which follows each chapter. References cited in the text will, of course, be found in the bibliography at the end of the book.

This book has profited from the readings given the manuscript by Professors Lyle Bourne and Leonard Berkowitz, the editors of the Scott, Foresman Basic Psychological Concepts Series. They have my gratitude. Dr. Berkowitz was charged with specific responsibility for this book, and his trenchant comments have improved the exposition markedly. We do not entirely agree with regard to certain issues, and I must accept the responsibility for the deviations from sound thinking which remain.

It is a pleasure to acknowledge the enormous help of Mrs. Esther Jordan, who typed the book from my manuscript, and who has the gratitude of one who can no longer pass the third-grade course in cursive writing. The final manuscript was expertly typed by Mrs. Beverly Stickler.

Charles N. Cofer
University Park, Pennsylvania

Table of Contents

1

Introduction

Motivation and emotion are terms which evoke great interest in college students in the United States. Just why these terms have the interest value that they do, in contrast to terms like *sensory processes, perception,* and *learning,* is not entirely clear. Perhaps it is because, in the popular vocabulary, motivation signifies the causes or the "why" of action. In the case of the emotions, of course, we have all experienced them and have sometimes been troubled over or mystified about the intensity or the uncontrollability of our emotions. Possibly the familiarity in this country of psychoanalytic and psychiatric thought, especially as translated into accounts often found in newspapers and mass circulation magazines and books, is a factor in the interest these terms, *motivation* and *emotion,* have for us. Psychoanalysis and psychiatry make extensive use of these terms, and they also point to significant relationships between motivation and emotion, on the one hand, and abnormality, such as in psychosis and neurosis, on the other. Perhaps we think that the differences among people or the different ways in which one person will behave on various occasions or at different points in time must have causes beyond those having to do with intellect or accurate perceptions of the world. This may be a way of saying that *motivation* and *emotion* are closer to what we mean by "human nature" than are words like *sensation, perception,* or *cognition.*

Whatever the reasons, *motivation* and *emotion* have had a wide currency in this century. It was not always so, for *motivation* at any rate. The word *motivation* does not appear in J. M. Baldwin's 3-volume *Dictionary of Philosophy and Psychology,* publication of which was completed in 1911. *Emotion* has a longer history and came to be used in the English language to refer to agitated or excited mental states of individuals in the eighteenth century, according to the *Oxford English Dictionary.* The word *motive* occurs in Baldwin's dictionary, but its use was in reference to a kind of conscious experience, rather than as a cause or as the why of behavior.

In psychology and several of the other behavioral sciences, the twentieth century, or at least the first half of it, may almost be termed the "motivational decades." It will be helpful to outline the reasons for this interest in motivation. They tell us a great deal about the shifting conceptions of man and how his behavior may be explained and about what the word *motivation* has meant and what it means today. (We will speak of the word *emotion* later.) A word of warning is perhaps in order here. Terms used in a scientific discipline, such as psychology aspires to be, are often taken from the popular vocabulary. In the process of such borrowing, however, the words are often given different, and sometimes more precise, meanings or connotations from those they have in common parlance. A word like *motivation* provides a good example of this alteration or narrowing of the common meaning.

As was said before, motivation is often used popularly to refer to the causes or the why of behavior. This assertion probably stems largely from the psychoanalytic heritage, which, in insisting that all conduct is determined, employed notions like unconscious energies and forces which direct behavior to serve the "purposes" engendered by the forces. We shall have more to say later about the conception of energies and forces but, for the present, must point out that an energy is really incapable of doing more than serving as the "motor" which underlies behavior. Take waterpower as an example. Water running over a fall is an energy source. But the energy must be harnessed to make it useful for some purpose. So we contrive a waterwheel, which, turned by the force of the water falling upon it, can rotate the mechanisms of a grinding mill or of a generator which will produce electricity. Mechanisms must be arranged, in other words, to direct or guide and to transform the force so that it may be employed. By itself the falling water can be beautiful and can erode the stones on which it falls, but it does not serve other purposes.

We can agree that behavior is determined, but in doing so we must go beyond the idea that it has an energic base. The directing, guiding, or steering mechanisms have importance equal to that of the energy in determining what will occur when or where. Psychoanalysis did not specify these mechanisms in any detail although it included them (ego-processes). But psychology is concerned with all the mechanisms that govern behavior—abilities and habits, for example—not just its energy sources. Psychology tends to limit the word *motivation*, then, to those factors involved in energy processes and to include other factors in the determination of behavior. And it is not at all clear that a motivational account which postulates "raw" energy sources is a useful one or even whether the motivation concept itself is a useful one. Robert Bolles (1967) has said that motivation is not a palpably observable fact of behavior or a direct aspect of experience. It is a term for conditions and processes, which, in a sense, we invent because the invention seems to bring some order or comprehensibility to the diverse phenomena of behavior and experience. Such inventions, being conceptual rather than real or existential, are subject to change, as the data of behavior and experience seem to require it. We shall see that the concept of motivation has taken numerous forms and various roles since its introduction early in this century. There are some experts today who feel that it is not a useful word or, better, that the concept is not useful or that it is unnecessary. Such a viewpoint suggests that alternative, perhaps better, ways can be or have been found to account for or to organize coherently the phenomena for which in the last half-century the concept of motivation has served as an explanation or as an organizing principle.

HISTORICAL BACKGROUND

There are, it is often said, two more or less incompatible conceptions of human nature. One holds that man is essentially rational, a choosing, willing being who knows the sources of his conduct or who is aware of the reasons for his conduct and hence is responsible for that conduct. The other viewpoint sometimes holds that man, by nature, is irrational and that his impulses and desires must be held in check by the force of society's sanctions. Another way of saying this is that man is pushed and pulled by the forces of his constitution and the stresses of his environment and that he is largely unaware of the sources of his actions. Personal responsibility is not emphasized by those who hold to this account.

Rationalism is the view which prevailed for hundreds of years in the great philosophical and religious systems which dominated Western thought from the days of the ancient Greeks (e.g., Plato) to relatively recent times. The alternative view began to receive credence in the seventeenth century, although it had surfaced before, even among the Greeks. However, it was not until the late nineteenth century and in the twentieth century that it achieved dominance. The concept of motivation has, in the main, been linked to accounts of man's nature as irrational; perhaps the concept could only achieve significant recognition after the sway of rationalistic conceptions had declined.

Rationalistic Conceptions

Motivational factors have little or no place in a rationalistic account of conduct, because man's reason is the overriding factor in the determination of what he does. His will is free to choose whatever course of action his reason dictates. If his choices are unwise, unethical, or immoral, he is responsible for them, because his reason and his will have freely selected them. Such a conception of man's nature underlay such events as the witch-hunts of the sixteenth century. Zilboorg has put it this way:

> Man, whatever he does, even if he succumbs to an illness which perverts his perceptions, imagination, and intellectual functions, does it of his own free will; he voluntarily bows to the wishes of the Evil One. The devil does not lure and trap man; man chooses to succumb to the devil and he must be held responsible for his free choice. He must be punished; he must be eliminated from the community. More than that, his soul, held in such sinful captivity by the corrupted, criminal will within the body, must be set free again; it *must* be delivered. The body must be burned (Zilboorg & Henry, 1941, p. 156).

Intelligence indicated what the will would choose. Although there was freedom of choice, there were and are, in philosophical and religious systems, good and bad choices, and choice of the good could be determined by proper knowledge. If one knows the good, he will choose it, and he may come to know it by education, contemplation, revelation, or authority. Animals, of course, were not endowed with the faculty of reason, but they did have "natural promptings" or instincts, which were placed in them by the Creator "for the guidance of the creature in the attainment of ends useful to it, in its own preservation or the preservation of the species, and the avoidance of the contrary (Wilm, 1925, p. 40)." This formulation, reached by the Stoics in the Greek period, is a precursor of the notion of instinct that was used in a somewhat different way in later centuries.

The Development of Motivational Conceptions

In the seventeenth century, movements away from rationalism began to have some force, as the more mechanistic ideas of the early Greek atomists, such as Democritus, and hedonists, like Epicurus, did not. Yet, it took a couple of centuries for motivational notions to come into full flower—in the motivational decades of the present century. (We shall see later that these blooms have tended to show signs of wilt or blight in the very recent years.) There are several important trends, those seen in philosophy, biology, psychiatry, and psychology. There have also been revivals of rationalism, although in a form somewhat different from that we summarized in brief a moment ago. To these developments we now turn.

Philosophy It was perhaps not a great departure from earlier ideas for René Descartes (1596–1650) to assert that animals are automata, whose actions arise because of forces, either external or internal, which moved their muscles. But it was a significant step when Descartes held that a somewhat similar mechanism operated in man. However, Descartes held that this mechanistic conception was not sufficient for man, who also possessed a soul which interacted with the body at the pineal gland in the brain and could influence the course of the "animal spirits" moving through the neural "tubes." These spirits were directly responsible for the movement of the muscles. The soul, which was reasoning and rational, placed man beyond a physical, mechanical conception. Thus, Descartes preserved the quality of the body and the mind, allowing them to interact at the pineal body.

A more thoroughgoing break with past traditions was made by certain English philosophers starting with Thomas Hobbes (1588–1679) and continuing with John Locke and David Hume to James Mill and his son, John Stuart Mill (1806–1873), to list the important names.

Central to the formulations of these philosophers, to one degree or another, were two ideas, those of associationism and hedonism. Neither idea was entirely original with these philosophers, as both date back to the Greeks. But their use in the hands of the British philosophers was and is influential.

Associationism went along with a rejection of nativism, the idea that many of man's characteristics, including innate ideas, are part of his natural endowment. These British philosophers rejected nativism and proposed that the ideas of the mind arise from experience. The figure of speech by which we liken the mind at birth to a blank tablet was used by Locke to say that the contents of the mind are acquired by experience. Some conception of innate ideas or of nativism usually accompanies rationalism, so in this sense the emphasis on the role of experience constitutes a break with rationalism. Further, the contents of the mind and the course of thought, the British philosophers believed, were molded by the laws of association. Thus, two or more simple ideas might, if they occur together contiguously in space or time, be interassociated with the result being a complex idea. The succession of thoughts or ideas one after another could also be attributed to our having experienced the events on which the thoughts or ideas were based in a similar succession. There were a number of laws of association, and the British philosophers did not always agree on what they were or which one, if any, was the most fundamental. Nor did they always agree as to how simple ideas were joined in complex ideas. Some seemed to speak as if the simple ideas were simply added together, others as if the simple ideas were joined as chemical elements are to form a chemical compound in which the qualities do not resemble those of the original elements. Despite these divergences, the important, common thread was that ideas arise from experience and are combined through association. The laws of association were conceived to work more or less automatically, whether one wants them to or not. Here, then, is a break with a pure rationalism.

Hedonism also represents a departure from rationalism. Hobbes believed that we behave in such a way as to achieve pleasure or to avoid pain and that, whatever we think, these are the real reasons that underlie our conduct. In this formulation, of course, Hobbes used hedonism as a motivational principle without moral, ethical, or rational features. In contrast to the rationalists, Hobbes took a rather pessimistic view of human nature, holding men to be naturally competitive because each man's desires to obtain pleasure and to avoid pain would conflict with another's. The hedonistic principle is a clear violation of rationalistic accounts, and hedonism, although not always in the form it took in Hobbes' thinking, is a central conception in the views of the British associationistic or empiricist philosophers.

Revivals of Rationalism The doctrines of Hobbes, Locke, and Hume were not accepted by everyone, and a number of philosophers opposed them. Immanuel Kant, for example, said that he was awakened from his dogmatic slumbers by Hume and espoused, in opposition, a faculty psychology in which feeling and willing were separated from knowledge.

In Scotland, the reaction was initiated by Thomas Reid, and this reaction had more effect than Kant's so far as the history of psychology is concerned. Reid also espoused a faculty psychology. He postulated a number of separate capacities and motivelike characteristics, such as will, courage, nobility, as intrinsic to man's mind, thus preserving a rationalistic and moral character for man. Important to us here, however, is the fact that Reid also included instinct in his scheme, using the word to refer to a force in the initiation of action. Bolles (1967) sees the introduction of this conception of instinct by the faculty psychologists (and it differs in a number of aspects from earlier uses of the term) as a concession made by this group in the face of the principle of hedonism. Instinct was said to be involved in only some behaviors, whereas hedonism functioned in all. This concession, of course, leaves room for rationality and for at least some freedom of the will.

Rationalism still exists in formulations concerning motivation, though it is no longer embedded in a faculty psychology. It tends to emphasize that man is aware of his goals or the ends of his actions and that these goals or ends are the basic stuff of motivation. One can determine, much of the time, the why or the motivation of an action by asking the actor his reasons (Peters, 1958). It is this writer's impression that since about 1950 this kind of account of motivation has received more and more favor, as psychology has tended to emphasize cognitive processes in preference to behaviorism and mechanical interpretations of the bases of conduct. Cognitive factors, for example, are seen as capable of modulating the force of bodily drives. This trend has been prominent especially in social psychology, where it has coexisted with a tendency to postulate needs or drives for knowledge of the world and for consistency among one's cognitions. These needs, in this writer's judgment, do not function according to entirely rational processes but also do not share the turbulent, disturbing character often attributed to the basic instincts by, for example, psychoanalysis. The influence of the emphasis on cognitive processes in contemporary psychology is perhaps responsible for the impression that the blossoming of motivational concepts in the first half of the century seems no longer as luxuriant today as it was then.

Biology

There are three major trends in nineteenth-century biology which are of importance. One was the rise of mechanistic biology. A second was the theory of evolution. The third, which we will develop in the next chapter, foreshadowed, in the work of the French physiologist Claude Bernard, the emphasis on homeostatic regulation of behavior.

Mechanistic biology arose in midnineteenth century in opposition to teleology and vitalism in biology. Teleology refers to the determination of events by their ultimate purpose or goal. Vitalism implies that the characteristics of living things cannot be reduced to physicochemical terms and that the characteristics suggest the existence of a force or entity which transcends the material or physical. Both of these ideas are compatible with rationalism, but neither seems consonant with the development of a scientific biology. In 1845, four young physiologists, all later to make distinguished contributions to this field, agreed to fight vitalism. Among them was Ernst Brücke with whom Freud later worked. He set forth the view that the principles of physics and chemistry are sufficient to account for the dynamic system that is an organism. This approach was, of course, antagonistic to the viewpoint of rationalism, and it had great influence on the attitudes of many physiologists and biologists.

More dramatic, of course, and, in a sense, more substantive was the theory of evolution, announced in book form by Charles Darwin in 1859. It is not too much to say that this theory revolutionized biology and that it made many things possible which, before it, were largely unthinkable, although Darwin's work, of course, had its antecedents. In psychology, the functional point of view seems to be a direct consequence of the theory of evolution, and to a great extent psychology in the United States may still be characterized as functional.

Darwin's theory was developed in the years following his voyage on the *Beagle*, which took him to many parts of the world, especially the tropics. In the almost five years he was away from England, he had an opportunity to observe many species of animals and, more significantly, to see that members of a species which had been isolated as a group from others of their kind for a protracted period showed changes. Especially striking were the changes found in "familiar" species in the Galapagos Islands in the Pacific. From these observations, Darwin took the notion of *variation* among the members of a species. Further, he saw that in a given environment some variations would be better able to survive than others. Consequently, in one environment, over the generations the successful variations would survive and multiply, whereas the poorly adapted ones would tend to die out. This point is epitomized in the phrase "survival of the fittest." Darwin's basic and most important conception was that through processes such as these species, including man, could evolve from other species. Hence, there was no need to postulate special acts of creation to account for the variety of animals, again including man, seen at any one time in a locality.

The impact of Darwin's theory was that an animal's characteristics may have *value* in the animal's struggle for existence. If the characteristic is favorable to life in a given environment, then the value will be positive to or conducive of survival. On the other hand, in a different environment, the same characteristic may be inimical to survival and thus have a negative value. Other characteristics, of course, may not matter either way in a given situation. The emphasis on survival- or adaptation-value of the characteristics of a species was critical; it placed the study of animals and of their behavior in a new perspective.

In psychology, this perspective led to the functional view and to the appearance of animal or comparative psychology and developmental or genetic psychology. We shall discuss these trends a little later, but, to reiterate, they were made possible by the two main fruits (for psychology) of Darwin's theory—that animals and men represent continuous species rather than discrete ones and that the characteristics of all animals and of their behavior have or may have functional value in adaptation to or survival in an environment. Motivation came to be an essential part of the analysis of how adaptation is effected.

Psychiatry The existence of mental illness had always been an embarrassment to the rationalistic philosophies except under the notion of demonic possession, to which reference was made a few pages ago in the quotation from Zilboorg. From the time humane treatment of the insane became fairly well established and notions of possession by the devil were discarded, there was a void in theoretical accounts of insanity. In the latter part of the nineteenth century, classification systems for mental illness were established, and work on certain kinds of mental illness by means of hypnosis had made some progress. In the late nineteenth century, Sigmund Freud developed a theory of neurosis and psychosis, which was a motivational one, emphasizing the irrational forces in man's nature.

From his work with the patients he treated, Freud formulated a number of ideas about how human behavior is determined and how it develops. He saw behavior as the outcome of basic energies, a life force or Eros and a death or destructive force, sometimes referred to as Thanatos. The first underlay man's life-maintaining and life-continuing activities and was chiefly discussed in terms of sexual motives and their vicissitudes. The second underlay the aggressive and destructive activities of man. Much more was written about the first force than about the second one.

Freud found, very early in his treatment of patients, that their symptoms had causes that the patients were unaware of and would even deny or sometimes reject with horror. For example, in the case of Anna O, treated by Josef Breuer, an early associate of Freud's, one of the many symptoms was a contracture of the right arm, a sort of paralysis. The patient was unable to explain the symptom or the circumstances surrounding its first appearance. The symptom was relieved when these circumstances were uncovered. They had included the experience of her arm going to sleep while she was in a very anxious condition when she was caring for her father alone during a serious illness. This kind of finding led to Freud's postulation of unconscious factors in the governance of our conduct, memories and the like. Freud likened the mind to an iceberg, most of which is underwater and invisible: most of the mind is unconscious.

Freud thought that the unconscious consisted of two parts, one that had never been conscious and one that had been in awareness but which had been repressed, i.e., forced back into the unconscious. The reason for the repression of some experiences lay in the anxiety and loss of self-esteem that continued awareness of them would bring. Repression, like the other mechanisms postulated by Freud and by others, functioned to protect the awareness from the anxiety that it would otherwise experience.

Freud thought of the Life and Death forces as instincts, although some writers have said that the word *drive*, rather than *instinct*, should be used in translating the German word *Trieb*. However that may be, it seems clear that in the case of the sexual urge, at any rate, the libido (or energy) was conceived to go through several stages during early life in the place and manner in which it sought to express itself. First, there was the oral stage, in which the pleasure arising from the expression of libido was achieved chiefly through the mouth and lips, as in sucking or other oral activities. This stage was followed by the anal stage in which the libidinal expression came to a peak in activities relating to defecation and urination. There was then the phallic phase, in which the genitalia became the zone of maximal pleasure. At this point sexual expression was largely repressed, permitting the latency stage which endured until about the time of puberty.

Space does not permit us to present the many detailed observations and arguments which Freud and his followers used as a basis and as a justification for this account of development. There have, of course, been alternative accounts and interpretations. Perhaps the most important aspect of Freudian theory, for our purposes, is the dynamic character of Freud's view of the personality.

The base of this view, of course, is the motivational forces in the instincts. However, Freud was fully aware that the uncontrolled expression of libido, in accordance with the pleasure principle, is not permissible either in the family or in the larger society of which the family is a part. Punishment and rejection, he thought, were often the consequences of direct and unbridled expression of the instincts. Yet, the energy of the instincts was seen as requiring expression or discharge: Freud seemed to propose a hydraulic model in which the energy of the instincts, like the level of water in a tank, would continue to rise and rise unless there was an outlet. The mental apparatus, Freud supposed, was developed largely to effect some discharge, while keeping hidden from the world and from the self the exact nature of the energies being expressed.

The structure suggested by Freud was the ego. This agency, arising from the id (the unconscious sources of the instincts), serves the purpose of permitting instinct discharge in disguised ways. The ego functions in accordance with the reality principle, i.e., it must take account of the consequences of the direct expression of the instincts and modulate the expression which it must permit so as to avoid the punishment, anxiety, and loss of self-esteem which unbridled expression would bring. Incorporated within the personality is another structure, the superego, which includes one's ideal self and the prohibitions and sanctions of parents and society. The superego serves as an internalized representation of external authority and prohibition. It is the ego's job to mediate between the demands of the id and those of the superego, allowing some discharge in the interest of the former but disguising the nature of the discharge in the light of the latter.

To perform its functions, the ego transforms the ways in which instinctual expression is accomplished, and the various mechanisms, like repression, reaction formation, and sublimation, are the means the ego uses to solve its dilemma. Thus, if anal impulses to be dirty and to soil things are dominant, the ego, not being able to allow such direct expression, might transform the expression of this energy into the opposite—excessive cleanliness and desire for order. This transformation is an instance of reaction formation.

The foregoing account can give only a glimpse of the nature of Freudian theory, but it should be clear that the theory is a dynamic or motivational one and that it denies a rational conception of man's nature. In Freudian theory, the impulses, anxiety, and fear of loss of self-esteem make the ego a sort of battleground in which some compromise among the warring forces is worked out. But the compromise is not reached rationally, as the entire drama occurs and the plot reaches a resolution outside of awareness. Thus, the overly clean and orderly person, the result of a reaction formation, would have no awareness of the reasons for his being the way he is, and he would resist, during psychoanalytic treatment, becoming aware of the forces in operation, because such awareness would bring great quantities of anxiety and severe loss of self-esteem.

Since Freud's time, and during it, there were many modifications of his theory, and certain aspects of the theory, especially its instinctual base, have come in for severe criticism and even rejection. Freud's theory has been said to be tied to or excessively influenced by the European culture in which he lived. Nevertheless, psychoanalysis continues to be an important account of personality, and in spite of changes and modifications in the theory, the notions of dynamic forces and of unconscious factors continue to be influential and widely accepted.

Psychoanalysis, then, clearly violates rationalistic conceptions of man, and it has directed attention away from intellect and to irrational forces, i.e., to a motivational account of behavior. Conduct, in this theory, has a function: it serves to permit discharge of motivational energies. In this sense it sees behavior as instrumental to the organism's needs, just as accounts of animal behavior, arising after the appearance of the theory of evolution, placed it in the role of serving the animal in its struggle for existence in and adaptation to an environment. Freud was familiar with the theory of evolution and was much influenced by it. The motivational character of the first half of the twentieth century is to no small degree due to Freud's theories and their wide influence.

Psychology The field of psychology emerged as a discipline separate from philosophy and physiology in the second half of the nineteenth century. In its initial manifestations its subject matter was well defined. It took as its province the study of conscious experience.

The goal of this study was to analyze experience into its elements. The idea was to discover the elements so that the laws of their combination could be elucidated; these laws would be the laws of association. The impact of the British associationist and empiricist philosophy on this enterprise should be evident. This psychology, identified with such names as Wilhelm Wundt in Germany and E. B. Titchener in the United States, employed the method of introspection. Stimuli were presented, and the observer's task was to describe his experience in terms of elements and their characteristics which were believed to be fundamental to the constitution of experience. Thus, to Titchener, at least at one stage of his work, the analysis yielded three primary elements—sensations, images, and feelings. Further characterizations were made, as, for example, in the case of sensations, which could be described with respect to their quality, their intensity, their duration, their extensity, and their clearness. Motivational terms and concepts did not enter into these descriptions to any extent and were largely outside the content of the discipline as it was seen from this point of view. One could epitomize the task of this group of investigators as being to determine what consciousness *is*. The observers used in the experimental work were adults, carefully trained in the introspective method.

Wundt's laboratory, usually said to be the first formal psychological laboratory in the world, was founded in 1879. The influences on Wundt, as we have said, were primarily philosophical and physiological. Evolutionary biology did not seem to have an important impact on the work of this laboratory and similar ones.

However, evolution did have an impact on psychology. This effect is seen first, perhaps, in studies of animal intelligence which appeared soon after the theory of evolution became well known. William James' *Principles of Psychology*, published in 1890, showed the effects of the evolutionary theory. James was a precursor of a new school of psychology which developed in the period 1890–1910 and was known as functional psychology. The mark of this school was that when it studied consciousness it wished to know what consciousness *is for*, what it does for the organism, how it helps in the adaptation to an environment. And, of course, behavior as well as consciousness became an important subject of study. One might say that the functionalists were interested in all means of adaptation available to organisms, not just in consciousness. Untrained observers—children, the mentally ill, and animals—could, in this view, be studied legitimately, because introspection, to the functionalist, was not the sole appropriate method of investigation.

The functionalist approach spread rapidly, especially in the United States, where it became and in some sense remains the dominant view. Motivational concepts were important to it, because of its emphasis on adaptation. We will trace the development of motivational concepts in the functionalist tradition in the next chapter. Before doing so, we will look, in the remainder of this chapter, at the concept of instinct, especially as it appeared in the writings of William McDougall.

James had said that man possesses more instincts than any other animal, and the functionalists included instincts as major sources of behavior. No one, however, with the possible exception of Freud, spoke of the all-powerful role of instincts as did McDougall. It is not too much to suppose that because of McDougall's advocacy of the role of instincts, motivational concepts became central to early twentieth-century general psychology, just as Freud's advocacy of his theory made such concepts central to clinical psychiatry and psychopathology.

McDougall regarded men's actions and thoughts as stemming from the instincts. Without the instincts, there would be no behavior, no mental life. Without these "prime movers" man would be an inert lump, an intricate mechanism with no motive power.

McDougall postulated a number of instincts, most of which had a corresponding emotion. In his *Social Psychology*, first published in 1908, McDougall spoke of the following instincts and emotions: flight and the emotion of fear; repulsion and the emotion of disgust; curiosity and the emotion of wonder; pugnacity and the emotion of anger; self-abasement and the negative self-feeling or subjection; self-assertion and the positive self-feeling or elation; reproduction and the tender emotion; gregariousness; acquisition; and construction. The last three instincts did not have associated emotions. In later writings the list of instincts changed somewhat and were ultimately called propensities. However, the basic stress on motivation remained.

McDougall thought of the instincts as irrational and compelling sources of conduct. He saw each "instinct as an inherited or innate psychophysical disposition which determines its possessor to perceive, and to pay attention to, objects of a certain class, to experience an emotional excitement of a particular quality upon perceiving such an object, and to act in regard to it in a particular manner, or, at least, to experience an impulse to such action (McDougall, 1908, p. 30)." Instincts were not reflexes or combinations of reflexes; instincts oriented the organism to goals—the ends toward which its striving was directed.

McDougall referred to his viewpoint as a "hormic psychology," the word *hormic* being derived from the Greek word *hormē*, meaning impulse or striving. Behavior serves the end or purpose of the instinct; thus it is instrumental to the instinctual requirements of the organism.

McDougall observed that in many accounts of men's conduct, especially those stemming from a rationalistic position, the problem is why does man ever behave irrationally? To McDougall, however, the question should be rephrased to ask, "Why does man ever behave rationally?" In other words, man, moved solely by his instincts, would be irrational and would show little or no self-control. For McDougall, the problem was to account for control over the instincts, and he regarded the personality as developed in the interest of such control. Society, McDougall argued, required constraints in the expression of the instincts, and this it achieved through the mechanism of the sentiment. A sentiment was a structure in which several instincts and their emotions were linked together in conjunction with an idea of an object or class of objects. Thus, the sentiment of self-regard, bringing together a number of instincts and emotions under the idea of the self and its status, was a major way of preventing the unbridled expression of the instincts. Moved, for example, to be pugnacious, one's action might be held in check by the fear that the action would cause him to receive negative evaluation from others; the sentiment of self-regard would be sensitive to such evaluations and as a consequence would inhibit or suppress the expression of anger.

McDougall's influence lay, not in his specific theory of instincts and their organization, but rather in the importance he accorded to motive forces in man's behavior. McDougall was a persistent and persuasive champion of a motivational view of conduct, and it is likely that the development of *drive* and other motivational terms was influenced to a large degree by his insistence on the importance of motivational forces. His ideas fit with the developing functionalist conceptions of organismic adaptation, so that they could be integrated, in a less extreme form, into the functionalist scheme. In the next chapter, we will see how motivational concepts developed and changed.

SUGGESTED READINGS

Atkinson, J. W. *An introduction to motivation.* Princeton, N.J.: D. Van Nostrand Co., Inc., 1964. Chapters 1, 2, and 3.

Bolles, R. C. *Theory of motivation.* New York: Harper & Row, Publishers, 1967. Chapters 1, 2, 3, and 4.
Boring, E. G. *A history of experimental psychology.* (2nd ed.) New York: Appleton-Century-Crofts, 1950. Chapter 26.
Cofer, C. N. & Appley, M. H. *Motivation: Theory and research.* New York: John Wiley & Sons, Inc., 1964. Chapters 1 and 2.
Hall, C. S. & Lindzey, G. *Theories of personality.* (2nd ed.) New York: John Wiley & Sons, Inc., 1970. Chapter 2.
Zilboorg, G. & Henry, G. W. *A history of medical psychology.* New York: W. W. Norton & Company, Inc., 1941. Chapters 5, 6, and 11.

2

Motivational Concepts and Their Theoretical Status

There was a negative reaction to the emphasis placed on instincts by McDougall and by others, and an alternative concept, drive, came to the fore as the leading motivational concept of the period from about 1920 to 1950. In the 1950's, however, when a number of difficulties with drive became evident, there was a consequent shift to the construct, incentive. This period also saw a renascence of instinct, especially in the work of certain zoologists, called ethologists, who studied animal behavior (see Chapter 3). Another trend has been to suppose that incentive may be replaced by reinforcement. We shall deal with these matters in the present chapter.

Yet another problem which has engaged the concern of psychological theorists, especially since about 1940, can be phrased as the question, "Just what is the function of motivational concepts in the description and analysis of behavior?" A number of answers may be and have been given to this question, and we will present and discuss these answers, also, in the present chapter. An alternative way of phrasing the topic of this discussion is to say that the problem is the theoretical status of motivational concepts.

THE NEGATIVE REACTION TO INSTINCTS

Once instincts were admitted, after Darwin, to accounts of the determination of human conduct, the number of instincts proposed, by one writer or another, became very large. We gave McDougall's list in the last chapter. William James said that there are human instincts of locomotion, vocalization, imitation, rivalry, pugnacity, sympathy, hurting, fear, acquisitiveness, constructiveness, play, curiosity, sociability, secretiveness, cleanliness, modesty, love, jealousy, and parental love.

In 1924, L. L. Bernard, a sociologist, surveyed the literature and found that several *thousand* kinds of behavior had been classified as instinctive in the papers and books (by many authors) that he reviewed. Two examples given by Bernard help to epitomize the situation as he found it: ". . . with a glance of the eye we estimate instinctively the age of a 'passerby'," and ". . . the instinctive morality developed by personal groups" (Bernard, 1924, pp. 132–134). The tendency to classify behavior as instinctive was so great as to lead to a paper by Ayres (1921), subtitled "The instinct of belief-in-instincts."

The problems with the instinct movement were that behaviors were classified as instinctive on the basis of no or very casual evidence and that once classified as instinctive there were no further questions to be raised concerning the nature of the behavior called instinctive. To call something instinctive was to "explain" it and remove the need for further inquiry about it. The easy and promiscuous use of the term in discussions of human behavior was the reason for its downfall. (In its return with the ethologists, instinct has a rather different usage and basis in evidence.)

The attack on instinct took several directions. One was to question the validity of casual observation in designating an act as instinctive. In supporting the case for the instincts he proposed, James used examples from the behavior of his own children, argued from analogy with infrahuman behavior, and pointed out the evolutionary advantage of certain instincts. Little experimental work or controlled observation was employed by writers advocating the instinctive basis for human conduct.

Another problem was the lack of agreed-upon criteria on which to base the classification of an action as instinctive or not. When such criteria were used, the evidence that a behavior met one of them was often questionable. Thus, McDougall argued that an aggressive instinct (pugnacity) exists in man because of the widespread existence of combat and war. Yet, it is not clear that combativeness is universal. There are peaceful societies and peaceful men. Have these people learned to suppress or control their aggression, or have aggressive men learned to be combative? The observations of the cultural anthropologists often did not fit with the universality claimed by the instinctivists for behaviors they said were instinctive. Too many of the instances cited by the instinctivists to support their case were taken from Western culture.

One of the major attacks on the instinct doctrine came from John B. Watson and other behaviorists. Watson's argument was empirically based. He and Morgan (Watson & Morgan, 1917) observed infants while they were being stimulated in a variety of ways. The evidence suggested that there are only three emotional reactions that are innate—fear, rage, and love—and that these reactions can be elicited innately by only a few stimulus situations. Fear, for example, was aroused by loud sounds and the threat of being dropped, rage by restricting freedom of movement. Watson (1924) went on, as a radical environmentalist, to deny human instincts. While later work has questioned the adequacy of Watson's and Morgan's observations and conclusion, their study was surely a major blow at the time to the instinct position.

Perhaps we have said enough to indicate why the instinct concept declined in the 1920's. Yet the decline was not complete, because the notion of instinct was a motivational one, and as we have seen motivational ideas seem central to functionalist and psychoanalytic thought. Instincts designated urges or forces in behavior that gave it a purposive cast. Although belief in instincts declined in the 1920's, the motivational aspects of instincts had to be preserved. The concept which preserved them was drive. As Peters (1953, pp. 665–666) has said, later writers "make great use of the concept of 'drive,' which turned out to be the objectively testable component of McDougall's more metaphysical concept of 'instinct'. . . ."

DRIVE

In *Paradise Lost*, John Milton (1608–1674) wrote: "A prowling wolf, whom hunger drives to seek new haunt for prey." In this line, the word *drive*, used as a verb, seems to connote much of what the word has been used to signify in psychology since 1918, when it became a part of the technical vocabulary (Campbell & Misanin, 1969, p. 58).

R. S. Woodworth in 1918 wrote of instinctive behavior and, in doing so, spoke of preparatory and consummatory reactions, following the English physiologist, Sir Charles Sherrington, with whom he had studied. A consummatory reaction, such as eating or drinking, brought an end to a behavioral episode which involved the preparatory reactions. The latter consisted of a series of acts which led to a consummatory reaction and seemed to occur when there was a readiness for a consummatory reaction, as, for example, in the hungry animal which is ready to eat. Here and elsewhere, Woodworth was concerned with two things—the mechanisms of action and the force which energizes the mechanism into action.

We have many potential acts or behaviors in our repertories, but they do not reach expression continuously or simultaneously in the typical case. They occur individually, sporadically, or episodically, yet the mechanisms which underlie them when they do appear are presumably always present in our nervous systems. It takes some special conditions for the mechanisms underlying a given act to be activated, and Woodworth used the word *drive* as one condition necessary to power the mechanisms into action. Woodworth was not content with a simple list of instincts; he thought also that mechanisms might develop their own energies, once they had been formed and had been employed.

The drive concept came quickly to use in reference to the physiological conditions which seem to underlie the occurrence of preparatory behaviors and consummatory reactions. Desire, Dunlap (1922) said, resides in tissues, and Dashiell (1928) held that tissue needs are the sources of drives. Tissue needs were induced by conditions of deprivation, like fasting, or of excess and served to instigate or energize acts which innately or through learning had been developed to rectify disturbances caused by tissue needs. Drive was sometimes equated to tissue needs, sometimes said to be established by the tissue needs.

Drive as a concept has usually taken one of two forms. One is to suppose that it is internal stimuli, correlated with states of tissue need, that instigate action. The other places either less or no emphasis on stimuli; it conceives of drive primarily as a central state which primes or sensitizes the structures underlying behavior into readiness for response in situations. Sometimes internal stimuli are said to accompany the central state, sometimes not.

Drive as Internal Stimuli

In this notion the idea is to find internal stimuli or sources of internal stimuli to accompany each of the drives usually postulated—hunger, thirst, and sex. In the case of hunger, the location of the stimuli has been placed in the stomach, of thirst in the mouth and throat, of sex in the genital organs. These accounts of the bases of drives are often referred to as the local theory of motivation, i.e., the general viewpoint guides one to find a locus or site where the stimulus consequences of a drive are to be found.

In hunger, the contractions of the empty stomach have long been suggested as an important basis of the drive. Two hundred years ago, Albrecht von Haller wrote that hunger arises from "the grinding or rubbing of the delicate and villoid folds of the gastric mucosa against each other . . . ." and that "the naked villi of the nerves on the one side (of the stomach) grate against those of the other, after a manner almost intolerable" (quoted by Boring, 1942, pp. 553–554). Evidence which seemed to support the idea that stomach contractions underlie hunger was reported by Cannon and Washburn (1912) and verified, in a long series of experiments, by Carlson (1916). Cannon had Washburn swallow a balloon which was attached to a recording apparatus in such a way that when the stomach contracted a mark was made on a moving paper (see Figure 1). Meanwhile, Washburn, who could not see the recording, pressed a key every time he felt a pang of hunger; these key presses were also recorded on the paper. Usually, the record showed that a contraction was followed by a pang. This correspondence seemed to verify the interpretation that hunger was due to contractions of the stomach. Cannon recognized that hunger is not always pronounced or present at all when people eat, but he felt that, in addition to hunger, there was appetite, which could account for such facts. He had relatively little to say about appetite, stressing, instead, his local theory of hunger and other drives.

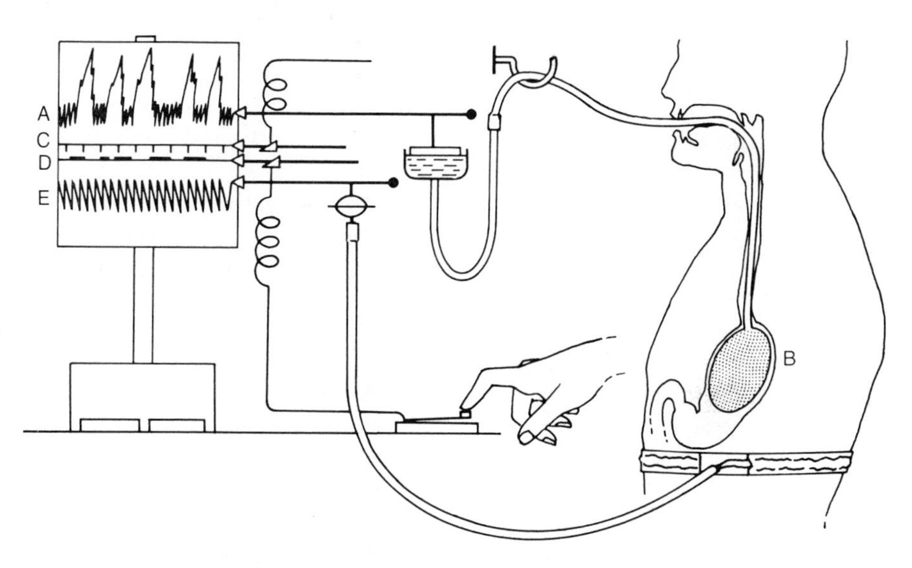

FIGURE 1 Diagram of the arrangements in the experiment by Cannon and Washburn. B refers to the balloon in the stomach, and the tracings on the kymograph are (A) the air pressure changes reflecting stomach contractions, (C) time, in minutes, (D) the occurrences of hunger pangs as reported by the subject, and (E) a record of respiration. From Cannon, W. B. Hunger and Thirst. In C. Murchison (Ed.) *Foundations of experimental psychology*. 1929. P. 437, Fig. 1. By permission of Clark University Press.

For thirst, Cannon proposed dryness in the throat and mouth as the local stimulus condition responsible; when the salivary glands "fail to provide sufficient fluid to moisten the mouth and throat, the local discomfort and unpleasantness which result constitute the feeling of thirst (Cannon, 1918, p. 295)." Cannon could cite evidence in support of this proposition—salivation decreases after much sweating or deprivation of fluids, and thirst occurs; atropine reduces salivary flow, and when it is administered, thirst results, except when novocaine, an anesthetic, is applied to the mouth–throat area. Cannon and others conducted a number of experiments which seemed to offer verification for the theory.

In sex, the local theory suggested sensations arising in the genitalia and related organs as the basis for the drive, and other local conditions were sought as bases for other drives. Tension in the mammary glands, for example, was seen as the reason a female animal would permit and encourage sucking by her young (see Cofer & Appley, 1964, pp. 176–177).

The overall point of view of the local theory can best be gained by quoting, again, from Cannon: "If the requirements of the body are not met . . . hunger pangs and thirst arise as powerful, persistent and tormenting stimuli which imperiously demand the ingestion of food and water before they will cease their goading (Cannon, 1939, p. 76)." E. B. Holt once put it that we are "scourged through life by stimuli." The local theory might almost be summarized as the theory of the devil in the flesh. Freud's death wish, an idea similar to that of Holt's, is the notion that organisms seek through death the termination of internal stimulation.

Evidence Against the Local Theory

It has never been entirely clear just how completely the local theory was intended to explain drives. As we said a moment ago, Cannon attributed many phenomena of food consumption to appetite, rather than to hunger pangs. However, the theory did stimulate a number of investigations, some of which found support for it, as we have seen. However, evidence not supporting it was also obtained, and no one holds seriously, any longer, to the belief that local factors are adequate to account entirely for any aspect of drive-related behaviors. Here we will summarize briefly some of this evidence in the cases of hunger, food, and sex.

Hunger There is even doubt today that the method used by Cannon and by Carlson is a satisfactory one. Some investigators have suggested that the balloon in the stomach instigates the contractions rather than simply measuring them. Davis, Garafalo, and Kveim (1959) measured stomach activity electrically by means of electrodes placed on the abdomen. They found no evidence for contractions in the empty stomach, except when a balloon was introduced there! Other evidence indicates that hunger persists when the stomach has been removed, following gastrectomy; when the stomach is full of food, but the passage into the small intestine is obstructed; and when sensory nerves leading from the stomach to the central nervous system are blocked or severed (Cofer & Appley, 1964, pp. 206; 208–210).

Following gastrectomy and the joining of the esophagus to the intestine, animals continue to show the usual behavioral signs associated with hunger. In human patients on whom similar operations have been performed, hunger persists, even including the experience of hunger pangs. In animals, cutting the nerves which deliver impulses arising from the contractions of the stomach has little effect on the animal's eating or other behavior associated with food deprivation. Some human patients have also been studied following vagotomy, the operation being carried out in cases of peptic ulcer. Most of the patients continued to experience hunger, although because of the vagotomy, there could be no contractions. The hunger they experienced was emptiness "allover" or in the abdomen, and there was weakness and a desire for food. Many of the patients reported no change in their sensations of hunger following the operation as compared to their preoperative experience of it (Grossman & Stein, 1948).

Thirst Here, too, the evidence seems to negate the local theory. Case studies of men suffering from severe desert thirst indicate that thirst continues after they have drunk substantial amounts of water and have certainly moistened the mouth and throat. Patients with diabetes insipidus continue to experience thirst and to drink normally even though drugs which stimulate (pilocarpine) or inhibit (atropine) salivation are administered. Similarly, they remain thirsty when the mouth and throat are anesthetized by spraying with cocaine. The nerves serving the region of the mouth have been severed with no effects on the drinking behavior of dogs. Sham-drinking experiments with dogs have also been performed. In these studies, the dogs drink, so that their mouths are wet, but the water passes through a fistula from the esophagus and outside the animal, rather than into the stomach. Such dogs continue to drink great quantities of water, though their mouths and throats must have been wet (Cofer & Appley, 1964, pp. 246–249).

Sex Again, in studies in which organs have been removed or denervated, a number of species, including man, continue to show sexual arousal and experience (Cofer & Appley, 1964, pp. 176–177).

These negative findings in the cases of hunger, thirst, and sex seem clearly to invalidate the local theory as a general account of the drives involved. No doubt, in many instances local stimulation is important to the motivation, but it is apparently not essential to the motivation. We turn next to central theories of drive which developed in the face of the inadequacies of the local, peripheral theory.

Drive as a Central State

Despite the failure of the local theory, various phenomena in behavior seemed, to many investigators and theorists in the 1920's, 1930's, and 1940's, to require a drive concept. It will be advisable, first, to review these phenomena and then to characterize the nature of drive as a central state which was developed to incorporate them.

The behavioral phenomena of concern show the central feature that conditions of deprivation of some sort tend to be associated with increased activity, either in general or in a specific, goal-object related way. Thus, it seemed to theorists that the drive conditions were sources of energy for such behaviors.

1. General or "Spontaneous" Activity Animals are often active, even when there are no obvious stimulus or incentive conditions in the immediate environment to which the activity can be attributed. This activity has been called spontaneous, and early investigations were concerned with factors leading to this activity; success in finding factors conducive to activity, of course, led to descriptions of the mechanisms that control the activity, which then could no longer be referred to as spontaneous. General activity is the term which came to replace spontaneous activity.

Very significant in accounting for general activity in motivational terms was the work of Curt Richter (1927) and his students and associates. They showed, for example, that the amount of general activity was reduced in male rats which had been castrated. More importantly, they observed that general activity seemed to occur cyclically or episodically.

In rats, Richter measured activity over 24-hour periods during which the animals were fed once a day, each time at the same hour. He found, as Figure 2 shows, that activity was greatest in the hour just before feeding; it dropped after mealtime, remained fairly low for several hours, and began to increase as the time for the next feeding approached. Wang (1923), who worked in association with Richter, found cyclic patterns in the activity of female rats, which he was able to correlate with the changes occuring in their estrous cycles. Richter's laboratory reported cyclicity in other, more specific activities, e.g., nest-building, drinking, and elimination, all in rats. While these activities are more specific than general activity, the rhythmicity they manifest suggests that, like them, rhythmicity in general activity is due to internal, motivational conditions, rather than being specifically motivated. Efforts were made in Richter's laboratory to correlate activity observed in sleeping medical students and in rats with stomach contractions. Some relationships were found, although their interpretation is not clear.

This work suggests that general activity may arise from a host of internal conditions, motivational in character. In his early work, Richter seemed to attempt to identify these internal conditions as being like stimuli (e.g., stomach contractions), but the observations could be and were also taken as evidence for an internal or central drive state.

2. Periodicity We noted periodicity in the general activity of rats a moment ago. Richter also observed that, with food freely available, rats did not eat all the time but did so, on the average, every two hours. Periodicity was also found for thirst and, as we have noted, for nest-building and elimination.

3. Consummatory Behavior The amount an animal eats or drinks is, in some cases at least, a function of how deprived he is of food or water. Hungry animals will typically eat more than less hungry animals (Skinner, 1938, pp. 343–351), as thirsty animals (Stellar & Hill, 1952) will typically drink more than those that are not thirsty. Given deprivation of food or water, a rat will, if experienced, eat or drink rapidly at first, gradually slowing down the rate of intake until he ceases eating or drinking. Variation in the amount taken with degree of deprivation and the slowing of the rate as intake proceeds suggest a quantitative determination of consummatory behavior by strength of drive.

4. Obstruction Box Studies Warden (1931) and his colleagues attempted to quantify and compare the strengths of different drives by means of an apparatus called the Columbia Obstruction Box. This instru-

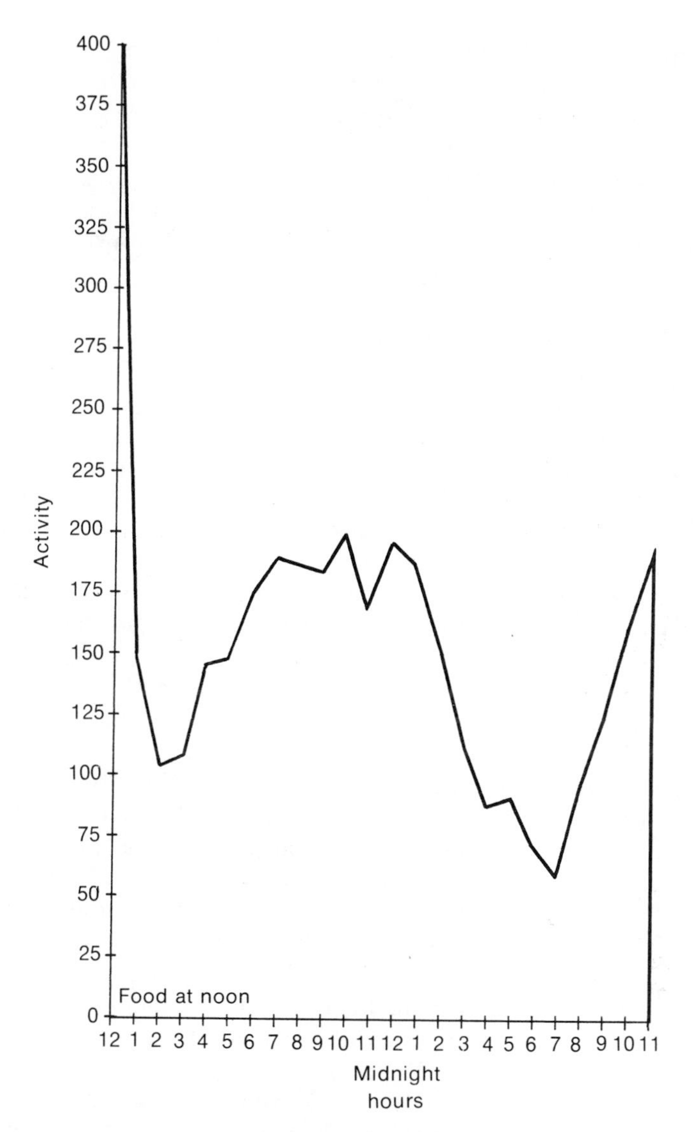

FIGURE 2 Mean activity of 40 rats over a 24-hour period. Activity was measured in a tambour-mounted cage starting at noon when food was given. The food was removed after 20 minutes, and most of the animals had stopped eating by the end of this interval. From Richter, C. P. A behavioristic study of the activity of the rat. *Comparative Psychology Monographs*, 1922, Vol. 1. P. 13, Fig. 6. By permission of University of California Press.

ment consists of a start box and an incentive or goal box separated by an electrifiable grid which the animal must cross to reach the incentive box. Number of crossings made in a standard time interval (20 minutes) was the measure employed. The animal would be deprived for a known interval of time (e.g., so many hours without food) and then be placed in the start box with an appropriate incentive (food, a receptive female, etc.) in the goal box. Warden found that as time of deprivation increased there was an increase in the number of crossings to the incentive; although the curves for all the deprivation conditions rose for the shorter deprivation intervals, not all continued to rise throughout the intervals used; some declined. Nevertheless, the evidence generally supported the idea that as drive increases, more behavior (the grid crossings) is undertaken. It was likewise possible to use this measure, Warden thought, for the comparison of drive strengths.

5. Specific Hungers Evidence that animals and men can, at least under some conditions, select a healthy diet when given free choice of a variety of foodstuffs has been known for a long time. When hogs, chickens, and rats were allowed to pick and choose from among a variety of foods, they showed weight gains superior to those of animals with fixed diets. Davis (1928) allowed newly weaned infants a daily cafeterialike choice of foods from among a variety of components necessary to an adequate diet. Although the infants did not consume a well-balanced diet every day, over a several-month period the diets they chose were satisfactory, according to nutritional requirements, and the infants were healthy and grew normally.

This evidence suggests that there are mechanisms which permit animals and men to choose foodstuffs in accordance with bodily needs. (To some extent, this has to be the case, as both animals and men have survived, grown, and been healthy, long before nutritionally desirable diets were afforded by experts.) Richter (1942–1943) and others have performed a number of experiments which give further support to these general findings.

Rats whose adrenal glands have been removed consume salty liquids at a high rate; doing so makes up for the salt deficiency which develops (and can be fatal) after adrenalectomy. They also prefer salty to nonsalty water, in terms of amount consumed. Parathyroidectomy causes rats to increase their intake of calcium, and removal of the pancreas leads to a reduction in sugar intake. Deprivations of many other specific substances, such as parts of the vitamin-B complex, fats, proteins, and carbohydrates, lead to compensatory changes in food intake (Cofer & Appley, 1964, pp. 228–236).

These studies of specific hungers were important in support of the conclusion that internal factors are involved in the regulation of behavior. The behavior here—compensatory eating or drinking—is seen to serve the needs of the organism and, in a sense, to maintain life and health by compensating for deficits that would otherwise lead to ill health and even death. Such evidence offered powerful and impressive support to the importance of drive in instigating behavior necessary to maintain the organism's internal economy.

6. Hormones Much behavior, especially in lower animals, occurs only now and then. Thus, maternal behavior and reproductive behavior do not occur all the time. In female rats, for example, the animal is sexually responsive to the male only episodically—at a certain period in her estrous cycle. The activities preparatory to the birth of offspring and following the birth are usually seen primarily in pregnant females and after parturition. In the male rat castrated in early infancy, sexual responsiveness to a receptive female is not likely to occur. However, injected with the male sex hormone, such animals will be responsive.

Here again, there is control of behavior by internal factors, at least in part. It was natural for theorists to postulate sex and maternal drives as the mechanisms underlying these behaviors.

7. Reinforcement This term refers to what we may more likely think of as reward. It is well known that learning is facilitated by administering rewards. Thus, a hungry rat will learn to press a bar or run a maze if it is rewarded or reinforced with food for doing so. However, in the absence of hunger, food is not so apt to be rewarding. The effectiveness of a reward, then, depends on the existence of an appropriate internal condition, i.e., a drive. This dependency, again, illustrates the importance of the internal condition so far as behavior is concerned; in this case, learning, an important adaptive device, is involved.

The Nature of Drive as a Central State As a central state, drive was regarded in no very specific way. It seems to have been imagined as a sort of "push" or force, activating the organism into behavior, either of a nonspecific sort, as in the case of general activity, or of a more specific sort, as in the cases of drinking, eating, mating, and maternal behavior. The accounts of the role of drive in activating behavior seem to imply automaticity, i.e., given mounting deprivation, the animal would become generally active or in the presence of an appropriate incentive become active specifically with respect to that incentive (Morgan, 1943, pp. 460–465).

Generally, the conception was a homeostatic one. The deprivation state induced an imbalance (the drive) which then motivated the general or the specific behavior. In the case of general activity, the idea was that an active animal in moving about its environment would be more likely, than if inactive, to encounter the appropriate goal objects. Where the behavior was specific with respect to an incentive object, the drive would lead to faster approach to the object and the consummation of an amount of the incentive consonant with rectifying the imbalance. Behavior, learned or unlearned, was considered to be functional, i.e., it persisted until it resulted in whatever consummatory behavior was necessary to allay the organism's needs. The implication was that without need, or drive, there would be no behavior; the organism, in principle, would remain inert. This account of behavior is, of course, squarely in the functionalist tradition, as outlined in the last chapter.

For a long time, there was confusion in theory between the idea that there were numerous drives, each one corresponding to a given kind of consummatory behavior (e.g., hunger and eating) and the idea of a more general, single drive state, contributed to by any or all deprivation states and capable of energizing any behaviors. The latter alternative was adopted by Clark L. Hull (1943) and was dominant for a number of years. Hull, of course, provided for some specificity by stressing the role of drive stimuli (e.g., stomach contractions) characteristic of each drive condition. The difficulty with the former alternative was that postulation of many specific drive states amounted to little more than having another name for a series of deprivation conditions—hunger named food deprivation, thirst named water deprivation, and so on. This alternative was not entirely abandoned, but it is safe to say that in the 1940's it was secondary to the concept of general drive.

Drive theory, as we shall term the ideas presented in this section, was proposed as a general account of motivation, human as well as animal. It was recognized, of course, that much of human behavior, unlike that of lower animals, could not be directly or even indirectly traced with ease to current conditions of deprivation of food, water, sex, and the like. Hence in addition to primary drive (hunger, etc.), a notion of secondary (or acquired or learned) drive was developed to provide the motivation for much of behavior, especially human behavior. The model of acquired drive was based on avoidance learning but was expected to apply as well to other situations.

Avoidance training goes as follows. Usually a box is employed which contains two compartments separated by a barrier. The floors of the compartments are composed of a grid of electrifiable rods. The animal, placed in one compartment, is shocked there and can escape into the other compartment, where he is not shocked. Rats and dogs learn this pattern readily. In addition, the onset of the shock is preceded by a tone or some other signal. If the animal jumps the barrier on hearing the tone, he can avoid the shock altogether. This skill is learned readily, so that the animal, at first only able to escape the shock, has now learned to avoid it. Such avoidance behavior is persistent, continuing for hundreds of trials even when the animal receives no shock (see Chapter 7, pp. 110–112).

The motivation for this persistent avoidance has been said to be fear (Miller, 1951), i.e., through the association of the tone and the shock the animal has come to fear the tone. Since prior to the learning the tone did not motivate avoidance of the compartment, the fear is learned. Fear in this case, then, is a learned or acquired drive. Since drive theorists, especially those influenced by psychoanalysis (e.g., Dollard & Miller, 1950), regarded fear and anxiety as a major human motive, this demonstration of avoidance was thought to be directly pertinent to human motivation, i.e., the learned drive of fear (or anxiety) was believed to underlie much human behavior not traceable to hunger, fear, or sex. In addition, it was suggested, other learned motives could be developed on the bases of associations with eating, drinking, and the situations involving the other primary drives.

This, then, was drive theory, and it was the dominant view of motivation in about 1950. Much of this theory seemed compatible, at least to the drive theorists such as Dollard and Miller (1950), with the psychoanalytic theory of motivation, although there were recognized differences in detail.

We shall be concerned in the next section with the downfall of drive theory, the current status of which Campbell and Misanin in a review published in 1969 summarize as follows: " . . . this has been a disquieting chapter to prepare . . . because of the disintegration of the drive concept (1969, p. 77)."

PROBLEMS WITH DRIVE THEORY

During the 1950's, three major kinds of difficulty with drive theory became apparent. One was that alternative interpretations can be made of the meaning of the seven kinds of evidence we reviewed a few pages ago as supporting the central drive state. Some of these new interpretations were based on new evidence. Some were based on further analyses of the meaning of drive in certain of the situations reviewed. A second was the discovery that much behavior is motivated by factors that did not fit with the homeostatic conception as it was developed in drive theory. The third difficulty was with secondary drive. We discuss each of these in turn, under the headings alternative interpretations, nonhomeostatic factors, and problems with secondary drive.

Alternative Interpretations

The major interpretive problem with the earlier work on general activity is that it did not take into account the role of learning in the activity patterns it described. Two experiments by Campbell and Sheffield indicate the nature of the problem. In the first (Campbell & Sheffield, 1953) rats were placed for seven days in cages in which their activity could be measured. The room in which the cages were housed was dark and soundproofed, and a masking noise was provided by a ventilating fan. Food was freely available during the first four days, but no food was present during the last three days. As may be seen in Figure 3, little change in activity occurred over the 72 hours of starvation, despite the mounting drive. This observation has been confirmed by other investigators. There was an increase in activity when once a day the experimenters entered the room, turned on the lights, and turned off the fan. The increase in activity was greater during the deprivation days under this stimulation than it was during the free-food days, suggesting to Campbell and Sheffield that deprivation increases sensitivity to stimuli. However, their findings without stimulation clearly indicate that drive does not automatically force the animal into activity.

How may the earlier, contradictory findings of Richter be explained?

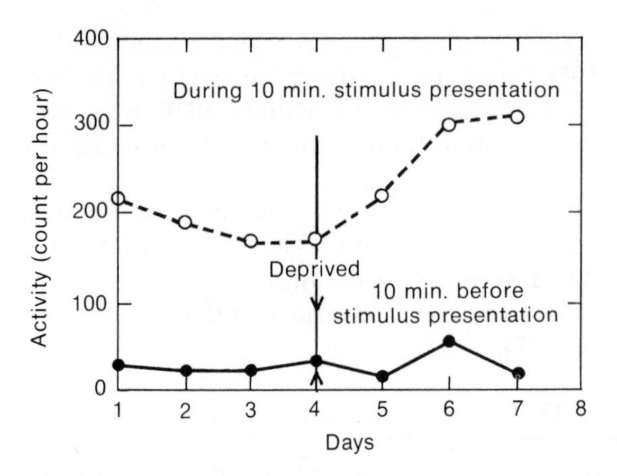

FIGURE 3 Mean activity records for two 10-minute samples over 7 days. Food and water were always available to the rats during the first 4 days, but food was withdrawn at the end of day 4. Stimulus presentation means that the experimenter entered the room, turned off the fan, turned on the lights, etc. From Cofer, C. N. and Appley, M. H. *Motivation: Theory and research*. 1964. P. 274, Fig. 6-1. By permission of John Wiley & Sons, Inc. (Cofer and Appley modified Fig. 1 in Campbell and Sheffield, 1953.)

In these experiments, the animals were fed periodically. Perhaps the animals became active when they anticipated that the time of feeding was approaching. Sheffield and Campbell (1954) performed another experiment to test this possibility.

After habituating their rats to the situation, Sheffield and Campbell starved the animals for three days. Then in one group, provision of food was always associated with a stimulus change (over several days), whereas in the other group it was not so associated. Activity tended to increase in response to the stimulus change in the former group but not in the latter group. This seems to suggest that animals learn to become active in response to stimuli which are regularly correlated with the occurrence of feeding. It seems likely, then, that Richter's animals learned to be active in anticipation of feeding, rather than that they became active because activity is an automatic effect of increasing deprivation. In many ways, the relation of general activity to time of deprivation was the best evidence for central drive state theory, as there were no obvious incentives present to elicit it. The fact that activity patterns are subject to learning, then, is a serious blow to drive theory as outlined at the end of the last section.

Another finding mentioned earlier that seemed to support the idea that behavior is regulated on the basis of tissue need was the periodicity observed in the animals' meal-taking, i.e., eating occurred every 120 minutes. Baker (1953, 1955) found the same average, but the variability of the intermeal times of individual animals around this average was very high, as illustrated by a standard deviation of 90 minutes. Baker analyzed the sequences of eating and noneating periods in his animals and could find no way of characterizing them except as random. Periodicity of eating, then, does not seem to be confirmed. (This conclusion, of course, does not mean that feeding rhythms cannot be learned.)

We will consider consummatory behavior and specific hungers together. Rats which have never experienced hunger or thirst (food and water having always been available) do not, after deprivation is introduced, show an immediate full utilization of eating and drinking periods. It takes repeated experiences of deprivation for the animals to begin to eat or drink immediately and to continue to eat and drink over the interval when food or water is made available (Ghent, 1951, 1957). This suggests that the animals may have to learn to be hungry or thirsty, although alternative interpretations are possible. Clearly, however, the initial experiences of deprivation are not followed immediately by eating and drinking adequate to make up for deficiencies. Animals seem to require time, sometimes several weeks, to adjust their food or water intake to new schedules of the availability of food or water.

Specific hungers, also, are not as automatically adaptive as earlier investigations suggested. Some deficiencies of diet are not made up. In other cases, a choice developed in a situation persists even when the choice is nutritionally bad for the animal. For example, in a choice situation, Young and Chaplin (1945) showed that rats preferred sucrose (a sugar) to casein (a protein). Casein was then removed from the diet over more than 30 days, and severe protein deprivaton was developed. Nevertheless, the animals continued to prefer sucrose over casein; however, when another method of testing in a different apparatus was used, the preference was reversed. But with the original method in the original apparatus, the nonadaptive preference continued. In one experiment, a learned preference for sugar over salt persisted following adrenalectomy (Harriman, 1955) and some animals died from salt deficiency as a consequence.

The picture of wisdom in dietary regulation portrayed in the earlier literature is, then, not entirely representative of findings in many cases. It is noteworthy that in many of the early studies, including the one with infants, the foodstuffs available for the subject to choose among included none really incompatible with a satisfactory diet from a nutritional standpoint. There is, nevertheless, some reason to believe that free dietary choice, while fallible, is compatible in many instances with good nutrition. The basis for satisfactory choice will be discussed later.

The obstruction-box studies did not measure "pure drive." One reason that we can say this is that, by the nature of the method, an incentive—food, water, a mate—was always present in the goal box. Another is that the animals received pretraining trials without shock before being tested with shock. Some learning to cross from the start box to the goal box undoubtedly occurred. Further, if the results for only the first five minutes of the test session are examined a picture different from the one based on the whole 20-minute interval emerges. The obstruction-box method, as used, was then fraught with complications and does not seem to yield clear evidence concerning the role of drive, alone, in the behavior observed (Bolles, 1967, 118–122).

The evidence from the studies involving hormonal control also tended to involve incentives, as well as the hormonal condition itself. Beach (1965), writing primarily about the male rat but generalizing beyond this animal, indicates that sexual behavior is not controlled by the internal hormonal condition alone. Stimulation, arising from the sexual partner, is necessary to effect the degree of sexual arousal which will eventuate in sexual behavior. There are other problems with the interpretation of sex and certain other hormonally controlled conditions in terms of the homeostatic drive conception, which we will discuss in the next part of this section. Likewise, reinforcement, interpreted as a process which reduces a drive condition (as food-intake may be said to reduce hunger, for example) has encountered difficulties which are summarized below.

Nonhomeostatic Factors

In the case of hunger and thirst, there is a depletion in the tissues, and appropriate consummatory behavior can make up for the deficits. However, with sex and very likely with other conditions involving some degree of hormonal control, this is not the case, and the homeostatic model may not be applicable as it is in connection with hunger and thirst. Thus, there is no depletion of tissue to instigate sexual behavior, maternal behavior, and similar states. Sexual and these other behaviors use up energy, whereas eating, on balance, restores it. It is not at all clear that hormonal levels in the blood stream are reduced by sexual or maternal behavior, so that a drive-reduction interpretation of these behaviors is not obviously relevant. It has been common to speak of homeostatic drives as relieving excesses, as well as deficits, and in excretory activities one can see how this can be. It is not obvious, however, that any excess exists or is reduced in female sexual behavior or in maternal behavior, and the male ejaculate is not hormonal. Observations like these have led Beach (1956) to suggest that sex is more an appetite than a drive, and, of course, sexual behavior is not essential to individual survival although it is for species survival.

It has often been suggested, on the homeostatic model, that reduction of drive is the basis of reinforcement for learning. However, a number of observations, in rats and other animals, have suggested that this conclusion is not necessarily true. Preferences have been learned when their consequences bring about an increase of stimulation in at least moderate amounts (e.g., Montgomery, 1954). Animals learn when the "reward" is incomplete copulation (Sheffield, Wulff, & Backer, 1951), when it is an increase in illumination (Kish, 1955) or sound (Barnes & Kish, 1961), when (Sheffield & Roby, 1950) it is the taste of saccharin (which does not reduce hunger drive), and when the response increases movement of the animal's cage (Barnes & Kish, 1957, p. 42). These observations suggest that not all reinforcement can be due to drive reduction. Electrical stimulation of certain parts of the brain (Olds & Milner, 1954), under some conditions, has considerable reward value, and this finding seems incompatible, also, with a tension or drive-reduction view of reinforcement.

Animals have been shown to exhibit curiosity and exploration even, or perhaps especially, when they are neither hungry nor thirsty and when no incentive objects are present which are appropriate goal objects for other motivational conditions. Thus, monkeys will manipulate objects, such as puzzles, and learn how to disassemble them with no motivation or reinforcement except that provided by the objects or the accomplishments themselves (Harlow, 1950). All of this evidence has been deemed to be incompatible with a homeostatic conception of drive involving stimulus or tension reduction. The early writers whose work displayed these phenomena, such as Harlow and Montgomery, were prone to speak of nonhomeostatic drives, like curiosity, exploration, or need for stimulation. We shall have more to say about these "drives" in a later chapter. Suffice it to say here that concepts of homeostatic drive and drive reduction were not compatible with these findings.

One dramatic example is provided by work with humans. Experiments were conducted under conditions of sensory deprivation or isolation in which the subjects were placed in sound-deadened rooms, with little visual, tactile, or other kinds of stimulation (Bexton, Heron, & Scott, 1954). Many subjects found such conditions after a brief interval to be intolerable, thus again suggesting that some degree of sensory stimulation is desirable and contradicting the view that a relatively stimulus-free situation would be sought and enjoyed.

The observations and interpretations just summarized have had a major impact on our conception of motivation, and we will discuss these matters much more fully in a later chapter. Evidence for nonhomeostatic factors along with the material we discussed a moment ago under "Alternative Interpretations" caused drive as a homeostatic, internal sort of push to be severely questioned.

Problems with Secondary Drive

Although the status of fear as an acquired drive or motive seems still to be relatively secure, it has not been possible to demonstrate acquired drives based on hunger or thirst, although many attempts have been made (see Chapter 7). Close parallels to the situation in which fear is learned have been studied with hunger and thirst as the drives on which secondary drives were to be learned. There has been little consistent success in this work. The failure to demonstrate acquired drives based on anything but fear has left a large void in the explanation, by drive theory, of much of human motivation. It is reasonable to wonder whether drive theory is worth pursuing if it cannot be extended to this important area of inquiry.

ALTERNATIVES TO DRIVE

Because of the difficulties with drive theory other processes have been suggested as replacements for drive. One of these is the concept of incentive. Another is to question whether motivational conceptions are necessary at all and to suggest that apparently motivational phenomena may actually reflect the operation of other factors, such as reinforcement. Perhaps this second alternative is another way of saying that when we can describe the processes and factors of which some behavior is a function there is little utility to invoking general notions, like motivation, to account for them. In this chapter, we sketch the nature of incentives and reinforcement, reserving to a later section of this book an evaluation of their status as well as of the status of motivation in general.

Incentives

Characteristically, incentives are regarded as objects, conditions, or stimuli external to the organism. They may be divided into positive incentives, which organisms tend to approach, and negative incentives, which they tend to avoid. Thus, food, water, or a mate may be characterized as incentive objects for the hungry, thirsty, or sexually aroused animal, and he will approach these objects. A situation in which pain has been experienced is a negative incentive, and it will be avoided. In the latter example, there is no negative incentive object, although it is easy to imagine instances in which such objects would be present, such as a predator. The avoidance reaction occurs to cues associated with the painful experience of shock. In the case of positive incentives, like food, cues of the situation in which food has been found and eaten may also develop incentive value. In a species like the human, in which symbolic processes are highly developed, it seems likely that incentive objects, situations, or states, both positive and negative, can be imagined. In such instances the incentive is internal, rather than external. In lower animals, however, we think of incentives typically as external.

We can think of an incentive as having two functions. One is to instigate approach toward it or avoidance (withdrawal) from it. The other is to evoke a state of arousal in the animal so that it will be moved (motivated) to approach or to withdraw from the incentive. The state of arousal is like that envisaged for drive in drive theory, but here the arousal is evoked by the incentive, rather than being due to conditions of deprivation, as in drive theory.

It is a fact that in all but one of the kinds of evidence listed earlier as supporting the conception of drive as a central state, incentives were present in the situations in which drive was studied. This is true of the studies of periodicity, consummatory behavior, specific hungers, the obstruction-box method, hormonal control, and reinforcement. It was not true of general activity because the incentives were not present when activity began to increase. However, we showed earlier that these increases in activity could be explained on the basis of the animal's learning to anticipate the occurrence of the incentive when feeding, for example, took place at a predictable time. Presumably, the cues associated with the arrival of mealtime acquired incentive value through their regularly being followed by food. Thus, we can say that in all of the situations in which evidence for drive was found, there was a confounding of incentive with time of deprivation, and we know from the study of Sheffield and Campbell that it was the cues, rather than the time of deprivation, which instigated the augmented activity.

Incentive, then, is a potential alternative to drive as the major motivational construct. We shall keep it in mind as we proceed through the rest of this book.

Reinforcement

Reinforcement refers to some condition which strengthens behavior which has preceded it. Another word for *strengthen* in this context is *learn*. Thus, a hungry animal which runs down a runway and finds food at the end and eats it will tend to repeat the performance at the next opportunity and do so more quickly than he did before. Food and similar objects which are approached are called positive reinforcers. A negative reinforcer is one whose removal strengthens behavior. Thus escape from or avoidance of electric shock is reinforcing because it terminates or eliminates the painful stimulation. (Note that this is not punishment. In punishment, the response itself would be shocked; it neither escapes nor avoids the shock.)

It is obvious that reinforcement involves incentives. Reinforcement has been proposed as an alternative to drive and also to incentive theory. How does it differ from incentive theory? The answer is that the reinforcement account of motivational phenomena is a nonmotivational one. It argues that the properties of behavior of interest can be explained in terms of the conditions existing at the time of reinforcement, i.e., that they are learned and that no special processes such as drive or arousal by incentives are necessary.

THE THEORETICAL STATUS OF MOTIVATIONAL CONCEPTS

We saw, in the first chapter, that motivation is a relatively new concept in psychological theory and that it entered the discipline as instinct only to be reformulated as drive. In the discussion of the evidence for drive, we saw that behavior was thought to vary in amount or quantity as drive varied. When drive increased, there was more general activity, consummatory behavior was enhanced, and so on. This kind of effect seemed to be adaptive, in the service of the organism's needs, just as instinct was. Another feature of instinct, for example in McDougall's account, was that it is purposive—directing or guiding the organism to suitable objects or actions in the interest of its needs. This aspect of instinct carried over somewhat to drive, as, for example, in specific hungers.

Motivational concepts, then, have had at least two major functions with respect to behavior. One is to energize responses, either in general or specifically, and to control their vigor and efficiency. The other is to guide behavior to specific ends, i.e., to give direction to behavior. (We could also say that motivation provides the conditions for reinforcing behavior or weakening it, but we will not pursue these functions here.)

The theoretical problem is that there are other mechanisms, especially learning, which are available to guide behavior. Thus, when an animal develops the tendency to turn one way in a maze rather than another, we say he has learned to go that way. Habits are viewed as structures which guide and control the direction of behavior, so that motivation is perhaps not necessary as a concept to account for directional aspects of behavior. Phenomena of choice and preference may be given an interpretation based on habit rather than on motivation.

What was meant by saying that reinforcement theory is a nonmotivational one is that the conditions under which reinforcement occurs are conceived of as those which control what is learned. If one can show that reinforcement conditions can cope with phenomena for which motivational concepts have been thought necessary, then it is perhaps redundant or unnecessary to speak of motivational terms. Whether reinforcement can achieve this state of affairs is at present an open question, to which reference will be made again later in this book.

The hallmark of the presence of and the need for motivational concepts in behavior is, the author thinks, the energization of responses and the control of their vigor and efficiency. As our discussion proceeds, we shall keep this criterion in the forefront of consideration so that by the end of this book we may have some supportable conclusion in mind as to whether incentive theory is viable or whether it can be replaced by reinforcement theory.

SUGGESTED READINGS

Beach, F. A. Characteristics of masculine sex drive. In M. R. Jones (Ed.), *Nebraska symposium on motivation 1956.* Lincoln, Neb.: University of Nebraska Press, 1956. Pp. 1–32.

Bolles, R. C. *Theory of motivation.* New York: Harper & Row, Publishers, 1967. Chapters 4 and 5.

Boring, E. G. *Sensation and perception in the history of experimental psychology.* New York: Appleton-Century-Crofts, 1942. Chapter 14.

Cannon, W. B. *The wisdom of the body.* (2nd ed.) New York: W. W. Norton & Company, Inc., 1939.

Cofer, C. N. & Appley, M. H. *Motivation: Theory and research.* New York: John Wiley & Sons, Inc., 1964. Chapters 2, 4, 5, and 11.

Dollard, J. & Miller, N. E. *Personality and psychotherapy: An analysis in terms of learning, thinking, and culture.* New York: McGraw-Hill Book Company, 1950.

James, W. *The principles of psychology.* New York: Holt, Rinehart & Winston, Inc., 1890. 2 vols. Chapter 24, Vol. II. Reprinted, 1950, in paper covers by Dover Publications, Inc.

Wolf, A. V. *Thirst: Physiology of the urge to drink and problems of water lack.* Springfield, Ill.: Charles C. Thomas, Publisher, 1958.

3

Biological Aspects of Motivation

All behavior is based in and determined by biological processes, but the importance of these processes can be seen more readily in certain activities—such as eating, drinking, and mating—than in others—such as human social behavior or motives, like achievement, affiliation, and power. In the present chapter, we concentrate on activities concerning which there is some understanding with respect to their neural and physiological control.

There are many activities of this kind, but knowledge concerning what behaviors are relatively closely controlled by specifiable neural and physiological factors varies a good deal across species. In some animals, like many birds and lower mammals, a fairly complete account can be given for some activities, such as parental behavior, for example. In others, including man, much less is known, and it is generally believed that the control of behavior in man is much more complex than it is in the simpler species. In considering this topic, one needs to maintain a healthy skepticism concerning sweeping generalizations made about many species from the knowledge based on the study of one or two.

Many activities, in one animal or another, seem to have a motivational base. Among them are nest-building and other behaviors associated with maternal behavior and parental activities in general, seasonal migrations, hoarding, sleep and rest, temperature regulation, respiration, and eliminative activities. There are perhaps two reasons that these activities may be said to be motivational in character. One is that they have adaptive and survival value and that they occur in relatively invariant patterns in a given species; learning plays a limited role in most of them in the majority of species. The other is that they are seasonal, episodic, or rhythmical, rather than being continuous, and appear to be instigated by internal glandular changes or homeostatic regulatory mechanisms. In seasonal migrations, for example, glandular changes, perhaps induced by variations in the amount of sunlight received during the day, are associated with the onset of migratory flights in birds. It should be pointed out, of course, that the course of the flight, determined as it is by complex patterns of stimulation, is probably best attributed to structural factors, rather than to motivational ones.

In the space available, it is not possible to discuss all of these behavioral patterns, and the ones chosen for presentation are those about which a good deal is known and which are found across many species. Before we discuss the control of these behaviors, however, it will be useful to discuss again the role of innate factors in the control of behavior.

THE RETURN OF INSTINCT: ETHOLOGY

We summarized, earlier, the counterreaction to the instinct doctrine, but the notion that there are innate behavior patterns did not entirely disappear. It came again into major importance, starting in the 1930's, with the work of a group of European zoologists who studied animal behavior. They called their field of work ethology.

The ethologists tended to concentrate their studies on birds and fish, though, of course, mammals were investigated as well. The instincts they discussed were behavior patterns, apparently unlearned and typical of a single species (species-specific). In many cases, if not all, it was observed that the species-specific behavior patterns occurred in the presence of particular stimulus patterns, i.e., the behavior patterns seemed to be *released* when the appropriate patterns of stimulation appeared. There was also a motivational part to the ethologist's account of the instinctive behavior, and it will be desirable, in discussing ethology, to keep somewhat separate the notions of species-specific behavior patterns, releasing stimuli, and the motivational theory.

Until relatively recent times (Beach, 1950, 1955), psychologists in the United States who studied animals did so in relatively narrow ways. They examined only a few species, and they concentrated their efforts on the investigation of learning processes. Furthermore, their purpose in doing animal work was to study learning in animals simpler than the human and under conditions that afforded better control of variables than is feasible with the human, so that the processes of learning over a wide range of animals (mammals, say), including the human, would be better understood. It is only a partial caricature of these workers to say that they studied learning in rats in order to understand human learning.

There were two assumptions that underlay this approach. One is that general laws of learning exist at some level and that the study of one or two species could uncover these laws. Once discovered the laws could be expected to hold true across many species so far as fundamental processes of learning are concerned. This assumption seems no longer to be tenable, as the papers by Seligman (1970) and Warren (1971) have demonstrated. The second assumption, not unrelated to the first one, is that virtually any response, if the animal was capable of making it at all, could be acquired. Bolles (1970), among others, has demonstrated that this assumption is probably invalid. Bolles points out that in the case of avoidance learning it is extremely difficult for some animals to learn to avoid a noxious stimulus by means of some responses, whereas they learn avoidance easily by means of other responses. Thus, for rats, pressing a bar as a means of avoiding shock is learned slowly and with difficulty, whereas the response of jumping out of a box is learned very quickly. Bolles argues that animals have species-specific defense reactions which are present innately. If one of these can be used in the situation, avoidance learning will be quick. But if some other response is required, and especially if it is incompatible with a species-specific defense reaction, learning of avoidance will be difficult. (See, also, Breland & Breland, 1961.)

Although the insistence of the ethologists on the importance of innate behavioral repertoires in learning was greeted initially by a good deal of skepticism on the part of comparative psychologists in the United States, the testimony provided by the papers of Bolles, Seligman, and Warren clearly indicates that the ethologists have "won the day" on this point. This is not, however, to say that all aspects of ethological theory, especially the assumptions about motivation, have been successful, as we shall see.

An example will aid understanding of fixed-action patterns and releasing stimuli, although neither is perhaps a motivational concept. A well-known illustration is provided by certain activities of the 3-spined stickleback (*Gasterosteus aculeatus*), a fish found in European waters. In the spring of the year, the males of this species migrate from the sea to rivers and go upstream. Presumably, hormonal changes are involved in the instigation of this migration. Their migration upstream continues until they reach a place suitable as a breeding area; prior to this point they do not behave aggressively toward other males, but once they reach the breeding site, they dig a pit in the sand and patrol a limited area of the stream, a "territory." In this stage, males develop a reddish color on their undersides, and if such a male approaches the territory of another stickleback, he will be attacked. Experiments in which wooden models have been used, including some which look very little like sticklebacks except for having a red-painted underside and being presented in a head-down position, show that the aggressive response is released by the red underbelly; females are not attacked or are not attacked very vigorously, but they do not have the red belly. However, their abdomens are swollen with eggs, when they are ready to spawn. This swollen belly, together with the more or less upright posture taken in swimming, seem to elicit in the male the initial part of a courtship sequence.

This part is the zigzag "dance," which may elicit approach on the part of the female. If she approaches, the male swims to the nest, the female following, and he indicates the entrance to the nest with his head. The female enters the nest, and "trembling" on the part of the male causes her to spawn. The male fertilizes the eggs, which he then aerates by motions of his tail and fins.

In this sequence of innate acts are seen a number of more or less specific actions, each released by a pattern of stimuli. The zigzag dance, the indication of the nest entrance, the trembling, the spawning, fertilization, and aeration are all instinctive acts, whereas the shape of the female, her following pattern, her spawning, and the eggs themselves constitute stimulus patterns which release the various acts.

Critical, of course, to the appearance of this pattern of behavior is the fact that the fish have undergone hormonal changes which ready them for reproduction. At times of the year other than the spring, these activities do not appear. This has suggested that there is a drive state which energizes the specific responses and sensitizes the animal to certain stimulus patterns.

Such a formulation is little more than another way of stating the basic observations. Two other kinds of observations, however, seemed to give support to the drive interpretation. These phenomena are displacement activities and vacuum activities.

The former are reported to occur in conflict situations, where two or more tendencies to respond block one another. Under these conditions, other activities may appear, like grooming, feeding, or sleeping. These responses are clearly normal responses in the animal's repertory, but they are said to be displaced when they occur during sexual or aggressive interactions with other animals. (Their form, however, in the displaced variety is sometimes reported to be distorted.) Vacuum activities are cases in which an instinctive act appears in a situation in which no adequate stimulus, so far as an observer can tell, is present.

Displacement and vacuum activities were taken, in early ethological writing, as evidence of the operation of a drive state, functioning in a manner not unlike that suggested by Freud. There is a buildup of drive energy, and, when its discharge is blocked in a conflict situation, the energy could spill or "spark" over to energize other responses, i.e., the displacement of activities. Or, it was supposed, the energy buildup could be sufficiently great as to cause a specific action tendency to occur even without a releasing stimulus. There is much in this formulation that resembles a hydraulic model of drive energy.

This theory may be criticized on three grounds. One makes the point that the assumptions involved do not accord well with our knowledge of the anatomical and physiological characteristics of the nervous system; for example, there does not seem to be any mechanism that could underlie "sparking-over." A second holds that appropriate stimuli, in the case of displacement activities, may well be present to explain their occurrence. A similar analysis can probably be made of vacuum activities, although it is difficult to investigate vacuum activities. Since they are supposed to occur in the absence of relevant stimuli, one can do little to study them except after the fact of their occurrence. The third questions the evidence on which the concept of specific releasing stimuli has been predicated. We consider the second and third points in some detail.

There are a limited number of activities which occur, in a given species, as displacement activities. Grooming, feeding, and sleeping are common ones, and it is noteworthy that these behaviors occur with high frequency in the animal in any case. One estimate for the rat, for example, is that grooming occurs 40 percent of the time the animal is awake (Bolles, 1960). These activities are then instances with high potential for occurrence under any circumstances. It is as if the animal, blocked in, say, a situation by the opposing tendencies to attack and to flee, resorts to doing things which he might well be doing anyway.

Another factor to be considered is that the stimuli which instigate grooming, for example, are almost always present. Thus, if grooming has been suppressed in an attack or sexual situation but then there is conflict, the stimuli are there to instigate it, while the blocking of the other behavior persists. This interpretation does not require one in terms of drive energy.

Rowell (1961) has afforded a test of this idea by augmenting peripheral stimuli experimentally and observing grooming behavior in both ordinary and conflict situations. He used the chaffinch and either sprayed the bird with water or provided a sticky birdseed; the former was designed to produce body grooming, the latter bill wiping. Rowell showed that both the frequency and the type of grooming, in both normal and conflict situations, paralleled the kind of peripheral stimulation he had augmented. This suggests that grooming is the product of the pattern and intensity of peripheral stimulation, at least in part. Another factor is the time available. Suppose grooming is observed to occur in conjunction with locomotion. Grooming occurs only when there are pauses in locomotion and only in those pauses which are long enough for it to occur. Conflict situations, of course, involve the cessation of other activities, so that there is time without interference for other responses like grooming to occur.

It is apparently unnecessary, then, to postulate drive factors in the explanation of displacement activities (cf. Zeigler, 1964). Peripheral stimuli and the absence of competing activities (due to conflict) are perhaps sufficient to account for them. For some displacement activities stimuli are always present, and the animal is sensitive to them. For others, the animal may not always be sensitive to relevant stimuli but may become so because of hormonal or other internal changes. The appearance of components of sexual or paternal patterns as displacement activities would be restricted to those periods of time in which hormonal states have sensitized the animal to respond to pertinent stimuli.

The example of courtship behavior in the stickleback included several instances of releasing stimuli. Another widely cited example is illustrated in Figure 4, in which a cardboard model of a bird is shown. If the

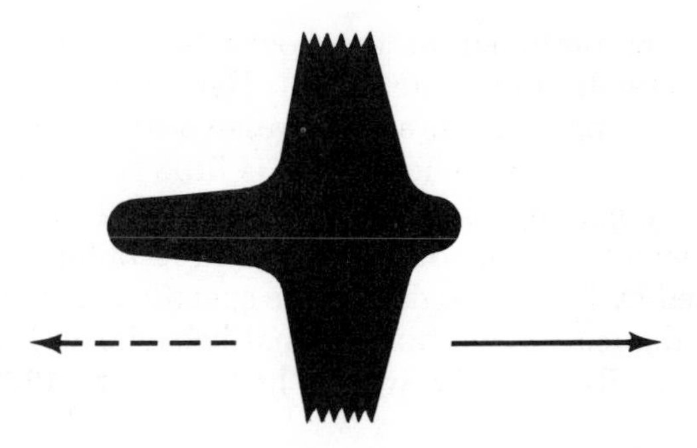

FIGURE 4 A model which when moved on a wire above certain birds is said to release an alarm reaction if moved to the right but not when moved to the left. Moved to the right, the silhouette resembles a bird-of-prey (a hawk). Reproduced from Tinbergen, N. *The study of instinct*. 1951. P. 78, Fig. 6-5. By permission of Clarendon Press, Oxford.

model is moved to the right, so that the short end is in "front," young turkeys exhibit a flight response, whereas they do not flee when the model is pulled in the other direction. The significance of the differential response is that if pulled to the right, the model resembles a hawk, a predator, whereas it resembles a goose if pulled the other way. Thus, it appeared that the particular hawklike visual pattern was a specific releasing stimulus for the alarm reaction in young turkeys (Hinde, 1970, pp. 63-66). Ducks and geese exhibited similar reactions to these stimulus patterns (Tinbergen, 1951, p. 77). Several other reports have failed to verify these findings (e.g., McNiven, 1960), and Hinde (1970, p. 510) says that "The earlier view that young turkeys respond differently to a model shaped like a hawk . . . and not to one shaped like a goose . . . was apparently due to pre-experimental habituation to geese . . . ."

Whether other examples of releasing stimuli, such as those described above in the account of courtship behavior in the stickleback, can be given an interpretation alternative to the notion of releasers—as seems to be the case with the alarm reaction in turkeys, chicks, and geese—is an open question. Some of the ethologists' concepts require further study under well-controlled conditions before their ultimate validity can be assessed.

These critical points apply primarily to the motivational theory proposed by the ethologists and not to their assertion that there are acts which have a largely innate, species-specific character. Whether a given act has a large native component can usually be assessed by experimental means. The kinds of instinctive acts postulated by the ethologists are very different from those suggested by a writer like McDougall. Yet, in some of their more popular writings and in writings influenced by ethology, in which the findings from lower animals are often generalized to man, the ethologists and their interpreters write almost as McDougall did. Examples are provided in the books by Ardrey (1966), Lorenz (1966), Morris (1968), and Storr (1968). Here, for example, ideas like territoriality, releasing stimuli, and aggressive drive are applied, largely by analogy, to human behavior. There is little scientific basis or merit in such applications, and the reader of Chapter 2 and the preceding pages of this chapter is aware of the lack of support for the kind of drive theory advocated by the ethologists. More specific comments concerning the validity of the extensions from animal behavior to human behavior are provided in a critical review written by Berkowitz (1969).

BIOLOGICALLY BASED STATES

In view of the developments, summarized in the second chapter, concerning the status of drive, it could be inferred that the investigation of the mechanisms underlying eating, drinking, and mating would no longer be concerned with the kinds of problems to which investigators were led by the theoretical framework of drive theory. This inference is justified by the evidence. Campbell and Misanin (1969, p. 60) describe the situation this way:

> Much of the research energy that was once directed at the complex of interactions between motivation and learned behavior is now focused on the analysis of the physiological and neurological variables that control hunger and thirst as well as other basic drives.

In the remaining parts of this chapter, attention will be devoted to this kind of work in the cases of hunger, thirst, sexual behavior, and pain. New technical developments, it may be added, and the discoveries they have permitted have been important in both the decline of drive theory and in the redirection of investigative interests.

Hunger

The critical discovery concerning the regulation of eating was that there are two areas in the hypothalamus (see Figures 5 and 6), one of which seems to control eating and the other the cessation of eating. Research has been devoted to the study of the anatomy and physiology of these areas, the participation of other parts of the brain in the control of eating, and the mechanisms by which the hypothalamic areas are activated by changes in the food supplies in the body. Much is known concerning these matters, but completely satisfactory accounts have not yet been achieved concerning any of them. On the other hand, little is known with regard to how the actual behaviors involved in eating are regulated (Grossman, 1967).

In a general way, animals monitor their food intake fairly efficiently in

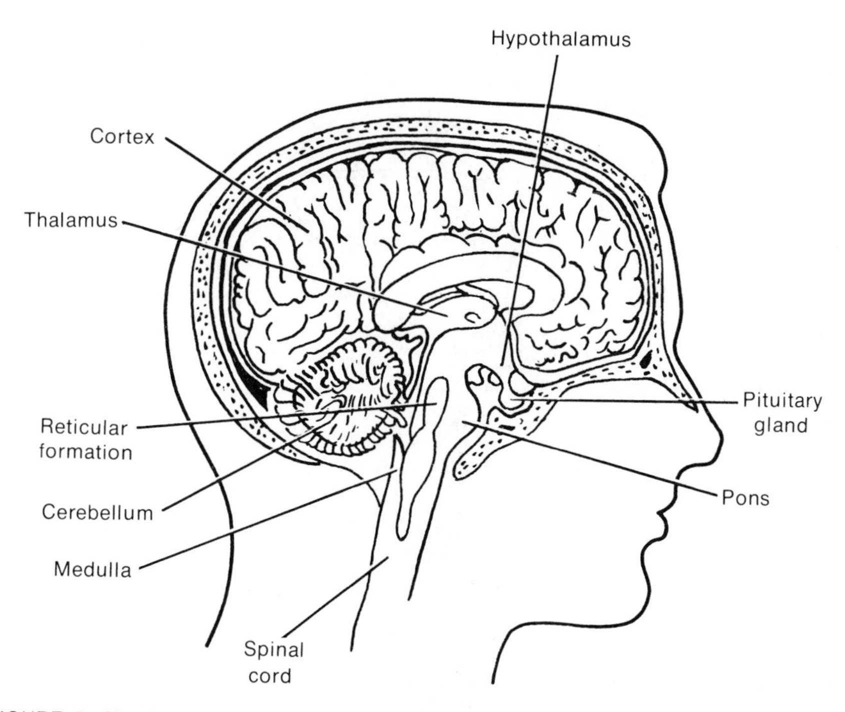

FIGURE 5 The hypothalamus in relation to other structures. Redrawn from Hokanson, J. E. *The physiological bases of motivation.* 1969. P. 150, Fig. A.2. By permission of John Wiley & Sons, Inc.

relation to bodily requirements. There are many mechanisms involved in this regulation, as the discussion which follows will suggest.

For over a century, it has been known that tumors or injuries in the general region of the hypothalamus are associated with overeating (hyperphagia) and obesity (e.g., Fröhlich's syndrome). Many workers believed that these disorders arose from dysfunction of the pituitary gland, but subsequent investigations have clearly disproved the role of this gland and have identified certain regions of the hypothalamus as the sources of these phenomena.

The clearest evidence became available after the development of the stereotaxic instrument, a device which permits fairly precise lesions to be made in fairly definite sites of the brain. When, with the aid of this device, bilateral lesions are placed in the area of the ventromedial nucleus of the hypothalamus (the locations of the lesions are verified at autopsy), hyperphagia and obesity result (see Cofer & Appley, 1964, pp. 217–222). The implication is that this area must be intact for an animal, like the rat, to stop eating; the implication is consistent with the fact that electrical stimulation of the area, a way of activating it, decreases the intake of food. Electrical activity of the nucleus increases when appetite

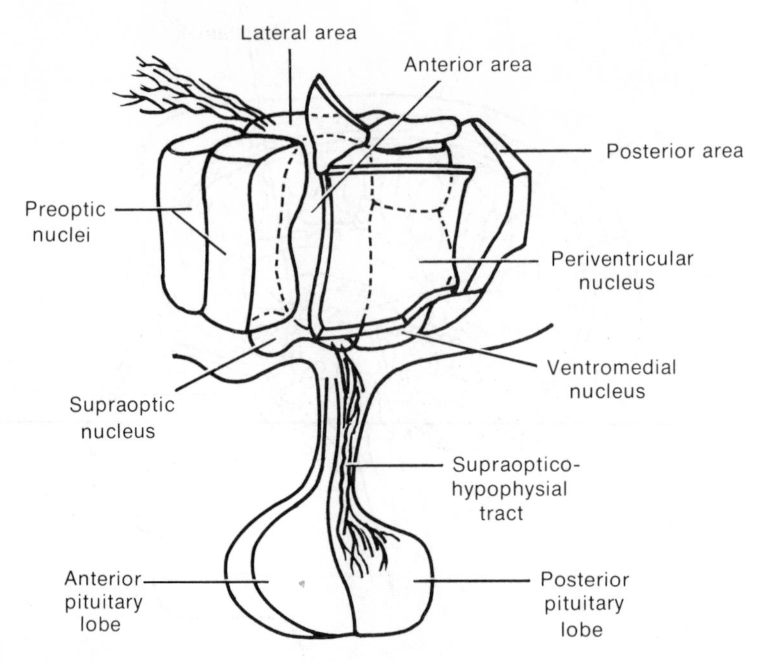

FIGURE 6 Nuclei of the hypothalamus. Reproduced from Hokanson, J. E. *The physiological bases of motivation*. 1969. P. 153, Fig. A.3. By permission of John Wiley & Sons, Inc.

depressant drugs are given intravenously, although such activity in other parts of the hypothalamus declines.

Animals with lesions in the ventromedial nucleus overeat substantially, the rate of eating increasing rapidly at first and then slowing down to a rather steady intake. Weight gains, correspondingly, are rapid at first and then slow down but weight remains high. Body weight may double over 50 or 60 days following the administration of the electrical stimulation used to make the lesion. The weight gain is due to the deposit of large amounts of fat, which, with other changes in the animal's organs, are associated with increased susceptibility to disease causing a shortened life-span (Grossman, 1967, p. 346).

One might think that the hyperphagic animal would be highly motivated for food, i.e., that he would accept almost any foods offered or that he would work instrumentally to obtain it. Such expectations would be predicated on the idea that the ventromedial nucleus contains a "satiety center," damage to which would make the animal driven to obtain and eat food. These expectations are not, however, supported. The hyperphagic animals are "finicky" eaters, eating little, for example, when their food is contaminated with quinine (which has a bitter taste to the human) in amounts that would not affect the eating of a normal rat. On the other hand, the hyperphagic animals respond with augmented eating when dextrose, which tastes sweet to the human, is added to their food (Grossman, 1967, p. 355). These animals will not work at tasks the performance of which leads to food as well as will normal animals, nor will they tolerate as much electric shock as will normal animals in order to reach food. The general interpretation of these behavioral data and the patterns of feeding is that the ventromedial lesions disrupt a mechanism that, when intact, stops the animal from eating after a time once he has started to do so. The mechanism of this control is not known.

Shortly after the discoveries summarized above, other areas of the hypothalamus, the lateral areas, were found to be involved in eating. Bilateral lesions cause animals to stop eating (become aphagic) and to refuse food; they also become adipsic (do not drink water). Unless animals with lesions like this are provided food and water by means, for example, of a stomach tube, they will die. However, recovery does occur after a time if the animals are artificially fed and watered, but it is a slow process. It is not known what the basis for the recovery is (Cofer & Appley, 1964, pp. 217–220).

Electrical stimulation of the lateral hypothalamus induces eating (Delgado & Anand, 1953), and the insertion into it of chemicals in crystalline form has different effects, depending on the chemical. Adrenergic substances (epinephrine and norepinephrine) produce voracious eating in animals that are well satiated for food; cholinergic substances (acetylcholine and carbachol) placed in the same location induce vigorous drinking (Grossman, 1960). There are probably two overlapping areas in the lateral hypothalamus, one related to eating and one related to drinking.

Control of feeding and drinking (see also the next section) clearly involves the lateral hypothalamus and the ventromedial nucleus of this structure, but other portions of the central nervous system are certainly involved. It is likely that there is a neural system, of which the hypothalamus is a part, which regulates eating. Extrahypothalamic structures in the system include the temporal lobe, the amygdala, the hippocampus, the frontal granular cortex, and the thalamus. A full account of the nature and the interactions of this system remains to be developed.

Much interest has been aroused in the question as to how the hypothalamic areas involved in feeding and the cessation of feeding are activated by the nutritional state of the body. The greatest emphasis has been placed on the notion that there are cells in the hypothalamus sensitive to certain features of sugar and fat in the blood. Also proposed is that the hypothalamic areas regulate food intake as a temperature regulating mechanism. We give brief attention to each of these ideas below.

However, peripheral factors cannot be entirely excluded from consideration, despite the evidence concerning the role of stomach contractions and the stomach itself summarized in Chapter 2. For one thing (Grossman, 1967, pp. 324 ff.), motility of the duodenum may underlie pangs of hunger. (The duodenum is that part of the small intestine just beyond the stomach.) Further, the stomach itself contains stretch receptors which could send impulses centrally indicating distension arising from the presence of food in the stomach (Paintal, 1954). Such signals may arise under normal conditions but could not operate when the stomach is removed. There is reason to believe that the ingestion of food leads to the release of chemical or humoral messengers to go elsewhere in the body. For example, a pouch made of gastrointestinal tissue and placed inside the body cavity shows contractions in rhythm with those of the stomach itself. Its contractions are inhibited when food is placed in the small intestine; as the pouch has no neural connections, this effect must be due to nonneural influences (Quigley, 1955, p. 11).

Jean Mayer (1953, 1955) has proposed that there are cells in the hypothalamus sensitive to the rate of utilization of sugar in the blood. The measure of this utilization is the difference in the concentration of sugar in the arterial blood supply in the brain and the concentration of sugar in the veins. Thus, there will be no activation of the cells (and thus no hunger) if the sugar concentration in arterial blood is much higher than that in venous blood, but as the concentrations drop to equality, the cells will be activated and hunger will occur. Mayer proposed this theory as a mechanism in the short-term regulation of food-intake and suggested a similar mechanism for fats in long-term regulation. The evidence for Mayer's gluco-static theory is both supportive and not supportive. (There is little evidence for the lipostatic or fat regulating mechanism.) It remains in contention as a plausible account, perhaps because there is no really adequate competitor, but since some evidence is not in accord with its expectations, it can hardly be wholly satisfactory.

Hunger as a thermoregulatory mechanism is the suggestion of Brobeck (1957). It is known that environmental temperatures influence eating, high temperatures depressing it. However, this effect is temporary. Eating increases body temperature, and Brobeck suggested that this temperature rise would warm the hypothalamic receptors in such a way as to inhibit eating. Cooling would, of course, have the reverse effect.

There is a good deal of evidence that is consistent with this theory, but it is probably not true that, as Brobeck once said, "animals eat to keep warm and stop eating to prevent hyperthermia." When suitable measurements are made, the variations in temperature in appropriate areas of the brain are very small, hardly enough to induce eating or fasting (Grossman, 1967, p. 372). Furthermore, the temperature changes that do occur do not seem to be correlated with intake, deprivation or absence of intake arising from satiety. These data seem to pose great difficulties for the thermoregulatory theory of hunger and eating.

At present, then, there is no fully satisfactory account of how the hypothalamic areas involved in eating and noneating respond to changes in the body's nutritional status. What has been accomplished in the research of perhaps two decades is to identify these areas and to implicate them, along with other central neural structures, in the control of hunger.

Before leaving the topic of hunger, we may comment that the mechanisms of specific hungers have been clarified in recent experiments. In the cases of many deficiencies, such as that for thiamine, the preference for the diet including the needed substance seems to be due to the novelty of the diet, rather than to the fact that it contains nutrients for which the animal has a need. In other cases, however, there may be an innate preference for the specific taste, in the case of sodium, the salty taste (Rosin & Rodgers, 1967).

Thirst

The intake of water is a central part of the complex fluid-balance mechanisms of the body and must, in the first instance, make up for water lost through respiration, perspiration, and excretion of urine. As in the case of food-taking, there are central neural structures which are involved in the occurrence of drinking, and there has been interest in their anatomical location and structure and in the mechanisms by which they are activated in the presence of imbalance of fluid.

The initial observations that pointed to hypothalamic areas as important in the regulation of water balance came from studies of factors involved in the secretion of the antidiuretic hormone (ADH) by the pituitary. When the secretion of this hormone increases, the amount of urine excreted is decreased (and the concentration of wastes in it is increased), whereas inhibition of the secretion of ADH allows excretion of greater amounts of urine in less concentrated form. The important observation, made by Verney (1947), was that control of the secretion of ADH was vested in cells in the hypothalamus; these cells, he thought, were sensitive to variations in the osmotic pressure of the blood in the area where the cells are located.

When injections of hypertonic saline solution were made into an artery serving this area, the secretion of ADH was increased, thus conserving bodily fluid. The saline content of the blood, after the injection, would be greater than that of the cells, and fluid would move from them into the blood, thus restoring the balance of tonicity. But in this process, the cells would become dehydrated, thus decreasing in size, and this change in some way could be the stimulus for increased secretion of ADH. On the other hand, hydration of the cells (which might arise from hypotonicity in the blood arising from water intake) would increase their size, thus causing a decrease in the secretion of ADH.

Bengt Andersson (1953; Andersson & McCann, 1955a) followed up these ideas by injecting hypertonic saline solution into the hypothalamic areas of goats. Many of the animals drank water after this treatment and would perform an instrumental task to drink water, even though they were not thirsty. When the hypothalamic areas were stimulated electrically by means of implanted electrodes (Andersson & McCann, 1955b), the animals also drank.

Comparable findings have been reported for other animals, although the exact anatomical locations involved differ slightly; in the goat the area underlying drinking seems to be separated from that involved in eating but in other species the two areas overlap (refer back to Grossman's findings with chemical stimulation in the lateral hypothalamus mentioned in the last section). Bilateral lesions of the suitable areas of the hypothalamus produce animals that do not drink water: they are adipsic.

The results of these experiments suggest cleary that a hypothalamic area is involved in drinking; it is an excitatory area. No inhibitory center comparable to the one that suppresses eating has been found. Other structures in the brain, lying outside the hypothalamus, are involved in the regulation of drinking so that there may be a complex neural system which underlies thirst.

On the basis of present evidence, it seems likely that cellular dehydration provides the basis for the excitation of the cells in the hypothalamus and elsewhere whose activity instigates drinking. Thermoregulatory processes may also be involved. It has also been suggested that there is another kind of thirst, separate from the osmotically based thirst arising from cellular dehydration. This thirst is due to variations in the volume of the intravascular fluids, a deficiency in which may induce drinking in the absence of cellular dehydration.

The mechanism that leads to the cessation of drinking is not clear. It cannot be cellular dehydration, because drinking stops long before fluid in significant amounts can reenter the cells. Water intake is probably metered in some way by stimulation of the mouth, and there may be some humoral secretion produced in the stomach because of water intake that, in some way, depresses the activity of the neural cells responsible for drinking. Our knowledge of thirst has advanced much beyond the stage at which the dry-mouth theory seemed to make sense, but it is still inadequate to provide a fully satisfactory account of the mechanisms of drinking.

Sexual Motivation

In accounts of sexual behavior, written when early drive theory was dominant, sexual motivation seemed to receive a treatment much like that given hunger and thirst. Local stimulation was thought to underlie sexual motivation and sexual activity to reduce it. It was pointed out in Chapter 2 that sexual motivation persists in the absence of local stimulation.

It has almost always been apparent, however, that sexual motivation differs from motivation based on food or water deprivation (Beach, 1956). In the latter cases, deprivation produces deficits in bodily tissues, and eating and drinking serve to reduce these deficits. In sex, however, there is no deficit (and there seems to be no reason to postulate an excess of some substance which is reduced by sexual activity), and sexual behavior uses up energy rather than restoring it, as eating does. Likewise, eating and drinking are necessary to individual survival, whereas sexual behavior is not. It is, of course, necessary to species survival. Hence, there are good reasons for thinking that sexual motivation differs from hunger and thirst. The same thing can be said for certain other behaviors—parental and migrational activities, for example.

Given intactness of the necessary neural structures, sexual behavior in many species arises because of two factors: an appropriate hormonal condition and external stimulation. Neither is ordinarily sufficient in itself; the presence of both is required (Beach, 1956). However, the degree of hormonal control does vary across species.

Sexual behavior in the male is controlled by hormones called androgens. Among these are testosterone and androsterone, with the former being the major one. Testosterone is secreted in the testes, but this process occurs under the control of the gonadotrophic hormones of the pituitary. Testosterone and other androgenic hormones control the growth of the genitals and the development of secondary sexual characteristics, such as the distribution of bodily hair, voice change, and a number of other features. In the absence of the testes, as, for example, in castration, development is hindered unless hormonal treatment is applied (Grossman, 1967, Chapter 8).

Many species exhibit seasonal or periodic sexual behavior, but this variation is primarily due to the female, as androgen levels in the male do not seem to vary in the normal case. Thus, the male (except in the prepuberal and senescent stages) is always hormonally ready to mate (Beach, 1956). That sexual behavior occurs only seasonally or periodically and that it does not occur constantly in the male are indications that hormonal "readiness" is not a sufficient condition for sexual behavior to occur, although it is a necessary condition.

The effects of castration vary across species and give us an idea of the degree to which the sexual behavior of a given species is under hormonal control. In many lower vertebrates sexual behavior declines as a result of castration; the decline tends to be less rapid in mammals, and in the human sexual behavior has been reported to continue indefinitely after castration in some cases, although the general rule is perhaps a decrease in sexual interest. Castration which occurs prior to puberty, however, tends to eliminate sexual activity, although it has been reported that sexual interest may remain to some degree. The effects of castration, including prepuberal castration, can usually be overcome in most species by means of hormone replacement, and in the normal male injections of hormone prior to the occurrence of puberty can accelerate its occurrence and the onset of sexual behavior. Hormone treatment can revive sexual behavior in aged animals. Hormonal replacement perhaps works best with nonhuman animals. There are, of course, many social and religious factors involved in sexual behavior in the human being (Beach, 1951; Grossman, 1967, Chapter 8; Ford & Beach, 1951).

Stimuli involved in controlling sexual behavior do so at three levels (Beach, 1951). One class controls the development of maturity. An example is temperature. Another class is more specific, for example, a territory. Some male animals do not mate except in their own territories or in situations in which certain environmental features, such as water, are present. Most important, and most widely necessary to male sexual behavior, is the third class. This is the presence of a mate and the stimuli emanating from her or which she provides. Male sexual behavior seems not to occur in the absence of such stimuli; in the human, of course, the stimuli can be symbolic ones. Thus, sexual behavior occurs only in season, in animals that mate seasonally, or in animals in which the female is receptive only during one phase of her estrous cycle, when she is receptive. Otherwise, sexual behavior does not seem to occur.

In many lower animals sexual behavior depends on rather specific stimuli, such as a scent, and elimination of this chemical sense will make sexual behavior unlikely. In higher animals, while stimulation is important and necessary, the stimulation required is not so specific, and sexual behavior can occur in the absence of almost any specific modality and in some higher species in the absence of more than one (Beach, 1951).

In the female, as we have suggested, the sexual behavior in most species, excluding certain primates and man, occurs either seasonally or episodically in conjunction with the estrous cycle. Sexual development is also under the control of hormones, arising in the ovaries. Sexual behavior in species with estrous cycles occurs during the period when the animal is said to be "in heat," and this period corresponds to that part of the ovulatory cycle in which successful fertilization of ova is most likely. This phase is under control of the hormone estrogen, which might be said to be the "sex hormone" in the female. If pregnancy occurs, or if it does not, the further changes which occur in the cycle are not conducive to sexual behavior in many species. However, in the human female and in primates, sexual behavior can occur at any time in the menstrual cycle. Stimulation is important to sexual behavior in the female, as it is in the male.

We see, then, that sexual behavior is an outcome of an interaction of hormonal factors and of stimulation, especially that arising from the partner. In at least some species, sexual behavior in the male can be maintained by replacing partners; apparently, the stimulation afforded by the new partner can rearouse flagging sexual interest (Cofer & Appley, 1964, p. 193). There is little utility in thinking of sexual behavior as the consequence of a "sex drive," modelled either on hunger and thirst or, it would seem, on the hydraulic model used by Freud and used also in early ethological theorizing.

Neural control of sexual behavior is complex, and there is a good deal of variation across species in the structures and mechanisms that influence sexual behavior (Beach, 1951; Grossman, 1967, Chapter 8). Some components of the sexual response are mediated at the level of the spinal cord in certain species, but regulation of sexual behavior seems to be lodged, to a great extent, in the anterior and other areas of the hypothalamus, where lesions, electrical stimulation, and chemical stimulation are found to have effects. Precise locations of regions which mediate sexual behavior vary across species, and the influence of the anterior hypothalamus may be exerted in part through direct control of aspects of sexual behavior and in part indirectly, through its influences on the hormones secreted by the pituitary gland.

Cortical damage has more effect on the sexual behavior of the male than on that of the female, but this difference may arise primarily because sexual behavior in the male is typically more active than it is in the female in which it is more passive, so that cortical damage may affect it more because of sensory and motor deficits than because of changes in sexual motivation per se (Grossman, 1967, Chapter 8). The extent of cortical lesions is important in the male, small lesions having relatively little effect, whereas lesions involving extensive areas of the cortex have great effects.

The role of experience in sexual behavior can be approached from two perspectives. One is that of sexual arousal. The other is that of the pattern in which sexual behavior occurs.

There is substantial evidence in rats of both sexes that experience has little to do with the development of the acts involved in mating behavior. Inexperienced animals perform these acts as well and as efficiently as do experienced animals. The innateness of sexual behavior patterns applies to many species. However, in the primates, including man, effective sexual behavior depends to a large extent on experience. Several detailed accounts of the development of patterns of sexual behavior in chimpanzees, for example, suggest a major role for trial and error in the emergence of copulatory skills in both the male and female. There is little doubt that the role of experience is important to human sexual behavior. The great variety in the conditions, positions, and conventions of sexual behavior, as well as the variation in attitudes toward sexual behavior between and among human societies (cf. Ford & Beach, 1951), attests to the role of learning and social factors in sexual behavior at the human level. It is possible, but still not certain, that some variations in human sexual behavior, such as homosexuality, may have a glandular basis, but experiential factors also, no doubt, have great importance.

In the male rat, there is evidence that experience can contribute to sexual arousal. Beach (1942) found that if sexual satisfaction repeatedly occurred in one cage, the cage itself was capable of inducing arousal on later occasions. In man, of course, all sorts of stimuli, including symbolic stimuli, are capable of instigating sexual arousal, on the basis of learning. The successful advertising of many products depends on this background of experience.

In monkeys, severely defective sexual behavior is known to accompany conditions of rearing in which social deprivation is the major feature. If the female animal is raised without its mother or siblings, and the deprivation occurs for a sufficiently long time, successful sexual behavior is difficult, if not impossible to achieve. Males, also, were badly affected by this sort of rearing experience. It should be noted, however, that the prolonged experience of social deprivation during important developmental periods has effects much more far-reaching than just those on sexual behavior. After this experience, the monkey is abnormal in many ways (Harlow, 1962).

Pain

It is obvious that noxious stimuli produce withdrawal and avoidance. Stimuli like electric shock, foul odors, loud and irritating noises, bright light, for example, often have these effects. In some of these cases, it is the sheer intensity of the stimulation, with or without pain, that is significant, but in others, electric shock, for example, it is that the stimulation is painful. Painful stimulation has long had a role in accounts of motivation, from concern with the effects of punishment and the nature of fear to the idea, seemingly held by Cannon, that the force of the basic drives arose from the goading, tormenting local stimuli they produced.

Many of the topics mentioned in the preceding paragraph receive discussion elsewhere in this book. Here we mention some of the physiological aspects of pain. Melzack and Wall (1965) have presented a "gate control" theory of pain (see Figure 7), which is an effort to take account of some of the known anatomical and physiological factors in pain and, at the same time, recognize that the notion that there are specific pain receptors in the body is not well supported and is also inadequate to account for many pain phenomena. They suggest that stimulation of the skin leads to nerve impulses which go 1) to the substantia gelatinosa (SG), a group of small, densely packed cells running through the length of the dorsal spinal cord; 2) fibers in the dorsal part of the cord which project to the brain; and 3) central transmission cells (T). They propose that the substantia gelatinosa acts "as a gate control system that modulates the afferent patterns before they influence the T cells" (Melzack & Wall, 1965, p. 974).

The letters L and S on the input side of the figure refer to large diameter and small diameter nerve fibers, respectively. There is evidence that T cells are activated by initial impulse volleys in L fibers but that with time the effects of these volleys are reduced. The impulses from S fibers, however, exaggerate the effect of impulses which come in. These decrements and augmentations occur in SG, the "gate," which is also influenced by ". . . brain activities, such as attention and memories of prior experience" (Melzack, 1967, p. 66). The output of the T system to the Action System is thus influenced by what happens at the gate, including the relative roles of the impulses transmitted along the L and S fibers

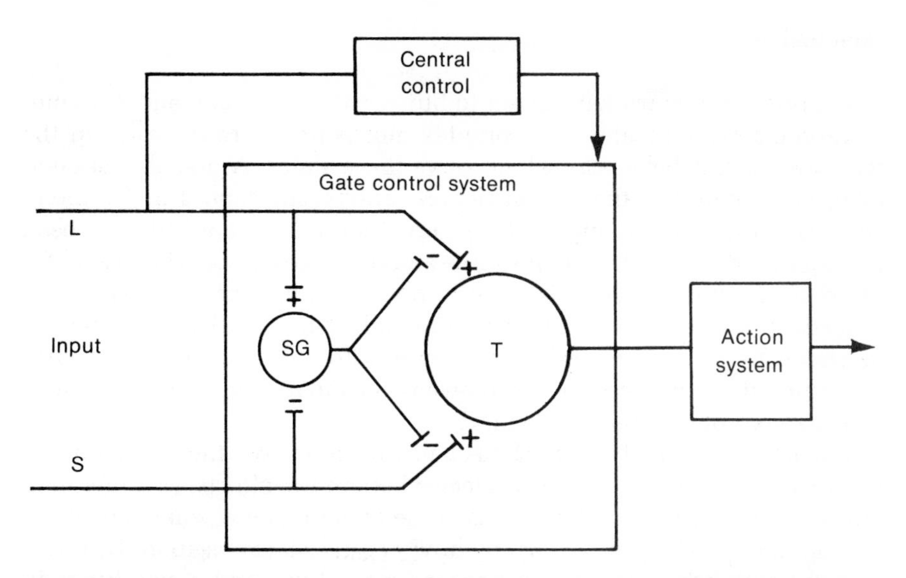

FIGURE 7 Diagram of the gate-control theory of pain. L refers to large-diameter fibers, S to small-diameter fibers, SG to the substania gelatinosa, and T to the first central transmission cells. The + and − signs refer to excitation and inhibition, respectively. From Melzack, R. and Wall, P. D. Pain mechanisms: A new theory. *Science*, Vol. 150, 971–979. P. 975, Fig. 4. November 19, 1965. © 1965 by the American Association for the Advancement of Science.

and by the impulses coming down from the central control system. The Action System will come into play "when the output of the T system reaches or exceeds a critical level" (Melzack, 1967, p. 67). This theory, employing the concept of the gate, is a way of accounting for the fact that experiences of pain are not in a one-to-one relationship to the intensity of external stimulation (i.e., weak stimuli can sometimes be painful, whereas very strong stimuli are sometimes not painful) and do not seem to be dependent on specific pain receptors but can occur in any sense modality.

The Action System is involved in two major processes: (1) the perception of pain in its various aspects, such as its location, magnitude, and the like and (2) the affective and motivational concomitants of pain. Because the output to the Action System is influenced by so many factors, we may expect the effects of "painful" stimulation to vary widely among people and in a given person, depending on his evaluation of the situation and his past experience with similar situations.

Considerable evidence supports this formulation, although, of course, it is tentative and many details remain to be specified. The evaluative and emotional reactions to the aversive stimulation are the ones of importance to motivation. Melzack's account helps us to understand why pain can sometimes be tolerated, whereas at other times severe reactions occur, even when the stimulation is not intense.

Conclusion

The brief review we have given to hunger, thirst, sexual, and pain motivation clearly indicates that complex mechanisms are involved in the regulation of the behaviors which serve these states. A notable deficiency in our account of the role of neural centers, substances in the blood such as hormones and sugar, and external stimuli is that little has been said about how these factors instigate and direct behavior. The reason for this deficiency is that little is known concerning how behavior is actually instigated and directed. In most, if not all, of the studies of the central mechanisms in hunger and thirst, for example, the animal's behavior was studied in the presence of relevant incentives, and he was free to consume or not to consume them.

It is not clear how the central mechanisms potentiate the consummatory processes, and it is even less clear what are the effects, say, of stimulating the eating and drinking areas of the hypothalamus when incentives are not present. The full story of how central states regulate behavior cannot be plotted without further work carried out under conditions in which incentives are not present. It is not possible for eating and drinking, anymore than it is for mating behavior, to occur in the absence of incentives. We do not know whether activation of eating and drinking centers will lead to behavior seemingly intended to locate appropriate objects for consumption; but it is at least possible that the presence of incentives will be found to be necessary for behavior relevant to the deprivation condition to appear.

The reader may wonder why we have concentrated on hunger, thirst, sex, and pain in this discussion, rather than on other states like parental behavior, nest-building, and migration. It is an interesting fact that hunger and thirst, especially, have been the conditions of choice which have been used in the psychological laboratory. This is perhaps because they are easily manipulated by the operation of deprivation, whereas maternal behavior, for example, seems to depend largely on the presence of young and on the prior occurrence of pregnancy and parturition in the animals usually employed in the laboratory. Further, much of the work involving deprivation of food and water was carried out to study the importance of motivational conditions on learning and on the performance of what is learned. It was probably the belief of investigators that hunger and thirst were representative of all motivational conditions and that, therefore, findings obtained with them would form the basis for general motivational theory. Since they are easy to work with, it made sense for them to be employed, rather than the other states mentioned.

The limitations that have been found in drive theory and the complex of factors now known to underlie hunger and thirst have, in a sense, liberated investigators to explore not only the mechanisms of hunger and thirst but also those of sexual and parental behavior. In addition, the influence of the ethologists has brought back to respectability the concept of innate behavior patterns and set the problem of how they are controlled. Such interests have changed the orientation of those interested in the biological bases of motivation. Rather than being concerned with the notion of general drive mechanisms, they now recognize that the study of each motivated behavior is worthwhile in its own right and that the complex network of regulatory processes involved in one case may be very different from the network pertinent to another.

It is the author's conjecture that the future study of motivation will see detailed accounts of the mechanisms underlying specific consummatory behaviors and that, for them, the notion of motivation will turn out not to be very useful.There are other areas in which, it seems now, more general information concerning motivation may be obtained, and they are discussed in the next four chapters.

SUGGESTED READINGS

Beach, F. A. (Ed.) *Sex and behavior.* New York: John Wiley & Sons, Inc., 1965.

Cofer, C. N. & Appley, M. H. *Motivation: Theory and research.* New York: John Wiley & Sons, Inc., 1964. Chapters 4 and 5.

Ford, C. S. & Beach, F. A. *Patterns of sexual behavior.* New York: Harper & Row, Publishers, 1951.

Grossman, S. P. *A textbook of physiological psychology.* New York: John Wiley & Sons, Inc., 1967. Chapters 6, 7, and 8.

Hinde, R. A. *Animal behavior: A synthesis of ethology and comparative psychology.* (2nd ed.) New York: McGraw-Hill Book Company, 1970.

Wolf, A. V. *Thirst: Physiology of the urge to drink and problems of water lack.* Springfield, Ill.: Charles C. Thomas, Publisher, 1958.

4

Emotion

Emotions are often linked with motivation, as they are in this book. The logic for this linkage is not entirely clear, but we can suggest a number of possible reasons, all involving the relation of emotional states to behavior. Fear, grief, anger, joy, elation, love, for example, may, when they are present, dominate our perceptions of the world and impart a special character to our behavior. In grief, for example, we appear to be sad, and our behavior may include weeping, loss of interest in many aspects of the world around us, slowed and diminished reactions to things and people to which normally we are reactive. We say that we are depressed. An emotion like grief, then, is associated with major changes in the way we act and in the way we say we feel. The emotional reaction may arise in connection with an external event, but it persists and involves internal aspects to which we refer when we describe our feelings.

These changes in behavior are not unlike those said to be associated with motivated states, although there are, of course, differences. Furthermore, both emotion and motivation seem to manifest an irrational character—one can "lose control of himself" in an emotional state, just as a strong motive may be said to offer the individual no choice concerning what he does. Many motives may have an emotional component, as would be the case if we say that the motive of aggression arises from anger or hostility or that the sexual motive contains the elements of love. Emotions, too, sometimes seem to be like motives, as would be the case when we say that the joy of accomplishment underlies someone's achievement. Motive and emotion, then, have relationships.

Emotion differs from motivation, however, in two ways. We say that someone looks angry, afraid, or as if he is in love. It is not common to say that one looks hungry or thirsty. Evidently, emotions receive expression in our faces, postures, and other movements. We say that we feel angry, sad, or joyous. We usually say "I am hungry" or "I am thirsty," not that we feel hungry or thirsty. The latter expressions probably do occur but seem, at least to this writer, less natural than the statements concerning emotions. We can say, in summary, that emotions are known by their overt manifestations and by statements of how we feel. Neither kind of evidence is especially pertinent to motives.

In what we have said so far in this chapter, we have characterized the states to which we apply the word *emotion*, but we have not defined this word. There does not seem to be a satisfactory way to define emotion, aside from its manifestations in act or verbal statement of feeling. Sometimes emotions have been defined as "stirred-up" states which disrupt behavior, but this definition seems too narrow. Sometimes the transitoriness of emotional states is emphasized in the definition, but it is also possible to talk about chronic emotional states.

If it is difficult to define emotion, why do we continue to use the term? The answer to the question seems to be that, uncertain as the referent for the term is, it nevertheless serves as a useful category of behavior and experience, one that we hesitate to try to eliminate from our vocabulary. It is probably the better part of wisdom to avoid disputes about terminology and to proceed to a discussion of what we know concerning the processes related to the broad category of events to which we apply the word.

Some psychologists, it may be noted, have attempted to discard the word emotion (e.g., Duffy, 1941, 1948). In its place they have substituted a dimension of activation which varies from little activation to a great deal (Duffy, 1962). The continuum of activation, they say, subsumes much of what we mean by emotion and what is left over is situationally determined anyway and therefore not a constant characteristic of the states we call emotional. We shall have more to say about this interpretation later in the chapter. Activation theorists have some important and interesting things to say, but their attempts to displace emotion from the psychological vocabulary have not been successful. Emotion continues to be used, as a "chapter-heading term," to use George Mandler's (1962) phrase, which collects together in one place phenomena, observations, and investigations which seem to be related to one another. In some sense, motivation is a chapter-heading term too, and the inclusion of both motivation and emotion in the same book serves to suggest that the diverse phenomena designated by both terms are thought to be interrelated in some way.

EARLY THEORIES

When we experience an emotion, we are often aware of sensations and feelings in various parts of the body. Thus, we may sense perspiration, contractions of the stomach and other viscera, tension in the skeletal musculature, and we may "shake" with emotion. The common sense interpretation of these changes is that they are caused by or accompany the emotion but that the emotion itself is something else. In 1884, William James suggested that the physiological changes are the basis for the emotional experience—that we are afraid because we run, we are sad because we cry. The perception of the bodily changes is the emotion, as James viewed the situation. A Danish investigator named Carl Lange came to somewhat similar conclusions at about the same time, although he emphasized vascular changes, and this view of emotions is now referred to as the James–Lange theory (see Figure 8).

An alternative view was espoused by Walter B. Cannon (1929), who offered a number of objections to the James–Lange theory. Cannon had a number of points to make against the view of James: emotional experience continues unchanged even though awareness of bodily changes is much diminished if not eliminated; the bodily events do not seem to differ from one emotion to another, despite the fact that we usually know what emotion we are experiencing; visceral activities are not sensed very accurately, and the viscera themselves are not well supplied with nerves; it takes time for visceral changes to occur, yet our experience of emotion is often swift; when changes in the viscera are induced, as by the injection of adrenaline, the resulting experience is not a true emotion: people will say, for example, "I feel as if I am afraid," but they are aware that they are not.

Cannon's objections to the James–Lange theory are not all well taken, but he felt that an alternative theory was necessary. He made essentially two suggestions. One is functional; the other concerns itself with the nature of emotion. As to the first, Cannon (1939) proposed that the sympathetic branch of the autonomic nervous system could discharge as a unit when on the occasion of some threat it was necessary for the body to prepare for vigorous muscular activity. This is his "emergency theory" of emotions, and the effect of sympathetic arousal was to release sugar, augment respiration, and shift the blood distribution from the viscera to the heart, brain, and skeletal musculature. The parasympathetic division of the autonomic nervous system, which tends to conserve bodily resources, was said to be inhibited under the conditions of threat. The emergency theory encounters difficulties, but, of course, it was not central to the theory of the nature of emotions.

Cannon's theory of emotion (see Figure 8) was proposed in 1927 (see also, Cannon, 1929) and extended in 1934 by Bard and is often referred to as the Cannon–Bard theory. Basically, it holds that impulses travel along sensory nerves to the cortex. There, if they are of an emotion-provoking nature, they can stimulate the cortex to release the thalamus from the inhibition in which it is normally held by the cortex. The thalamus can then discharge both to the cortex to produce an emotional experience and also, of course, to the viscera to produce emotional behavior. The thalamic inhibition can also be overcome by impulses set in motion

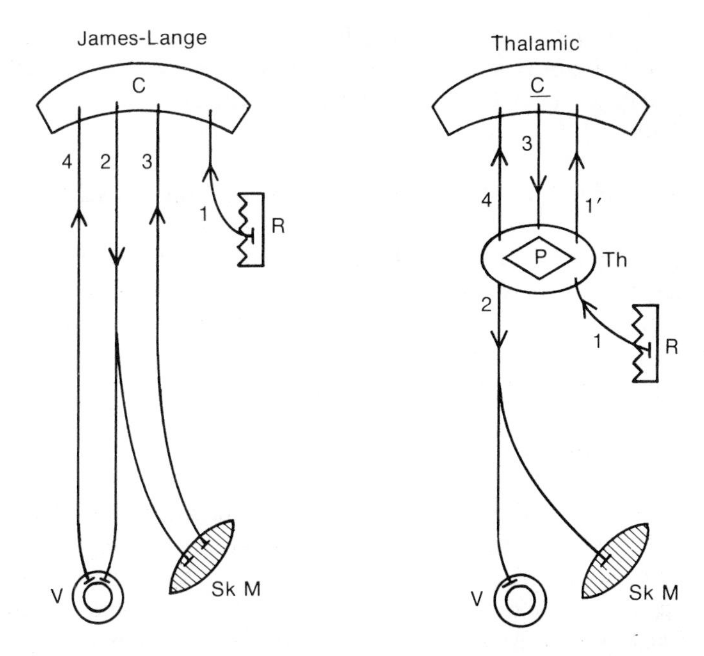

FIGURE 8 Diagrammatic representations of the James–Lange and thalamic theories of emotion. R refers to receptor, C to the cerebral cortex, V to viscus, SKM to skeletal muscle, Th to the thalamus, and P to pattern. The lines represent nerve pathways, with the arrows indicating direction of impulses. The line on the right in the diagram for the thalamic theory is inhibitory in function. Taken from Lindsley, D. B. Emotion. In S. S. Stevens (Ed.), *Handbook of experimental psychology.* New York: John Wiley & Sons, Inc., 1951. Pp. 473–516. P. 502, Fig. 8. Originally from Cannon, 1931.

by very strong stimuli, which reach the thalamus directly. In this case, then, the thalamus discharges to the cortex and to the viscera.

There are objections which can be raised to the Cannon–Bard theory, but it, like the James–Lange theory, has stimulated a great deal of investigation, some of which we review in this chapter. Another point of view has now emerged in the field of emotion which bids fair to replace these older theories, as we shall see. There are other, later theories which have interest but will not be reviewed here because their impact has not been as great as that arising from the views we consider.

Another theoretical issue which received attention early was the question whether emotions are innate. McDougall, it will be recalled, spoke of innate emotions, each one in association with an instinct. But in 1920 Watson and Rayner reported observations that suggested to them that only three emotional patterns—fear, rage, and love—are innate and that each one can be innately elicited by only a few stimuli—fear, for example, only by loud noises and loss of support. They looked to learning as the means by which other emotional patterns were developed and as the process by which other stimuli, in the case of the emotional stimuli, could come to elicit them. Learning is still regarded as important to the development of emotions and the stimuli that evoke them, but unlearned components now seem to have greater significance than was given to them by Watson.

PHYSIOLOGICAL PATTERNS AND NEURAL MECHANISMS

The James–Lange theory in pointing to visceral changes as the "stuff" of emotion required that different emotions be associated with different physiological response patterns. The Cannon–Bard theory pointed to thalamic activity as central to emotions. Both ideas have led to a great deal of investigation to which we now turn.

Physiological Patterns

Of Cannon's five points against the James–Lange theory, three seem most disabling, and we discuss two of them here, reserving to a later section analysis of the third point. Cannon's first argument was based on the observations made on a woman whose neck was broken in a fall from a horse (Dana, 1921). As a result of her injuries, she was paralyzed and received no skin or visceral sensations from the neck down. Thus, she had no awareness of visceral changes. Yet, in the year she lived following the accident, she reported normal emotions of grief, joy, displeasure, and affection. Patients who have experienced sympathectomies still report emotional reactions. Such evidence appears to invalidate the James–Lange theory.

However, this evidence comes from people who have, before their accident or surgery, been normal, and it is possible that prior learning has in some way maintained their experience of emotion in the absence of full and appropriate visceral sensory feedback. Some support, though indirect, for this interpretation comes from experiments with animals in the avoidance learning situation. If the sympathetic nervous system has been rendered nonfunctional by surgery, avoidance is difficult if not impossible to learn (Wynne & Solomon, 1955). The sympathectomy, however, does not interfere with the maintenance of avoidance behavior if it was learned prior to the operation.

Another point of Cannon's is that the qualitatively different emotions cannot be differentiated from one another on the basis of visceral reactions. A substantial amount of effort has been devoted to the attempt to discover patterns of such reactions which are unique to each of several emotions. The kinds of reactions studied include electrical responses of the skin, activity of the heart and vascular system, breathing, muscular tension, metabolic rate, pupillary dilatation, and the like. There has been little success in finding either in responses or in patterns of responses distinctive differences between emotional states. There have been reports that anger and fear show different, but subtly different, physiological patterns, but beyond this distinction nothing can be said in support of the James–Lange theory (Grossman, 1967, pp. 502–515). One reason for the failure to find general patterns shared by individuals is that people differ in their reactions to stress (Lacey, 1950). For example, one person may react mainly through the reactions of his heart, whereas another responds in terms of activity in his stomach. It is also the case that the stimulus situation may control, at least to some extent, the pattern of physiological response.

A number of investigators still hold the expectation, however, that physiological patterns which differentiate the emotions may be found. The question, then, is not settled. However, an interpretation of emotion, based on nondifferential physiological patterns, has been made and will be presented in a later section.

Neural Mechanisms

The Cannon–Bard theory, of course, pointed to the importance of central nervous system factors, especially the thalamus, in emotion. A great deal of effort (see Grossman, 1967, pp. 518–550, who is followed in the ensuing account) has been expended in the effort to unravel the contribution of various neural structures to emotion, and the results, on the whole, reveal a very complex situation which is not at all clear. One point is, however, fairly certain. It is that the thalamus, which Cannon emphasized, is not essential to emotion. Another certain point is that the influence of the cerebral cortex is or may be excitatory, in addition to being, as Cannon thought, inhibitory in emotion.

In spinal animals and in those in which the medulla oblongata also remains, some responses mediated by the autonomic nervous system can be elicited and can be referred to as "emotional." However, the decerebrate animal, in which many more neural centers are spared, manifests an emotional response referred to as rage. It is called rage because that is what it resembles, but the patterns of attack which are involved are not well coordinated or well directed. Stimuli elicit the reaction, but the response is brief. It must be remembered that we speak here of a manifest behavior pattern which looks something like the expression of rage. With animals, of course, there is no way to determine whether there is also an experience of the emotion.

Decorticate animals also exhibit "rage" reactions, even to innocuous stimuli. The term *sham-rage* has been applied to this behavior, but it is rather like rage in the normal animal save that it is poorly directed with respect to the eliciting stimulus. It seems likely that these responses are mediated by hypothalamic structures, and direct electrical stimulation of portions of the hypothalamus evokes rage reactions with attack and also defensive and flight reactions. It appears that the hypothalamus is more important to emotion than the thalamus.

Hypothalamic structures are certainly involved in emotion, but in general it seems to be the case that higher levels of the brain are also involved in the regulation of emotional behavior (and it is suggested by some that the "experience" of emotion occurs there, too). No entirely satisfactory account can, however, be given at present concerning the cortex and emotion. Stimulation of and lesions in various cortical areas and structures have diverse effects on emotional behavior, in some cases augmenting it and in others diminishing it. Obviously, cortical involvement in emotional behavior is too complex to be understood in terms of our present limited information.

ACTIVATION OR AROUSAL THEORY

As we admitted early in this chapter, there is no satisfactory definition of emotion. For years, writers have argued that the word is useless without a definition and have asserted that it should be replaced. It is usually agreed that when we use the word emotion we often wish to designate the fact that someone is aroused in some degree. And it has been suggested by Elizabeth Duffy (1962), Harold Schlosberg (1954), Donald Hebb (1955), Robert Malmo (1959), and Donald Lindsley (1951) that level of arousal (or activation) provides the framework in which emotional phenomena can be discussed without invoking the word *emotion* at all or to any extent.

Something of what arousal means can be understood by referring back to the discussion of physiological patterns. We said there that little success has attended efforts to find patterns characteristic of the several emotions, but implicitly we indicated that there are physiological changes which occur when we say we are having an emotion. Thus, there are changes in breathing, heart rate, blood pressure, muscle tension, electrical conductivity of the skin, and so on, and these changes are indicative of what is meant by an aroused or activated state.

The clearest expression of activation theory, however, is the account of it given by Lindsley (1951) in conjunction with the electroencephalogram (EEG). The EEG is a record of the electrical activity of the brain. It is obtained by attaching electrodes to the scalp, amplifying the potentials, and making a record of them. The record shows an irregular line consisting of oscillations or waves. The waves can vary in frequency as well as in amplitude or size.

A characteristic wave pattern or rhythm is the alpha rhythm. The frequency of this rhythm is from 10 to 14 waves per second, and the waves are of moderate amplitude. There is a fast rhythm of low amplitude, and there are several other rates and amplitudes found in EEGs under given conditions.

The alpha rhythm is obtained, typically, from a person who is lying down with his eyes closed. He is awake but mentally relaxed and subject to little external stimulation. The fast rhythm appears when the subject tries to solve a problem in his head or when he is subjected to stimulation as with a light or a sound. Emotional states are also associated with the fast low-amplitude rhythm. The slower rhythms of large amplitude begin to appear as the person drifts into drowsiness and then into deep sleep. Lindsley pointed out that there are these various EEG patterns and that they parallel degrees of arousal (see Figure 9).

From this point of view then, emotion is an aroused state, as indicated by the fast rhythm in the EEG and by other physiological measures like those mentioned earlier. The different emotions cannot be distinguished on the basis of the EEG any more successfully than they can be distinguished by means of the other physiological patterns. The activation theorists, like Duffy (1941, 1948), who were concerned about this, appealed to the person's knowledge of the situation in which he experienced arousal as the basis for his experiencing one emotion rather than another. We shall have more to say on this point in a moment.

It is clear that in highly emotional states, such, say, as mania, our behavior is not very effective or well organized. Likewise, when we are relaxed, drowsy, or asleep, there are few things that we can do well. Thus, the activation theorists suggested (see Schlosberg, 1954; Hebb, 1955) that there is a level of arousal which is optimal in terms of behavioral efficiency and that level is an intermediate one, lying between the extremes of drowsiness and excitement. When plotted on graph paper, the curve for this relationship is an inverted U. Furthermore, they proposed, the optimal level would be more pleasant, more desirable than the levels on either side of it. Hence, we should seek and be rewarded by increases in arousal level when our current level is low but seek and be rewarded by a decrease in arousal level when the current level is above the optimum.

Activation theory, then, is a way of thinking about emotions, and in the next section of the chapter, we will discuss the situational factors which determine what emotion we feel that we are experiencing. It is also an approach to defining conditions which govern reward, a matter which will concern us in the next chapter and in Chapter 7. Activation theory also proposes some conditions for effective performance; it is also tied in with a view of the nervous system. We discuss these two points here, the second one first.

In 1949 Moruzzi and Magoun discovered that electrical stimulation of the reticular formation of the brain stem produces a change in the EEG from a relaxed or drowsy pattern to the fast rhythm of alert attention. Lesions in this structure produced the opposite change, i.e., converted the fast pattern to slow waves and, with the most extreme lesions, a pattern characteristic of sleep (Lindsley, Bowden, & Magoun, 1949). The reticular formation is a network of neurones which is found in the brain stem and which extends from the medulla to the thalamus (see Figure 10). It sends nerve impulses upward to the cortex and down to the musculature and autonomic nervous system, and it receives impulses from the major sensory nerves (via collaterals) and from the cortex. The importance of this structure in activation theory is in its diffuse stimula-

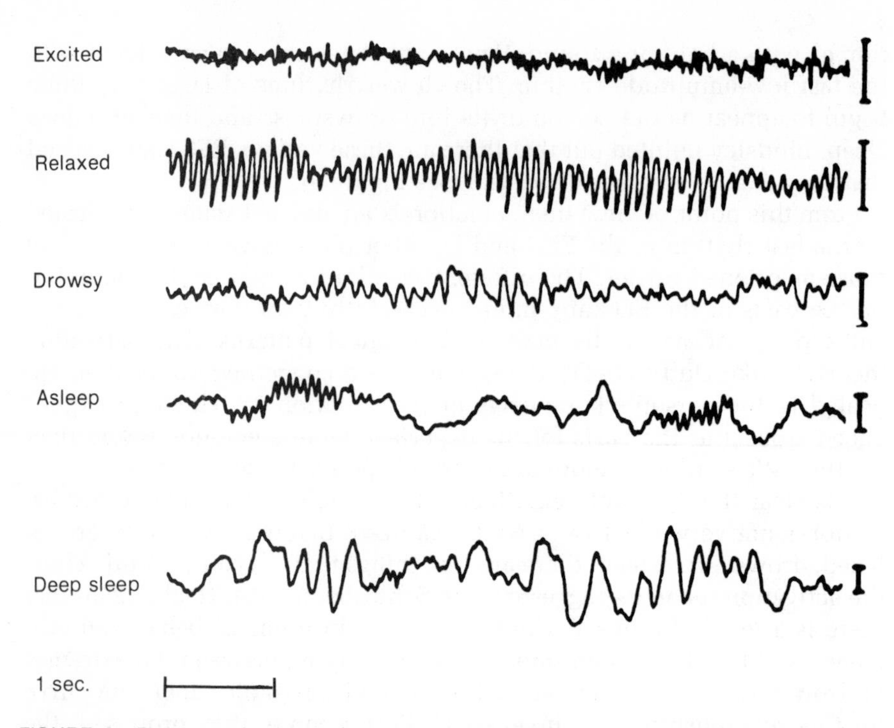

FIGURE 9 Patterns of normal EEG, from deep sleep to wakefulness to excitement. From Lindsley, D. B. Psychophysiology and motivation. In M. R. Jones (Ed.), *Nebraska symposium on motivation 1957*. P. 67, Fig. 5. By permission of University of Nebraska Press.

tion of the cortex, i.e., impulses from it are believed to stimulate or arouse the cortex. Furthermore, and most importantly, effective cortical function is thought possible only in an aroused condition produced by reticular activation. This set of notions gave a neural underpinning to the arousal theorists' idea of the relation of arousal level to behavior efficiency.

Knowledge which has accumulated in the decades since the discovery by Moruzzi and Magoun has indicated that the reticular formation is more complex than it had been thought to be and that it is not the only means by which the cortex can be activated (Grossman, 1967, Chapter 5). Nevertheless, the theory had and still is having considerable impact on a number of motivational problems, as later chapters will show.

There is evidence that behavioral efficiency does vary with arousal level as activation theory predicts, although there are also problems. Thus, Freeman (1940) found the expected inverted U-shaped relationship between skin conductance, a measure of arousal, and reaction times, a measure of efficiency. Stennett (1957) had his subjects perform a tracking task under several degrees of arousal, induced by instructions. Better performance was obtained with intermediate than with extreme levels of arousal. In several experiments with animals, investigators (Bé-

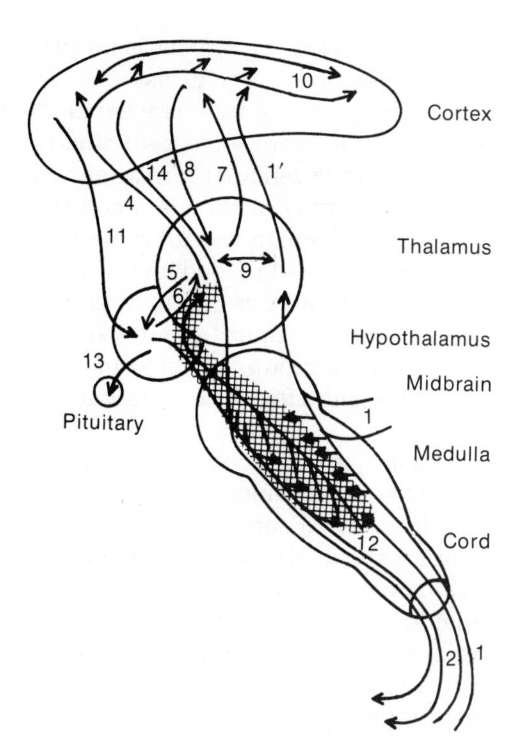

FIGURE 10 Location of the reticular formation. The crosshatched section is the reticular formation. The numbered lines refer to various pathways and interconnections. Reproduced from Lindsley, D. B. Emotion. In S. S. Stevens (Ed.), *Handbook of experimental psychology*. 1951. P. 507, Fig. 9. By permission of John Wiley & Sons, Inc.

langer & Feldman, 1962; Dufresne, 1961) have measured arousal by means of heart rate and efficiency by means of bar-pressing and have taken both of these measures under varying deprivation conditions (food or water) and degrees of electric shock (Ducharme & Bélanger, 1961). Heart rate increases with deprivation and with shock, thus showing increasing arousal. However, bar-pressing rises up to an intermediate degree of arousal and then drops off. Fuster (1958) had monkeys learn a discrimination between pairs of objects. Then the monkeys were tested on the discrimination with the objects being illuminated only very briefly. During some of the tests, the reticular formation was stimulated by means of implanted electrodes, and correct choices and speed of reaction were improved under this stimulation as compared to control tests without stimulation.

These results offer substantial support for the expectations of activation theory, but as already mentioned there are problems (see Lacey, 1967; Malmo & Bélanger, 1967). One problem is that the various measures used to index arousal do not agree with one another very well. Clearly, they are not just alternative ways of measuring the same arousal state, but at present there is no satisfactory basis for preferring one rather than another. It has also been possible to disassociate activation and performance. For example, in one study lesions were made in the posterior hypothalamus; many of the cats were somnolent after this treatment, and they remained so even when the reticular formation was stimulated (and the record of the electrical activity of the brain consisted of fast waves). In another experiment, meprobamate was given to one of two groups of animals; both groups were deprived of food and their heart rates and bar-presses were recorded. Heart rate increased in both groups with deprivation, and the bar-pressing in the control group varied with deprivation. However, in the meprobamate group, bar-pressing was constant across deprivation intervals, thus showing disassociation from arousal as indexed by heart rate.

The simple neural basis for activation theory and the predicted relation between arousal and performance are only partially supported by recent developments. In the next section, we discuss the way activation theory would account for the qualitatively different emotions.

Before going on to the next section, however, we may mention briefly the fact that norepinephrine, a substance similar to epinephrine or adrenalin, is found in the brain. There is reason to believe that this substance is involved in affective reactions of a generalized kind. Thus, as Schildkraut and Kety (1967, p. 28) have put it,

> Those drugs which cause depletion of norepinephrine centrally produce sedation or depression, while drugs which increase or potentiate brain norepinephrine are associated with behavioral stimulation or excitement and generally have an antidepressant effect in man.

Kety (1967a, p. 107; see also 1967b) has pointed out that these effects of norepinephrine (or other amines) are general, i.e., they are not associated with specific emotional states. He cites the work of Schachter, which we review in the next section, as pointing out the importance in producing particular emotions of cognitive factors in association with interactions among amines at given sites in the brain.

SITUATIONAL DETERMINANTS OF EMOTION

One of Cannon's objections to the James–Lange theory was that the artificial induction of physiological arousal, as by an injection of adrenaline, does not produce a true emotion in most people. Following such injections people report "as if" states, i.e., they say they feel as if afraid or as if a great happiness were about to occur. Stanley Schachter (Schachter & Singer, 1962; Schachter, 1964) has performed a number of experiments using such injections, but he has also contrived the situation in such a way as to permit the subject to interpret his state of arousal as an emotion. Under these conditions, the subjects seem to experience emotions and to act emotionally. Schachter suggests, then, that for an emotion to occur there must be a state of arousal *and* a way of interpreting the state in emotional terms. The interpretation comes from the situation. This formulation does not require, of course, that there be distinctive patterns of arousal for qualitatively different emotions: the same or a similar arousal state will be interpreted as one or the other emotion, depending upon the situation.

In one of Schachter's experiments (with Singer), subjects were told that their vision was to be tested to determine the effects of a vitamin supplement called Suproxin. The subjects, with their consent, were injected with Suproxin and were asked to wait with another subject for 20 minutes for the drug to enter the bloodstream. Their vision was to be tested after the waiting period.

In fact, some subjects were injected with adrenaline whereas others received a placebo, an injection of saline solution. Further, the subjects receiving adrenaline were divided into the following three subgroups. One was told what symptoms they would experience as side effects from the Suproxin; these were the actual effects usually produced by adrenaline. This group is the informed group. A second group was told nothing about the effects of the injection; this group is the ignorant group. The third subgroup was misinformed about the effects of the injection, the misinformed group. It was said that they might have a mild headache, feel their feet becoming numb, and experience itching. None of these effects is produced by adrenaline which typically produces tremor, pounding of the heart, and warmth in the face.

The informed group, of course, had an adequate explanation of the symptoms they would experience, whereas the ignorant group had none, and the misinformed would actually experience symptoms different from those they would have. The latter two groups then would have a problem of interpreting their reactions. Schachter contrived social situations which would allow these two groups to give an emotional interpretation.

One set of groups was asked to wait under conditions designed to evoke euphoria or good feeling. The person with whom the subject was to wait for 20 minutes was actually a stooge of the experimenter's. In the euphoria condition, the stooge said he felt good and performed various high-spirited acts, such as shooting baskets with wads of paper and sailing paper airplanes which he made. For another set of groups, the stooge acted angrily, his anger being induced, presumably, by the requirement that he and the subject complete a highly personal questionnaire (there was no misinformed group in the anger condition). Following the 20-minute interval, the subject was asked, on a pretext, to fill out some rating scales, including ratings of his mood. In addition, he had been observed through a one-way mirror during the waiting period to assess the extent to which he had joined the stooge in expressing either euphoria or anger.

In general, the result (see Figure 11) supported the expectations. The informed group showed little shift to a mood like that of the stooge and no tendency to act like him, whereas the ignorant and misinformed groups did so. Although the overall results with the placebo group were not as different from those for the ignorant and misinformed groups as had been anticipated, various other analyses of the data, involving elimination of subjects from the ignorant and misinformed groups who had attributed their reactions to the injection, show more reaction in the ignorant and misinformed groups than in the placebo group.

In another experiment with Suproxin, subjects were asked to watch an excerpt from a slapstick comedy, and their reactions to the humor were observed and evaluated. In this case, there were three groups, one receiving the placebo, one adrenaline, and one chlorpromazine, a drug which depresses activity in the sympathetic nervous system. The results again supported expectations. That is, there was more reaction to the humor in the adrenaline-injected subjects than in the placebo subjects, who in turn reacted more than the subjects given chlorpromazine. Here the same external situation induced different emotional reactions in people whose state of physiological arousal varied.

Schachter's experiments indicate a strong, critical role for our interpretations of why we are aroused in determining what emotion we report that we have. Thus, emotion is a joint product of physiological arousal and a cognitive evaluation of the situation in which the arousal takes place. This formulation does not exactly support the James–Lange theory but does not reject it either. Although the arousal does not have to be different for qualitatively distinct emotions, nevertheless emotion is an interpretation of physiological reactions. Had James emphasized situational determinants more than he did, his theory would fit Schachter's findings fairly well. On the other hand, it does place stress on physiological reactions. It avoids some of Cannon's criticisms because the arousal can be the same for different emotions, great sensitivity of the viscera is not required, and induced arousal is interpreted as an emotion given the situation in which it occurs. The presence of emotions without visceral components, as in the accident case mentioned earlier and in sympathectomized patients, may be explicable in terms of prior learning in these cases, a point made in conjunction with the findings on avoidance learning in animals sympathectomized before or after the learning of the avoidance problem. The short latencies of the emotional experience in contrast to the longer latencies of visceral reactions constitute a problem for Schachter's formulation which again may be resolved by appealing to prior learning. We have learned to describe certain situations as emotional ones and can do so quickly. It is, of course, a common report that

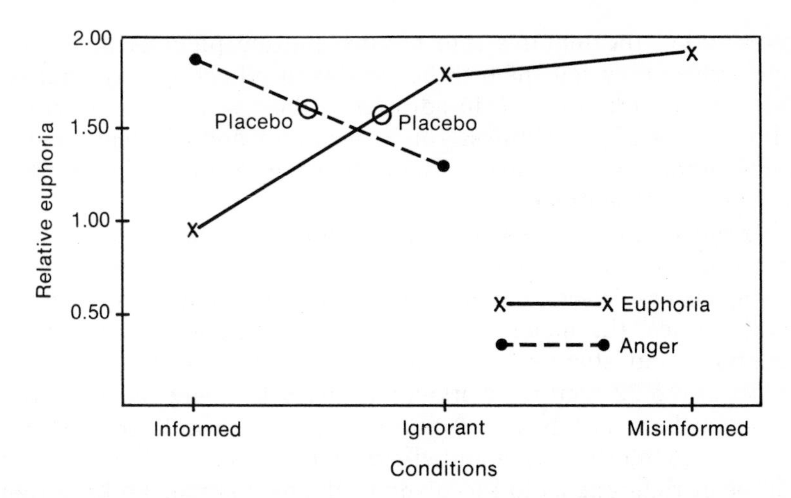

FIGURE 11 Plot of the findings from Schachter and Singer. The ordinate shows relative euphoria, i.e., degree of reported happiness less the degree of reported irritation. For further description, see text. Reproduced from Mandler, G. Emotion. In R. Brown et al. *New directions in psychology.* 1962. P. 282, Fig. 1. By permission of Holt, Rinehart, & Winston, Inc.,

the full emotional experience in conjunction with a situation does not appear immediately but takes some time to develop.

DIMENSIONS OF EMOTION

In a language like English, there are many words which designate emotions and shades of feeling. Davitz (1969), for example, found 400 words in Roget's *Thesaurus* which seemed likely to be used as the name of an emotion. There are also many facial expressions of emotion. In one series of posed facial expressions, there are 72 pictures, each one presumably illustrating a different emotion or shade of emotion. Several writers have wondered how many dimensions of emotion there are, presuming that many emotion words refer not to separate emotions but rather to degrees of one or the other of the basic dimensions. We can consider two such attempts to find the dimensions of emotion here, one dealing with facial expressions, the other with emotional names. In passing, we should mention that similar analyses could probably be carried out for posture, gait, and gesture, all of which may provide indications of emotion, but no adequate analysis of these forms of expression is available, to the writer's knowledge. In speech, there are also signs of emotion, as in hesitations, repetitions of words, variations in rate, and the like. Space limitations do not permit a discussion of these features of speech in the present work.

Schlosberg (1954) has worked with sets of posed pictures made to represent a variety of facial expressions thought to occur in emotion. His subjects sorted the pictures into groups, putting pictures in the same group because they felt them to be similar in reflecting a general emotional category, like disgust. In addition, subjects rated the pictures on the dimensions of pleasantness – unpleasantness and of attention – rejection. Preliminary work suggested these two axes as probably basic to the sorts previously mentioned.

The results show that certain basic emotional categories into which the pictures were sorted (contempt, love – mirth – happy, surprise, fear – suffering, anger – determination, and disgust) fall around the perimeter of an oval surface, the major coordinates of which are pleasantness – unpleasantness and attention – rejection. This surface is shown in Figure 12. Most of the 72 pictures worked with by Schlosberg's subjects find a place somewhere on this surface. Consequently, it would seem that two dimensions (Schlosberg later added a third dimension, activation, which would be at right angles to the plane of the oval surface) offer a framework in terms of which facial expressions, as represented by posed pictures, can be located.

Davitz has attempted to determine the dimensions in terms of which emotion words might be placed. He began by asking a large number of people to describe emotional experiences they had had. Then he extracted and refined from this material a list of 556 statements which provide a sort of checklist of aspects of emotional experience. A few of the statements follow: "my pulse quickens"; "I'm at peace with the world"; "my thinking is rapid"; "I feel outgoing"; "I seem to be fighting myself."

From the list of 400 emotion words obtained from the *Thesaurus* as mentioned above, Davitz chose 50 to represent a wide and varied range of emotional states. He asked each of 50 subjects to think about each of the 50 words and to check items in the checklist which described an experience he had had in reference to each of the 50 words.

There are several outcomes of Davitz's investigation, but we must be content here with presenting the more general findings. One outcome is a dictionary for the emotional meaning of the 50 words. Another is a set of clusters into which the 50 terms seemed to group themselves in terms of the checklist items which were used to describe them. There are 12 such clusters, the names of which are listed below with an illustrative checklist item for each one:

Activation: "I'm excited in a calm way."
Hypoactivation: "I feel mentally dull."
Hyperactivation: "My pulse quickens."
Moving Toward: "I want to help, protect, please another person."
Moving Away: "I want to withdraw . . . be alone . . ."
Moving Against: "Fists are clenched."
Comfort: "A sense of well-being."
Discomfort: "There's a lump in my throat."
Tension: "I'm wound up inside."

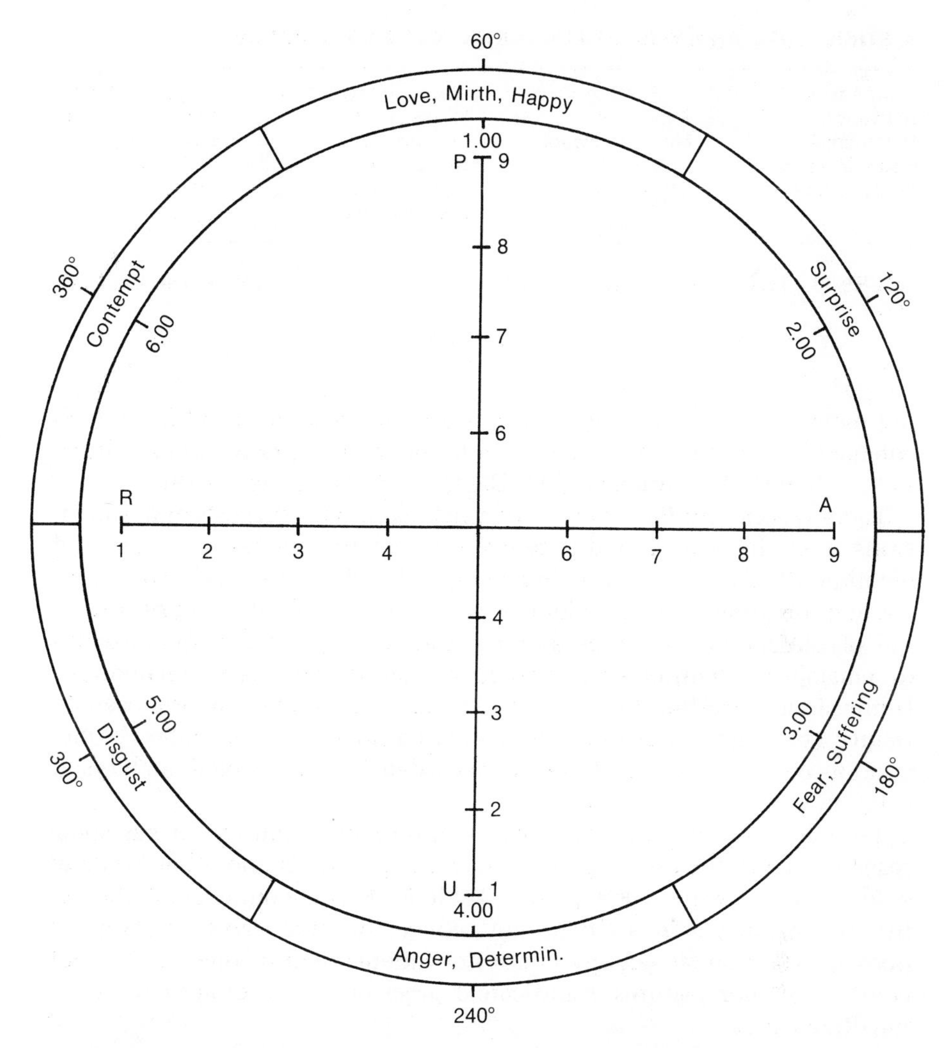

FIGURE 12 Judgments of the emotional values of pictures located on an oval surface. P and U refer to pleasant and unpleasant and R and A to rejection and attention. Modified from Schlosberg, H. The description of facial expressions in terms of two dimensions. *Journal of Experimental Psychology*, 1952, Vol. 44, P. 232, Fig. 1. By permission of the American Psychological Association.

Enhancement: "I have a sense of sureness."
Incompetence–Dissatisfaction: "There's a sense of weakness."
Inadequacy: "I feel vulnerable and totally helpless."

The clusters are, of course, interrelated, and further analysis led Davitz to suggest four basic dimensions, activation, relatedness, hedonic tone, and competence. They relate to the clusters as shown in the accompany-

A STRUCTURAL ANALYSIS OF EMOTIONAL MEANING CLUSTERS

Dimension	*Posture*	*Negative: Type 1*	*Negative: Type 2*
Activation	Activation	Hypoactivation	Hyperactivation
Relatedness	Moving Toward	Moving Away	Moving Against
Hedonic Tone	Comfort	Discomfort	Tension
Competence	Enhancement	Incompetence: Dissatisfaction	Inadequacy

FIGURE 13 Taken from Davitz, J. R. *The language of emotion.* New York: The Academic Press, Inc.

ing figure. In Figure 13 the clusters are grouped under headings which emerged from the statistical analyses of the intercluster relations, whereas the dimensions were added by Davitz to characterize the rows.

There is some similarity in the dimensions Davitz suggests and dimensions others have suggested in terms of which to organize the domain of emotion. Thus activation is a dimension with which we are already familiar, and the dimension of hedonic tone is similar to Schlosberg's continuum of pleasantness–unpleasantness. Davitz suggests that Schlosberg's dimension of attention–rejection is similar to the one of relatedness. Dimensions suggested by other writers also resemble those proposed by Davitz, competence, for example, which has arisen in the context of motivation but has not been typically recorded in dimensional analyses of emotion.

That there is some order among emotion words and that it has some resemblance to the order found in facial expressions and other kinds of evidence (see Davitz, 1969, p. 132, Table 5–1) is encouraging. Although the dimensional analysis does not reduce the number of emotions, it does suggest that the emotions are not independent of one another but contain common features or indicate degrees or aspects of basic underlying dimensions.

SUGGESTED READINGS

Arnold, M. B. *Emotion and personality.* New York: Columbia University Press, 1960. 2 vols.

Cofer, C. N. & Appley, M. H. *Motivation: Theory and research.* New York: John Wiley & Sons, Inc., 1964. Chapter 8.

Davitz, J. R. *The language of emotion.* New York: Academic Press, Inc., 1969.

Duffy, E. *Activation and behavior.* New York: John Wiley & Sons, Inc., 1962.

Grossman, S. P. *A textbook of physiological psychology.* New York: John Wiley & Sons, Inc., 1967. Chapters 5 and 9.

Mandler, G. Emotion. In R. Brown, E. Galanter, E. H. Hess, & G. Mandler, *New directions in psychology.* New York: Holt, Rinehart & Winston, Inc., 1962. Pp. 267–343.

5

External Stimulation

A major problem for homeostatic drive theory, as pointed out in Chapter 2 (p. 31), was evidence that exploratory, manipulatory, and curiosity behavior exists in many animals and that a reduction in external stimulation seems often to have aversive properties, rather than attractive ones. The first demonstrations which revealed this kind of evidence were advanced mainly in opposition to homeostatic drive theory but were interpreted as suggesting drives additional to those usually postulated by homeostatic drive theorists. As additional observations have become available and as the old ones have been assimilated, alternative interpretations have arisen, alternatives which owe much to activation or arousal theory, which we summarized in the last chapter.

In the present chapter the evidence concerning these developments is summarized, and the theoretical interpretations are examined. The phenomena considered seem to arise in conjunction with variations in external stimuli and point, therefore, to an independent role for such stimuli in motivation which was not envisaged in classical homeostatic drive theory. The word *curiosity* is sometimes used in connection with these phenomena to designate a class of stimulus characteristics which arouse exploration, manipulation, and inspection of stimuli.

ACTIVITY AND PLAY

Before we explore the major topics of this chapter, it seems worthwhile to devote a little space to discussing play and to the question whether there is a drive for activity.

One may raise the question whether there is a motive for play. Observation of children and of the young of many species of animals certainly suggests that play is a major enterprise in their lives, and, of course, leisure and recreational activities of the adult support major industries in many societies, especially in the United States. Yet, play is not often listed in discussions of motivation, and where it is treated it is often seen as serving some other motive, rather than as arising from a motive for play itself.

It is probably the case that the acts we refer to as "play" are too varied and, to some extent, too arbitrary to support the notion that they express a specific motive. One man's play may to another be a drudgery, and, likewise, one man's work may be another's hobby or avocation. To a child, play may simply be his "work" role; such an idea is perhaps epitomized in the comment of a small child after he determined what was to occur at home one morning: "Daddy has to work (in the yard), mommy has to clean (the house), and I have to play." Play can probably be defined only in contrast to work and perhaps represents only the fact that in his waking life the human, of whatever age, wishes to be busy, to be occupied, to be doing something, to be active.

A question does exist as to whether there is a motive or a drive, independent of any others, to be active. It is difficult to establish such a motive in a pure form because to do so requires that all other sources—motives, incentives, stimuli—that might themselves be responsible for the activity be eliminated or be held constant. With animals, some attempts to study this question have been made.

Activity is usually studied by means of an activity wheel, by means of a cage which tilts when the animal moves about it, or by observing the animal and recording his movements as he moves around or as he does other things, such as grooming himself. There does not seem to be a general trait for activity, as measurements of the same animal in more than one of these situations do not correlate well one with another. However, by selective breeding, active and inactive strains of rats can be developed (Cofer & Appley, 1964, pp. 269–277).

If activity expresses a drive, then deprivation of activity for a period of time should result in an augmentation of activity following the deprivation. Deprivation has been induced by confining the animal (usually a rat) in a very small cage for various time intervals. There is some evidence that short periods of confinement are followed by increased activity, as a drive conception would predict, but that longer periods have an opposite effect, the animals being less active after confinement than are suitable control animals (Hill, 1958). There is not, then, clear evidence for an activity drive from these studies, although its existence cannot be entirely ruled out.

There is evidence, as was mentioned in Chapter 2, that variations in activity can be produced by learning. This evidence indicated that activity increased with food deprivation when the regular feeding schedule employed permitted the animal to anticipate the approach of feeding time. In a recent experiment, Bindra and Palfai (1967) confined rats in a plastic device which essentially immobilized the animal. Attached to the device was a small water cup. Stimuli were presented while the animal was restrained either (1) with water in the cup, (2) with electric shock to the rear legs, or (3) without any special condition. Later, in a cage, the same stimuli were presented while the animal, no longer restrained, was mildly thirsty. The group given water became more active, that given shock became less active, and the third group showed no change when the stimuli were presented. This, of course, suggests that learning can be a factor in activity, but it is noteworthy that the activity in the cage could hardly have been specifically learned as a response to the stimuli while the animal was restrained. Aside from the demonstration that learning is a factor, the interpretation of the results found is not entirely clear, but Bindra (1969) suggests that the stimuli associated with water or with shock have attained the capacity to arouse a central motive state (see Chapter 9).

Clear evidence for an independent activity drive is sparse, and it may be that the safest interpretation is to say that activity perhaps reflects general arousal rather than a specific drive and that the stimuli of the situation may be important to changes in activity. Arousal would account for the increased activity in the group in the Bindra–Palfai experiment which experienced the pairing of the stimuli with the water. In the group that experienced shock, however, there should have been arousal too. In this case, perhaps, the animals moved their legs into a crouching position when they experienced shock in the restraining device. If the stimuli associated with shock elicited a crouching posture in the cage, then activity would not be expected to increase, despite the arousal.

STUDIES OF EXTERNAL STIMULATION

In the study of the motivational significance of external stimuli, several procedures have been used. One studies exploration by means of locomotion, another by means of manipulation of objects. A third uses choice and inspection time to gauge the value of stimuli and of stimulus parameters for exploration. Finally, the fourth determines the effects of reduction of stimulation on various aspects of behavior. We discuss each of these in turn.

Locomotory Exploration

Animals move about their environments and when encountering again a situation where they previously turned in one direction will often turn, the next time, in the opposite direction. These behaviors could be called exploratory or could be regarded as expressing a motive to experience variety, but they could also arise from other factors. Considerable effort has been extended to determine whether these behavioral tendencies reflect an independent motive for exploration.

Systematic study of these tendencies began in the early 1950's. In the case of alternation, the question was investigated by determining whether an animal alternated his response from right to left (or the reverse) in order to vary the response he made or to vary the stimulus situation he would encounter (Glanzer, 1953). Consider a simple maze in the form of a cross (+). Suppose the animal is started from the bottom leg of the cross and that the upper leg is blocked so that he cannot enter it. He will then turn to the left or the right as he leaves the bottom leg. On the next trial he is started from the upper leg with access to the lower leg blocked. Which way will he turn when he reaches the choice point? The evidence indicates that he will turn left if he turned left from the bottom leg, right if he turned right from the bottom leg. Thus, he repeats the turning movement on the second trial but in doing so moves into the arm of the cross which he had *not* explored on the first trial. This result suggests exploration or the importance of encountering a variety of stimulation. (No rewards were used in these experiments, and the animal was not motivated by hunger or thirst.)

The other task used to study exploration was an elevated maze. The top of this kind of maze is elevated above the floor of the room, and the animal is placed on the top, which has no sides and is open above him. Such a maze can be made into several shapes, a straight one, one in the form of a T, and one in the form of an L, for example. When the number of 15-inch segments traversed was measured (Montgomery, 1951), it was found that more segments were entered when the shape was that of a T than when it was that of an L, and that more segments were entered for the L than for the straightaway. In general, the findings can be summarized by the statement that the rats tended to avoid the places which they had already visited.

In the elevated-maze studies, as in the cross-maze experiments, the animals were not rewarded by the experimenter, and they were neither hungry nor thirsty. There is evidence, which is not entirely consistent, concerning the effect of hunger and thirst on exploration. Probably, the weight of the evidence is that these motives and also the motive of fear tend to suppress exploration (Cofer & Appley, 1964, pp. 290–291). This finding supports the notion that exploration is independently motivated.

Exploratory behavior declines as the length of time spent in the situation increases. If the animal is given the opportunity to explore a second maze after a first one, he will do so, but the extent of his exploration is a function of the similarity of the two mazes. He explores the second maze less as its similarity to the first one increases (Montgomery, 1953). Animals will explore objects on the floor of the apparatus or patterns on the walls by nosing or sniffing them. The complexity and newness of objects lead to their being investigated, in preference to familiar objects, and more time is spent in a box whose walls are painted in complex patterns than in boxes with bare walls (Cofer & Appley, 1964, pp. 291–294).

There is also evidence that the opportunity to explore can serve as a reward and lead to learning. Thus, if one choice in a simple maze leads to a complex maze, whereas the other one leads to a plain blind alley, the animal, over trials, will develop a consistent preference for the turn which leads to the complex maze (Montgomery, 1954). If the positions of the blind alley and the complex maze are reversed, the animal will unlearn his pattern of choice and develop the opposite choice, the one that now leads to the complex maze.

There is, then, good evidence that animals will explore, and it is buttressed by systematic observations made in natural settings, although in the latter case other factors such as hunger or thirst cannot always be ruled out. Exploration, or at least response alternation, has been observed in the laboratory in both lower and higher animals from planaria to human beings.

Manipulation of Objects

It is easiest to observe manipulation of objects in animals like primates which do not remain most of the time on all fours and which have manual dexterity. One can, of course, see manipulation of objects in other animals, such as squirrels, dogs, and kittens, but most of the work has been done with primates. Monkeys, for example, were placed in cages with mechanical puzzles attached to the walls (Harlow, 1950; Harlow, Harlow, & Meyer, 1950). The puzzles consisted of a hinged metal piece with a slot at one end. The metal piece, as shown in Figure 14, was flush against the wall and through the slot projected a metal ring through which a hook could be inserted. In this hook and eye arrangement, the metal piece was "locked" against the wall when the puzzle was "assembled." The monkeys disassembled the puzzles, i.e., they removed the hook from the eye and moved the hinged metal piece away from the wall. There was no reward (other than manipulation itself) for their doing so, and disassembling puzzles had never been rewarded or associated with satisfactions in their past lives. The monkeys had 12 days of experience with these puzzles, and then their skill at disassembling the puzzles was compared with that of inexperienced monkeys. Evidently the experienced monkeys had learned from their experience (they had disassembled the puzzles frequently over the 12 days), as their performance far surpassed that of the naïve animals.

Manipulatory behavior here is not attributable to other motives or rewards. Monkeys show it at an early age (from 20 to 30 days), making it unlikely that it is a learned pattern (Harlow, Blazek, & McClearn, 1956).

With young chimpanzees, manipulation of objects is observed, and the more heterogeneous in color and shape a set of blocks is the more manipulation takes place (Welker, 1956). Infant monkeys make more hand, mouth, and lip contacts with food when there is a variety of foods or when a given food is presented in a variety of colors than when there is a single kind of food and all instances of it have the same color (Mason & Harlow, 1959).

One would expect that children would exhibit exploratory behavior, and the laboratory evidence available confirms this expectation. In one

FIGURE 14 Monkeys "disassembling" a mechanical puzzle. Picture provided by Wisconsin Regional Primate Research Center.

study, for example, a novel object was used in a relatively bare room, although other toys were available. The object was a red metal box on four legs with a lever protruding from one end. The lever could be moved, and arrangements could also be made so that its movements were registered on a visible counter or were accompanied by the sound of a bell and buzzer. Observations were made in the absence of visual or auditory consequences, in the presence of both, and in the presence of either one. The subjects were nursery school children, 3 to 5 years of age (Hutt, 1966).

Exploration of the object, including the manipulation of the object, was observed over several ten-minute sessions. When there was no or only a visual consequence of moving the lever, exploration of the object fell off rather sharply after the first session, but when either auditory or both auditory and visual stimulation was produced by moving the lever, exploration of the object continued with no decline over five sessions, falling only at the sixth session. The auditory stimulation was apparently responsible for this continuation of exploratory activity.

Exploratory behavior, in the absence of motives or rewards other than those arising from exploration itself, seems to be well established.

Choice and Inspection Time

In a sense, choice has already been mentioned in the discussion of exploration and of alternation, in which a selection of one of two turns was seen to be influenced by the opportunity to explore. Also, one could interpret the time animals spend in complexly patterned environments as a measure of inspection. However, the studies we review under the present heading have rather specifically manipulated parameters of the stimulus situation and have gauged their influence on choice and inspection time measures.

There have been several studies with infants (Berlyne, 1958a; Fantz, 1958). In these experiments, patterns are presented, and the measure is which one the subject looks at first. The patterns with greater amounts of contours attract the infant's gaze first, in both human and chimpanzee infants. Thus, a checkerboard pattern is more attractive than a simpler one. This result implicates choice.

With college student subjects, Berlyne (1957) employed the following situation. The subject sat before a tachistoscope in a darkened room and pressed a key to expose a picture. The exposures were very brief (.14 sec.), but the subject was permitted to expose a picture as many times as he wished. The number of times he pressed the key for a given picture was the measure of inspection time Berlyne employed. There were several sets of pictures. One was a set of pictures of birds and another of animals, and inserted in each of the series of seven pictures were two which were incongruous, e.g., an elephant's head on a lion's body and a bird's head and wings on a four-legged body. Another series began with a circle, and in successive pictures details were added to make a bear in the final picture (another series shifted from a circle to a clown). A further series consisted of six pictures containing patterns of red triangles, then five of green circles, and then one of violet squares. Finally, there were three series of cards, one of which contained nine figures in a regular arrangement and one of the same figures in an irregular arrangement (e.g., nine crosses in a 3 x 3 matrix and one set of crosses irregularly spaced over the area). The sequence of cards was presented randomly.

More responses were made to the incongruous than to the congruous pictures, to the cards (numbers 7 and 12) in which the pattern changed in the series of triangles, circles, and the square than to those in which no change occurred, and to the cards containing irregular arrangements of figures than to the cards bearing regular arrangements. (There were no significant differences associated with the sequences circle to bear or to clown.) Berlyne suggests that the significant effects in this study, which involve inspection time, show that curiosity or exploration is evoked by such stimulus factors as incongruity, surprise, and uncertainty. In a somewhat similar experiment (Berlyne, 1958b), he found again more fixation time for incongruous than for congruent pictures and for complex pictures than for simple pictures. Complexity was varied by introducing irregularity into the arrangements of pictures, by increasing the number of parts, by using irregular shapes, or by making parts of a figure different from one another (e.g., using a square, circle, triangle, and diamond instead of four squares). Figure 15 illustrates these features. With 10- to

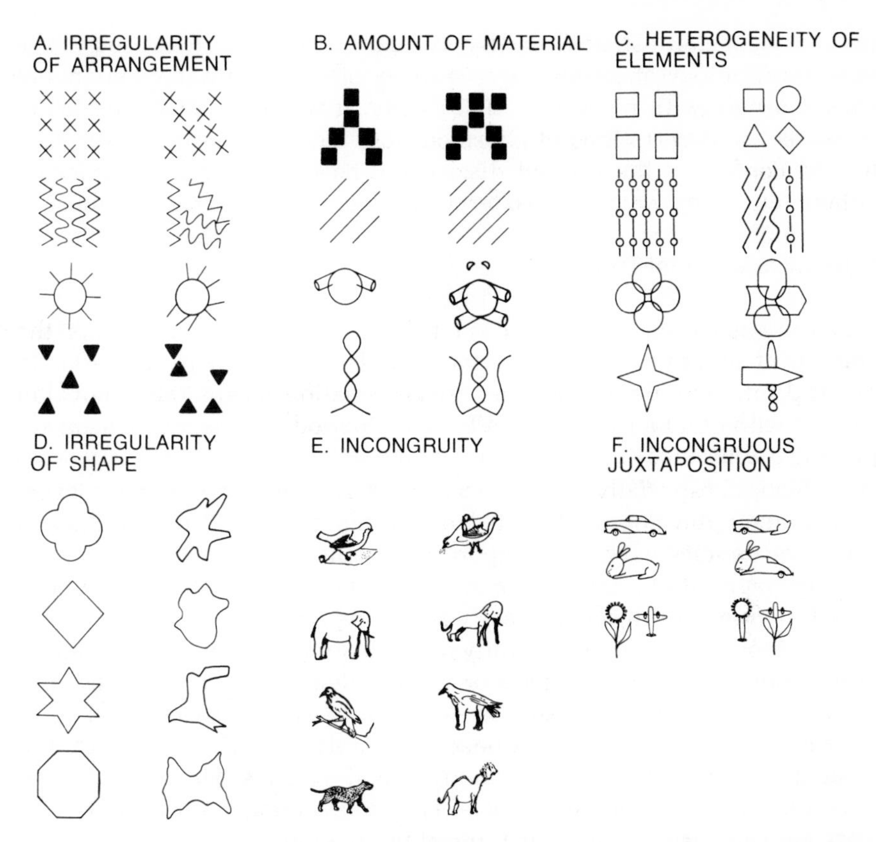

FIGURE 15 Visual stimuli used by Berlyne to arouse curiosity. Reprinted from Berlyne, D. D. The influence of complexity and novelty in visual figures on orienting responses. *Journal of Experimental Psychology*, 1958, Vol. 55, P. 291, Fig. 1. By permission of the American Psychological Association.

12-year-old children, preference for block designs increases within limits as a function of their scaled complexity.

All of this work (and there is too much of it to be brought together in the present space) indicates an important role for various parameters of the stimulus in getting a subject to orient himself to the stimulus and to inspect and examine it (see Welker, 1961). In none of these experiments were any other drives active, and there were no rewards aside from inspecting the stimuli themselves. Perhaps a name for choice and inspection of stimuli would be curiosity, but this word might also apply to locomotory exploration and to manipulation of objects.

A time-honored word that could also be used to refer to orientation to and inspection of stimuli is *attention*, and stimulus properties are often mentioned, among other things, as factors which can draw or capture attention. Among them are size, intensity, color, motion, position, repetition, change, contrast, and novelty. Attention, however, was used in the older terminology of psychology as a way of classifying the contents of consciousness with respect to their clarity. It was thus a term useful in introspective descriptions of consciousness. For this reason, perhaps, it has, in context of the present discussion, been displaced by curiosity, although in many ways the two terms designate much the same things.

Sensory and Social Isolation

Sensory isolation or deprivation refers to a situation in which the amount of external stimulation received by an organism is markedly reduced for some period of time. Social isolation means the removal of contact with other animals, again for some period of time, but it need not include the absence of other sensory stimulation. Prolonged sensory or social isolation, especially when it occurs in early life, may have very severe effects upon development and functioning. Sensory, perceptual, and cognitive deficits have been reported as consequences of severe early sensory deprivation, and severe emotional and social effects have been found in animals subjected to early social deprivation.

From the standpoint of the study of motivation, we shall have nothing to say about many of the effects of sensory deprivation but will be concerned with studies of sensory isolation only as they seem to relate to the question whether there is a need or a motive for stimulation. On the other hand, the disturbance of motivational systems has been of paramount concern to students of social isolation, so that a summary of this work has great relevance to the topic of motivation.

Sensory Isolation In the early 1950's, rather dramatic effects were reported to occur as the result of periods of sensory deprivation in human subjects (Bexton, Heron, & Scott, 1954). The first studies were reported from McGill University of Canada. The subjects (college students) were paid for their participation ($20 per day) and were asked to remain in a lighted, partially sound-deadened cubicle in which they were to lie on a cot (see Figure 16). The subjects wore translucent goggles, which prevented pattern vision, and wore gloves and cardboard cuffs, designed to reduce tactile stimulation. An air-conditioner provided a constant masking noise, and the subject rested his head in a U-shaped pillow. Time-outs were provided for meals and toilet needs (other experiments have provided eating and toileting facilities in the restricted environment). The subject was free to terminate his service at any time.

The result was that after two or three days the subjects quit the experiment, despite the wage, because they found the situation intolerable. Later, the experimenters themselves served as subjects, remaining in isolation for six days. A substantial number of similar investigations have been carried out, and the number of variations on the procedure just outlined have been substantial (cf. Schultz, 1965; Zubek, 1969). The results

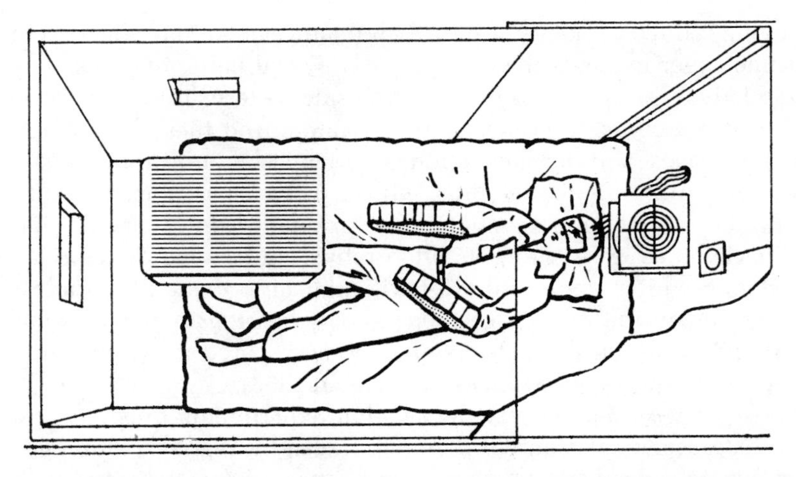

FIGURE 16 Diagram of a sensory deprivation chamber, showing the subject lying on a cot with goggles over his eyes and cuffs over his hands and forearms. Above his head, there is an exhaust fan and above his feet an air conditioner. A microphone and speaker are also shown. Redrawn from Heron, H. Cognitive and physiological effects of perceptual isolation. In P. Solomon et al. (Eds.), *Sensory deprivation*. Cambridge: Harvard University Press, 1961. Pp. 6–33. P. 9, Fig. 2-1.

obtained have not been entirely consistent, perhaps because of the varying experimental conditions, but, in general, significant effects have been observed to arise during the period of isolation and sometimes to continue for a while after the period of isolation is over.

From a motivational standpoint, the most interesting result is that the reduction in stimulation tends to be aversive. There are boredom, restlessness, irritability, emotional lability, and a desire to leave the situation. It is noteworthy that according to some accounts of the nature of motivation this relatively stimulation-free situation should have been an attractive one, especially as through it the subject not only made money but contributed to science. The fact that the reduction in stimulation is aversive, if it goes on long enough, offers a serious problem for any theory, such as homeostatic drive theory or classical psychoanalytic theory, which sees freedom from stimulation as the goal of the motives it postulates.

The isolation situation, however, seems to be stressful, rather than comfortable, and suggests that there may be a need for some level of stimulation. It has a number of effects (Schultz, 1965; Zubek, 1969), which are more specific than those we mentioned. There are EEG changes, in the direction of lower frequency rhythms, and there is sometimes a carry-over of this change for several days following the return to a normal environment. A number of changes in the effectiveness of intellectual performance have been reported, as in verbal fluency, abstract reasoning, recall and recognition tasks. However, the results on these skills show considerable variation, probably due to the various conditions employed for achieving reduced sensory input. A dramatic perceptual effect reported for some experiments is the occurrence of visual hallucinations, varying from relatively simple rows of dots or mosaic patterns to scenery, people, and bizarre architecture. Not all investigators find these hallucinations or vivid images, and perhaps much significance should not be accorded them. However, other perceptual effects have been reported, such as impairments in color perception, in performance on reversible figures, and in vigilance tasks. Subjects often relish, under sensory deprivation, stimulation which would not ordinarily appeal to them. For example, in one experiment the subjects seemed to enjoy hearing an old stock market report and a talk on the dangers of alcohol prepared for young children (Cofer & Appley, 1964, pp. 278–284; Hebb, 1955).

The evidence from sensory deprivation experiments thus clearly suggests that absence of external stimulation can be aversive, although this generalization is subject to many qualifications. The qualifications arise from the fact that there are individual differences among people in their reactions to sensory isolation, some tolerating it much better than others, and that there are a variety of conditions which may ameliorate or heighten its effects.

Sensory isolation has been studied in monkeys in the context of the question whether the opportunity to receive stimulation would be a way of maintaining and reinforcing behavior. After a time spent in a dimly illuminated box with opaque walls, monkeys learned to discriminate (on the basis of color) which one of two windows that when pushed would open and reveal for 30 seconds a view of the laboratory environment (Butler, 1953). Learning thus occurred on the basis of an increase in stimulation, and the response was very persistent, continuing over ten four-hour testing sessions. More responses occurred the longer visual deprivation continued. Isolation from sounds also leads monkeys to learn to prefer the one of two levers whose depression was accompanied by 15 seconds' worth of noise from the monkey colony (Butler, 1957). This evidence suggests that sensory deprivation not only motivates behavior but that stimulation can reward behavior.

Social Isolation A substantial body of research has grown up on the topic of the social isolation of infant monkeys. In these experiments, chiefly the work of Harry Harlow (1958) and his associates, the infant monkey is removed from his mother and raised in a cage with a substitute mother or mothers. One such substitute was made out of wire. The other was similarly constructed but was made with wood covered by foam rubber which in turn was covered with terry cloth; this second mother was therefore soft. Both mothers were heated by means of an electric light bulb and could be arranged with a nursing bottle. When both mothers were available, the infant monkey spent much more time on the terry cloth mother, even though its feedings could be carried out only on the wire mother. Infants having contact with the cloth mother were more adventuresome and willing to explore the environment than were those infants having contact with the wire mother. Harlow concluded that he had established in these experiments that there is a need for contact stimulation and that it is independent of other needs and their reinforcements, such as those for hunger and thirst.

Despite the apparent advantages of the cloth mother, studies of the monkeys at later points in time indicated that, in the absence of social stimulation, their behavior was aberrant in many respects. Four main areas of disturbance have been suggested by Mason (1968, pp. 81–82). Many of the monkeys show (1) abnormal postures or movements, for example, rocking, pacing, and staring into space; (2) excessive fearfulness; (3) disturbances of motor patterns including those involved in motivated patterns (neither male nor female monkeys responded normally in sexual situations at maturity, and those females that were successfully impregnated were woefully inadequate in their maternal behavior); (4) deficiencies in social communication. A threat from another animal might not elicit withdrawal as it ordinarily does, and a male, solicited sexually by an experienced and receptive female, might ignore her, begin to groom her, or initiate playful behavior.

Some alleviation of the abnormal patterns shown in later life was provided by allowing motherless monkeys to interact with age mates during the early development period. Mason has shown that monkeys differ in the way they develop if the artificial mother remains stationary or moves about (on wheels). The mobile mother is better for development than the static one.

It is clear, then, that a suitable social environment is important to the normal development of monkeys, including areas of behavior (sexual, maternal, fear) which are usually classified as motivational. Contact may be involved, but there are also interaction with peers and the effects of a mobile mother. Consequently, at the present time, it is not entirely clear just what deficiency in the environment of the socially deprived animals was responsible for their unusual behavior either in infancy or at maturity. One can be reasonably certain, however, that social isolation in early life can have some ill effects.

THEORETICAL INTERPRETATIONS

The first reactions to the findings that external stimulation or its absence has motivational significance were these: (1) the evidence seemed to contradict expectations based on homeostatic drive theory and thus seemed to refute that theory in its most general form; (2) it was suggested that there are additional, nonhomeostatic drives such as exploratory drive, manipulation motives, curiosity, and a motive for stimulation. The latter reaction was unsatisfactory on two counts: it continued the tradition of drive theory by adding new drives; the new drives were unlike the old ones in that their antecedent conditions were largely unspecifiable, and it was not certain whether they were general energizers or rather specifically limited to the situations in which the behavior they were to explain appeared.

An alternative account was couched in terms of a "boredom drive," the condition for the establishment of this drive being a monotonous stimulus situation. Such a drive could be reduced by the variation in stimulus input arising from exploration, the occurrence of stimuli in the case of sensory deprivation, and the stimulus features we have mentioned before—incongruity, surprisingness, novelty, and the others. Sometimes the boredom drive is said to constitute a state of arousal, which augmentation of stimulus input reduces. Such a formulation has some consistency with traditional drive theory, although it does, of course, postulate a new drive, one which underlies all of the behaviors involved in exploration, manipulation, curiosity, and leaving the situation of sensory deprivation.

This formulation in terms of a boredom drive has not been popular, perhaps because it is dfficult to test and because it seems to be designed primarily to save the old viewpoint.

Subsequently, a more general formulation has been reached, and it is organized around the ideas of arousal-activation theory with its corollary that there is an optimal degree of arousal. The notion of an optimum has been broadened to include not only the kind of physiological arousal proposed by the activation theorists but also other things. Examples are optimal degrees of stimulation, of complexity, and of information. There is an implicit commitment here to the notion of arousal, but it is not always specifically assessed (Hunt, 1965).

The notion of an optimal level of stimulation, for example, gains some credibility from Helson's notion of adaptation level or AL (Helson, 1964). This is a level of stimulation to which we have become accustomed or adapted, and when stimulation is in this range, no adaptive response is required. The adaptation level is an average of past and present background stimuli, and a current stimulus which does not deviate much from this average does not require us to do anything. But when stimuli deviate from the average, i.e., exceed it or are less than the average, adjustments have to be made. The AL is not fixed, of course, and can change with experience. When a country dweller first goes to the city, for example, the noise there may be annoying to him and disturb his sleep. If he stays long enough, however, so that his AL changes, he will no longer be troubled by the noise, asleep or waking. The city dweller, on the other hand, may be kept awake by the quiet of the country, again until his AL changes.

If we assume that lack of sensory variation represents a level below that of AL, then the organism will be moved to explore or to leave the situation in order to get stimulus input back to a satisfactory level. On the other hand, input that is too far above the present AL may initiate withdrawal to a stimulus situation less deviant from the AL. The latter situation has been supposed to be the case in certain reactions of fear to novel objects that are reported. For example, young laboratory-reared chimpanzees will react with fear to the model of the head of another chimpanzee, to an anesthetized infant chimpanzee in which, of course, the usual movements and expressions are absent, and to the investigator wearing a Halloween mask or wearing the animal caretaker's jacket. At an earlier age, such stimuli would probably not arouse fear, and it is believed that the accumulated experience of intact and active chimpanzees and of the face and attire of the investigator have established an AL from which the fear-arousing stimuli deviate. Fear of strangers, usually absent in human babies, may appear as they grow older, probably as a result of similar processes. Such a formulation, of course, differs from that given fear by Watson and Rayner (p. 59). In general, all we have said about the exploratory and investigative responses of animals and people to novel and unusual stimuli must be tempered by the statement that the novelty and unusualness be not so great as to arouse fear.Fear seems to be incompatible with the expression of exploration and curiosity, although it is not beyond reason that some exploration can be motivated by fear when the fear is not very great.

Incongruous, surprising, and informational stimuli too, if they do not deviate too far from AL, may be said to have their effects on behavior because of deviation from AL.

A theory of the kind we have just sketched differs markedly from a drive theory. This general way of thinking characterizes the ideas of many investigators today, who see exploration, curiosity, and information processing as processes of central importance in behavior but as not being readily understandable in terms of the concepts of drive theory. There is a certain danger in the kind of theory we have just described, because its component aspects are loosely defined and therefore applicable, after the fact, in the explanation of almost any result or phenomenon. It would be difficult to set up an experiment to test a precise derivation from this theory, because precise derivations, in the loose terms of the theory, would be difficult to make.

SUGGESTED READINGS

Berlyne, D. E. *Conflict, arousal, and curiosity.* New York: McGraw-Hill Book Company, 1960.

Cofer, C. N. & Appley, M. H. *Motivation: Theory and research.* New York: John Wiley & Sons, Inc., 1964. Chapter 6.

Fiske, D. W. & Maddi, S. R. *Functions of varied experience.* Homewood, Ill.: Dorsey Press, 1961. Chapters 5, 6, 7, 8, 9, 10, 12, and 13.

Schultz, D. P. *Sensory restriction: Effects on behavior.* New York: Academic Press, Inc., 1965.

Zubek, J. P. (Ed.). *Sensory deprivation: Fifteen years of research.* New York: Appleton-Century-Crofts, 1969.

6

Incentives and Reinforcement

Drive theory and instinct theory emphasized the role of internal pushes or forces in determining behavior. We have seen, however, in discussing hunger and sex, for example, that external stimuli and events have much importance in inducing the behaviors often attributed to drive or instinct, and, for the ethologists, releasing stimuli, which are external, were given a large role in the occurrence of innate behavioral patterns. Emotions, as Chapter 4 brought out, are aroused by or in situations, and the last chapter stressed the role of external factors in such phenomena as exploration, manipulation, and curiosity in general. Clearly, there is an important role for external stimuli in motivated behaviors, and it can be suggested that perhaps all motivated behavior is the consequence, directly or indirectly, of external stimuli.

Such a view has received increasing credence in recent years, and the result is incentive theories of motivation. Such theories hold that external events, either through learning or innately, have the capacity when they occur to induce states of arousal in organisms, i.e., to motivate them. One task of the present chapter is to discuss incentives and incentive theories of motivation.

External events, however, have another function which seems to be related to motivation. This function is to "strengthen" the behavior which has preceded the occurrence of the external event. If a hungry animal presses a lever and the lever press is followed by the delivery of food, there is an increased tendency for the animal to press the lever in the future in that situation. This increase in the tendency to press the lever is what is meant, at least in part, by the phrase, increase in strength.

An event, such as the delivery of food, which increases the strength of some response, is called a reinforcer, and the operation of providing for the occurrence of the reinforcer is called reinforcement. One reason for thinking that reinforcement has something to do with motivation is that many reinforcers, such as food, for example, have their most potent effects when the animal has been kept on a deprivation schedule. Another reason is that some authors (e.g., Bolles, 1967) have suggested that perhaps all motivational phenomena can be accounted for in reinforcement terms, i.e., that the notions of drive and incentive can be replaced by reinforcement. This suggestion proposes, essentially, a reinforcement theory of motivation. The second task of this chapter is to discuss reinforcers and reinforcement and to consider a reinforcement theory of motivation.

Incentives and reinforcers share the property that both are or may be external events. Incentives lead to arousal, reinforcers to changes in strength. There is an interesting point that one and the same event may both arouse and reinforce an animal. Thus, giving an animal a bit of food before he runs in a runway may arouse him so that his running speed is augmented. On the other hand, giving the food after the running has occurred may also augment running speed on the following trial. The prefeeding operation seems to be one of incentive motivation, the postfeeding one of reinforcement. It is often difficult to differentiate incentives and reinforcers on the basis of what they are and yet they have or may have different effects. Because there are these links between incentives and reinforcers they have been brought together for discussion in the same chapter.

INCENTIVES AND INCENTIVE THEORIES

Effects and Characteristics of Incentives

The most effective way in which to indicate the value of incentives is to consider the results of an experiment. Zeaman (1949) ran an experiment with rats which illustrates the role of incentives in two ways.

The animals were trained, after deprivation of food, to run down a straight alley to a food box. The measure Zeaman took was the latency or starting time of the running response. One group of animals ran to a food reward of 2.4 grams, another to a food reward of 0.05 grams. Nineteen trials were given to both groups, and by that point the latencies for each group had become constant. However, the average latencies of the two groups differed, the one running to the large reward having a very short latency, the one running to the small reward having a much longer mean latency, as Figure 17 shows. This is one effect of incentives, i.e., the quantity of the incentive has an effect on behavior. At the next trial, Zeaman switched the food rewards, so that the group which had earlier received the small reward now received the large one, and the group which had received the large reward during training now received the small amount of food. Figure 17 shows that there was an immediate change in the latencies on the trial following the switching of rewards. The group changed to the large reward reduced its mean latency drasti-

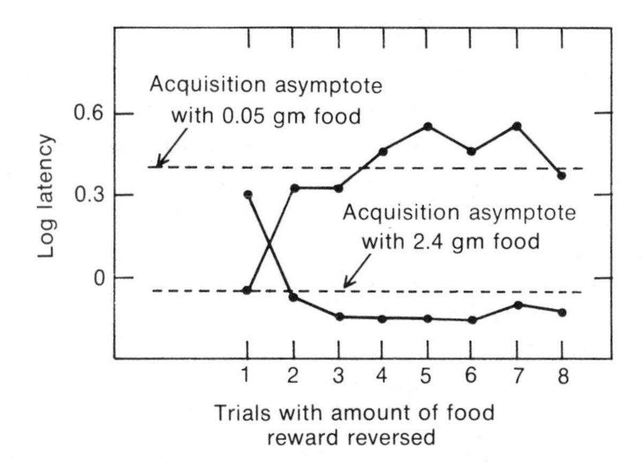

FIGURE 17 Shifts in the latency of running as a function of changes in the amount of reward administered after an asymptote for latency had been reached under the prior reward. Reproduced from Kimble, G. (Ed.), *Hilgard and Marquis' conditioning and learning.* (2nd ed.) Copyright 1961 by Appleton-Century-Crofts, Inc. Reprinted by permission of Appleton-Century-Crofts, Educational Division, Meredith Corporation. Kimble adapted this figure from Zeaman (1949).

cally, whereas the group switched to the small reward increased its latency by a large amount. Zeaman's results are consistent with those reported earlier by Crespi (1942), and the rapid changes in running performance following the switch in rewards have been confirmed by several other investigators. This change in performance is the second effect arising from the manipulation of incentives.

It is important to note two things about these results. One is that the approach to the stable latencies (asymptotes) during training occurred at the same rate for the two groups. This suggests that habit formation, despite the different asymptotic latencies, was proceeding in a comparable fashion and that the habit strength at the end of training was the same. The second point is that after the switch of rewards the change in performance was immediate. Our conception of habit and habit-formation is incompatible with such rapid changes. The learning of habits occurs slowly. Hence, the rapid changes are not due to alterations of habits. Since drive did not change with the incentive changes, we must conclude that the alteration in performance arose because of incentive changes.

Given the argument just presented, one is forced to the conclusion that incentives can have an important role in the control of performance. The case we have discussed, of course, concerns the amount or the size of the incentive. Are there other characteristics of incentives which have parallel effects?

We can answer this question affirmatively with respect to several other features of incentives.

For example, in one study (Simmons, 1924) it was found that different food rewards were not equivalent in promoting learning in rats. The most effective reward was a combination of bread and milk, together with return to the home cage; next most effective were bread and milk alone, then, in order, sunflower seeds, return to the home cage, and escape from the maze. Rats are known to prefer a bran mash food to sunflower seeds. Elliott (1928) gave the bran mash reward over the first nine days of training in a maze and then switched the reward to sunflower seeds. Performance deteriorated after the switch, becoming worse than that of a control group rewarded throughout with sunflower seeds. In monkeys, performance is disturbed if the reward is shifted from a piece of banana to a less preferred piece of lettuce.

The running speeds of rats to a reward are fastest when the reward is a sugar solution, next to a wheat solution, and slowest to casein (a protein). Shifting rats from casein to sugar increases running speed.

Incentives can also motivate behavior if the animal has a taste before he performs the task. Small amounts of food or water (appropriate in each case to the current state of deprivation), given before performance on a runway or a maze, augment performance. (Large amounts, of course, would negate the effects of deprivation, and if given prior to the run, would depress performance.) Chicks will run faster to four one-quarter pieces of popcorn than they will to a whole piece, despite the identity of the quantities in this case. Delay of reward impairs performance as contrasted with performance followed by immediate reward.

These effects of incentives are most readily seen in situations in which time (speed or latency) is the major dependent variable studied. The results are considerably more complex and less consistent when errors or correct responses are observed. It seems likely that the cases where speed or latency can be observed in uncomplicated tasks may give us the best index of the role of incentives as motivational factors. With the more complex measures and situations, other factors may obscure the motivational effects of incentives.

In human motivation, we speak readily of incentives. A way of characterizing human motivation, which seems plausible to us, is to discuss it in terms of goals or objectives. One can also speak in terms of drives, needs, or motives, but, as we shall see in Chapter 7, the presence of goals or goal objects is often an important if not the most important condition which leads us to use terms like *need* or *motive.* Since goal objects are incentives, we may say that an account of human motivation based on incentives is a natural or plausible one.

In Chapter 7, then, we will discuss incentives in human motivation. Here, however, we may observe that many practices in dealing with human behavior involve the manipulation of incentives. Some examples are as follows: grades for academic work, wage systems geared to output, prizes for exceptional and meritorious performances, various kinds of social recognition for achievement or service, membership in exclusive or elite groups or organizations, diplomas and certificates, and abundant amounts of verbal praise for various accomplishments. These are positive incentives. We also use negative incentives, those we hope will instigate behavior that will not be destructive, ineffective, or ill-guided. Negative incentives follow behaviors which we wish to avoid, and our threats and systems of discipline and the like presumably function as negative incentives.

This brief excursion into the role of incentives in human motivation serves merely to indicate that animal work is not the only locus where incentives may be used and be found to be effective. But we shall discuss the human case in Chapter 7 around topics often discussed also as human motives.

Incentive Theories

It will be recalled that in hungry rats when the occurrence of feeding was regularly associated with a stimulus change, activity increased in response to the stimulus change (Sheffield & Campbell, 1954). One can suppose that anticipatory feeding responses become conditioned to the stimulus changes and that they serve to arouse the animal so that he becomes active. Another possibility is that frustration occurs when the stimulus change which induces the anticipatory reactions is not followed immediately by food. One could argue either way, although there is some evidence (Amsel, 1962) that frustration of a feeding response does arouse the rat. Amsel and Roussel (1952) ran hungry rats in two connected straight runways, both of which led to food reward. The animal ran to the first goal box (at the end of the first runway) where it received food and then along the second runway to the second goal box, where it received more food. After this pattern was well established, food was removed from the first goal box (frustration). The important observation is that frustration in the first goal box augmented running speed in the second runway. Amsel has conducted a large number of experiments which seem to show that nonreward is a frustrating state of affairs and that the frustration has arousing effects on other behavior.

The stimulus change and the effects it produces in the experiment reported by Sheffield and Campbell can serve as an example of the kind of event an incentive may be said to be and of its role in motivating behavior. Presumably, the effects of properties of incentive objects, which we summarized in the last section, can be interpreted in terms of the arousal produced by the anticipations these incentives induce or in terms of the frustration arising from the delay of the reward or in the failure of the reward to occur.

A further example of how incentives might work is afforded by the work of Young (1959). Young, as we mentioned earlier, carried out a number of experiments with rats in which he measured running speed to get to incentives, choice between incentives, and amount of an incentive consumed. He found, for example, that rats running to a sugar solution do so quickly with no hesitation and accept the food at once. In contrast, rats run more slowly to casein, often exploring the area before accepting the casein. Young thinks that for the rat sugar is a much more palatable or preferred food than casein, i.e., that it produces more affective enjoyment and thus arousal than does casein.

Young suggests that when the animal has had experience with this situation, he begins a new trial with a "proprioceptive tension" in anticipation of running to food. The situation activates this tension which is motivational; the tension arises "from the muscles, tendons, and perhaps the joints" (Young, 1959, p. 107). Presumably, Young says, there is more of this tension when the animal runs to the preferred food than when he runs to the less preferred food. Incidentally, the animals in Young's experiments were neither hungry nor thirsty; they ran to the foods presumably because to taste and ingest them occasioned "affective enjoyment," i.e., pleasantness. That the animals anticipated the effects of their running seems evident from Young's description of their state of tension. Whether there was frustration involved is not clear, although the period of restraint before the animals were allowed to run may have produced frustration.

David C. McClelland and his associates (1953) have proposed a theory of motivation which is rather like Young's, although it is directed toward human motivation. Fundamentally, the notion is that motivated behavior takes the form of approach to a situation or to a stimulus or of withdrawal from stimuli. The basic mechanism underlying the approach or the withdrawal is the *anticipation* of what commerce with the situation will bring. If there is an anticipation of pleasure, there will be approach, but if the anticipation is one of unpleasant affect (e.g., pain, fear, or anxiety), there will be withdrawal.

To put this formulation somewhat differently, we can give the following example:

> Let us suppose that a man is experiencing a very pleasant affect or emotion. While this experience is occurring, he is also receiving various stimuli or cues from his environment, his body, his thoughts, and his emotional state itself. Through this contiguous occurrence with the emotion, any one or more of these stimuli or cues may become associated with the emotional state; that is, they can, on later occasions, reactivate some part of it. This fractional reactivation of the emotional state is apparently motivating; that is, the man will now engage in instrumental activities which will bring him to approach the circumstances under which he experienced the pleasant affect or emotion (Cofer & Appley, pp. 374–375).

It must be emphasized that the cue activates only a part of the emotional state and that this provides for the anticipation that getting into the situation will permit the experiencing of the entire emotion. Thus, the man is motivated to do what is necessary to reexperience the entire emotion. Were the cue to do more than this and induce the experience of the total emotion, there would be no motivation to carry out instrumental acts, because experiencing the whole emotion is the goal state.

In the case of cues which evoke an anticipation of unpleasantness on the reexperiencing of a situation, of course, the anticipation will trigger instrumental behavior which will avoid contact with that situation, thus producing withdrawal.

Affective processes (pleasantness and unpleasantness) are made fundamental to motivation, and affective processes, as we saw in Chapter 4, may be given an interpretation in terms of arousal. In McClelland's view, all motives are learned, because they depend on the anticipation of affective outcomes. These anticipations are evoked by cues which develop their capacity to do so because of their prior association with the experiencing of the full affective state. This is, of course, an incentive theory of motivation, as is Young's.

McClelland and his associates developed their theory because, among other things, they were dissatisfied with the drive concept. Their choice of pleasantness-unpleasantness as the relevant affective variable is consistent with the long history that hedonism has had in analyses of human behavior. The account they offer for the conditions which determine affective arousal, however, is not the traditional one of hedonistic theory.

The condition necessary for the arousal of affect, according to McClelland et al. (1953, p. 28), is a discrepancy "between expectation (adaptation level) and perception . . ." This means that the expected, the predictable, the routine are not emotionally arousing. We become adapted, with time, to a given level of stimulation and activity and experience affective neutrality. This idea corresponds to Helson's notion of adaptation level (AL), an idea developed briefly in Chapter 5. It is deviations from the AL or anticipated deviations from it that bring reactions of affect. The cue which evokes the anticipation of pleasure (or of unpleasure) from interaction with another situation is one which signals a change in adaptation level. This formulation is compatible with what we know from the last chapter about the conditions for the occurrence of curiosity and stimulus-seeking behavior.

The degree of discrepancy from expectation or AL, it is proposed, determines whether the experience will be pleasant or unpleasant. If the discrepancy is small, pleasure will occur, if large, unpleasantness. It must be noted that the changes can be in either direction from AL, that is, the change can be an increase or a decrease in stimulation with respect to present AL. Whichever direction the change takes, its size determines whether the consequence will be pleasure or unpleasure.

Stated in its basic terms, the theory seems to be fairly simple. In actuality, it is complex, because to apply it or to test it one must know the current AL in order to estimate whether a situation will produce a deviation from it and the size of the deviation. In addition, events contain many dimensions, and variation from expectation can occur on any or all of these dimensions. Experimental tests, therefore, are difficult to contrive. So far as the writer knows, there is one major experiment which seems to meet the requirements for a suitable experimental test. The results of this test confirm the basic postulates of the theory concerning the conditions for the occurrence of positive and negative affect. This is the experiment reported by Haber (1958) and discussed below. Several other tests of the theory in situations much more complex than the one employed by Haber have not given full support to it (cf. Verinis, Brandsma, & Cofer, 1968). It is difficult to be sure, however, whether these experiments have constituted appropriate tests of the theory.

On the basis of the theoretical analysis, the occurrence of positive and negative affect and of affective indifference should vary with discrepancies from AL in the manner shown in Figure 18. Haber's experiment produced results in conformity with these expectations. Haber had his subjects place their hands in water at a given temperature, and a subject kept his hands there until he said the water felt neutral (AL). Then each subject placed each of his hands at the same time in different buckets, the water in which was at different temperatures. The subject then removed his hand from the bucket in which the water felt "less pleasant." A set of judgments was obtained for a number of temperatures and ALs.

Preference for water temperatures was maximal for moderate deviations from AL and declined on either side of these maxima, a result which the theoretical analysis predicts. Thus, one can say that in this situation the analysis of the conditions of pleasantness and unpleasantness receives confirmation.

The statement was made a moment ago that all motives are learned. The reader may have wondered whether this assertion is to be taken seriously, and in McClelland's view it is. As an example, consider hunger. At the beginning, according to the theory, this condition is not a motive. Only after internal cues arising from the deprivation state and other, external cues have become associated with the pleasures of food-taking can the cues evoke an anticipation that entering an eating situation will be pleasurable. Only then can we say that there is a hunger motive. It is a very dependable motive, because the cues arising from deprivation and cues from eating situations occur with great regularity, but the motive itself is learned.

The McClelland theory, then, rejects the idea of drive but provides that cues (external or internal) may trigger off affective reactions which provide the energy for the occurrence of behavior. The cues, of course, provide direction or guidance for behavior in the case of these "motivational associations." There are other associations, not motivational in character, which lack affective arousal, so that affective arousal seems to be the hallmark of the motive. In its rejection of drive and adoption of a

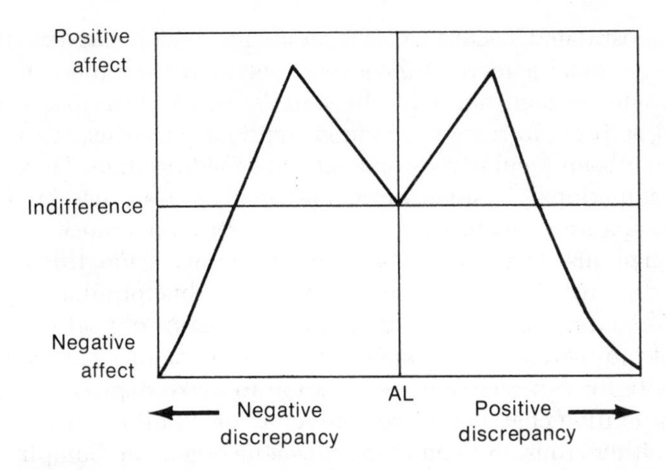

FIGURE 18 Hypothetical relations between judgments of affect to deviations of stimulation from Adaptation Level, according to McClelland's theory. From Haber, R. N. Discrepancy from adaptation level as a source of affect. *Journal of Experimental Psychology*, 1958, Vol. 56, P. 371, Fig. 1. By permission of American Psychological Association.

cue-arousal mechanism for motivation, the theory is an incentive theory of motivation. Like Young's it holds that the mechanism of incentives lies in affective arousal, initiated by cues, on the dimension of positive and negative affect.

There have been several proposals of incentive theories, most of them of much more limited scope than McClelland's. Included among these formulations are notions stressing anticipatory goal reactions, such as feeding responses. We mentioned these ideas briefly in discussing Sheffield's and Amsel's formulations which stressed frustration of anticipatory feeding reactions as the basis for motivation in certain situations.

Cofer and Appley (1964, Chapter 16) have generalized these views in a theory of motivated behavior based on reactions to incentives. They have taken as their starting point the notion that the essence of the motivation concept lies in its role of regulating the *vigor* of behaviors, i.e., motivation serves to invigorate behavior. In making this judgment, they have accepted the notion that the unique function of the motivation construct is to energize responses through states of arousal, leaving to other factors the guidance of behavior, i.e., its direction (see Chapter 2, p. 34).

The arousal is induced by stimuli, either external or internal ones, but Cofer and Appley suggest that two mechanisms are required to account for the induction of arousal by stimuli. One mechanism depends on learning and is referred to as the anticipation-invigoration mechanism (AIM). The other does not require a history of learning and is called the sensitization-invigoration mechanism (SIM). It is possible that the two mechanisms would often work in concert, as the arousal in many situations may be the result both of learned and unlearned processes. In discussing AIM and SIM, however, we shall consider them separately.

AIM is postulated because of the evidence which has led so many writers to propose a learned-incentive mechanism of motivation. Perhaps the major reason that led Cofer and Appley to turn to it is the evidence that activity, in response to food deprivation, seems to arise when stimuli have been regularly associated with feeding time. These stimuli evoke anticipations, of some kind, that feeding time has arrived, and these anticipations themselves or their frustration arouse the animal and energize his responses. Many observations, aside from the ones having to do with activity, are compatible with this formulation. Among them are the effects of prefeeding, of characteristics of goal objects, persistence of motivational phenomena in the absence of local stimulation, the necessity for experience of deprivation to make deprivation motivating, the appetitive character of sexual behavior. In all of these cases, the incentive either arouses or comes to arouse the organism. Complex human motivational phenomena, as Chapters 7 and 8 will suggest, seem to require an interpretation in which incentive stimuli play a major role.

Cofer and Appley are not specific with regard to what mechanisms may underlie anticipation, although they are sympathetic to the idea that components of the goal reactions may form the basis for the anticipation.

The directional aspect of behavior is treated by Cofer and Appley as arising from the stimuli of the situation, including those which induce the arousal. Incentive theories, in general, tie arousal to situations; and situations, of course, contain many stimuli to which reactions of approach and avoidance, for example, have been associated. What the animal does is attributed to the control such stimuli have over his reactions—choice, preference, patterns of movement previously learned, and, as just mentioned, whether he will approach or withdraw from the situation. The motivational component—the arousal—governs only the vigor with which such learned reactions occur.

The foregoing account suggests that incentives may function in relatively specific situations, and one may wonder how more general motives, such as those we often presume the human organism to have, would be coped with in this formulation. The answer lies in the suggestion that what we call general motives arise because many and diverse stimuli have come to evoke arousal and that these same stimuli (and perhaps others) have, through learning, become equivalent in the sorts of behavior they control—acts related to achievement, for example, or to aggression, anxiety, and the like.

The other mechanism, SIM, was introduced by Cofer and Appley in recognition of the evidence that some stimuli seem to have the capability of arousal without prior learning. The examples come from hormonally based activities, including the releasing stimuli discussed by the ethologists in hormonally prepared animals.

The model for SIM was taken from the proposal of a sexual arousal mechanism by Beach (1956). It differs from AIM only in that certain stimuli, e.g., those associated with a receptive female, can apparently without learning arouse a hormonally ready male rat. Similarly, the male rat will arouse the female, but only when she is hormonally ready to be receptive. This kind of mechanism seems to underlie a number of behaviors; for example, rat pups are most effective as stimuli for maternal behavior when the female has just given birth; hormonal factors (among others) are involved in nest-building; they also seem implicated in the migratory flights of certain birds.

It is not clear what the mechanisms are that result in the effect that at certain times the male rat, for example, is an arousing stimulus for the female and at other times is not. Some change in sensitivity in the female is perhaps involved, but details are lacking. The basis for this selective sensitization to stimuli remains to be worked out.

At any rate, the arousal occurs, and as with AIM the situation provides many cues for the behavior which takes place. In these cases, the animal's innate structure provides the mechanics which underlie the behavior. Learning may not be involved at all or, if it is, probably contributes much less to the pattern of behavior in the case of SIM than it does in the case of AIM. Situations, as Beach has observed, may through experience come to evoke sexual arousal in the male rat, but this process merely extends the variety of situations in which arousal can occur. In rats anyway, learning seems to be essential neither to the occurrence of arousal in the presence of hormonal states and adequate stimuli nor the pattern of behavior which eventuates. Needless to say, in other species the role of learning is much more extensive.

Episodes of motivated behavior stop, in the Cofer and Appley hypothesis, when the arousal function of the incentive stimuli is reduced. This presumably comes about because of consummatory (or escape) behavior which must change the arousal potential of the stimuli or the capacity of the response mechanism to support the behavior. In some cases, of course, as in the hunger-free rat's running to a sugar or a saccharine solution, however, the animal continues to run to the incentive for many, many trials.

REINFORCERS AND REINFORCEMENT THEORY

Motivation, as we have seen already, has referred historically to internal factors which govern behavior and may be likened to a push, i.e., behavior springs from internal "pushes." The many difficulties with this idea have led to an alternative interpretation in terms of incentives which we have just reviewed; the latter may almost be said to "pull" behavior to (or away) from them. But perhaps it is possible to get along without any motivation concepts at all. Such a view has been proposed. Its current major manifestation is in a reinforcement theory. Before we discuss this theory, we should become more familiar than we are with reinforcement.

Many years ago, E. L. Thorndike (1911), on the basis of the research which he had performed, proposed what is usually referred to as the law of effect. This law states that those responses which occur in a situation and which lead to "satisfaction" will tend to be repeated when the situation recurs, whereas those responses not leading to satisfaction will not be strengthened. Thorndike defined satisfaction as anything ". . . which the animal does nothing to avoid, often doing such things as attain and preserve it" (1911, p. 245). At one time Thorndike thought that punishment weakened the responses made in a situation, but he gave up this idea because his data did not support it.

The law of effect has a great deal of descriptive validity, although it is likely that there are cases of learning to which it does not readily apply. The major theoretical discussion has centered on the mechanisms of the law, rather than on its empirical validity.

Although terms like *satisfaction* and *pleasure* were sometimes used in early formulations of the law, they were eventually supplanted by alternative accounts which spoke of drive reduction, need reduction, or drive-stimulus reduction as the event or process essential to the occurrence of reinforcement. For our present purposes, we can speak simply of drive reduction as the basis for reinforcement, not entering into the question how this term differs from need or drive-stimulus reduction.

Clark L. Hull's (1943, 1952) systematic behavior theory made extensive use of the concept of drive reduction. In brief, this idea is that reinforcement occurs, as in the case of food for a hungry animal, because the reinforcer reduces, in some measure, the prevailing drive condition.

This principle was a popular one for a number of years, but it has been troubled by a number of difficulties. One of its implications is that the reduction of a prevailing drive involves a reduction in stimulation, i.e., a tension reduction. (In this implication it seems comparable to some of Freud's notions.) It is this aspect that has been attacked, and the consequence is that reinforcement, in the generality, cannot be equated with drive or stimulus reduction.

The idea of drive reduction is not one that seems compatible with the work reviewed in Chapter 5, in which it became obvious that novel stimulation seems to be motivating and that conditions of sensory isolation or deprivation appear to be aversive. In addition, learning seems to occur when the consequence of a response is augmented stimulation, as the following discussion indicates.

Rats will learn to go into that arm of a Y-shaped maze which leads to another maze which is complex and which offers them the opportunity to explore, in preference to the arm which leads to an ordinary goal box (Montgomery, 1954). Monkeys will learn to press a distinctive panel on the side of a box, which, when pushed, opens and allows them a view of the laboratory environment. This environment is presumably more stimulating than that provided by the box in which they are confined (Butler, 1953). Auditory stimulation is also reinforcing to monkeys (Butler, 1957). If one goal box contains novel objects in it, rats will learn to go to that goal box rather than to one that is empty (Berlyne & Slater, 1957).

The onset of a relatively dim light serves as a reward (Roberts, Marx, & Collier, 1958) for rats. Apparently, movement in a part of an apparatus can be reinforcing for these animals. Placed in an enclosure in which there is a platform in each corner, rats will spend an increasing proportion of their time on the one platform of the four which moves from their weight (Kish, 1955; Barnes & Kish, 1957).

Other kinds of rewards are also effective though they do not involve drive reduction. Thus, rats will learn the correct response in a T-maze, when the reward is saccharin (which tastes sweet to the human), a nonnutritive substance (Sheffield & Roby, 1950). Saccharin was a more effective reinforcer than dextrose, a nutritive substance not so sweet as the saccharin. Male rats will learn to increase their speed of running in a runway when the reward is incomplete copulation with a receptive female (Sheffield, Wolf, & Backer, 1951). The rats were sexually inexperienced, and the fact that the copulation was incomplete should have raised the stimulation level, rather than reducing it. All of these findings give clear support to the notion that drive reduction is not a necessary condition for reinforcement, although, of course, they do not indicate that drive reduction, when it occurs, is not reinforcing.

Some attempts have been made to propose a mechanism of reinforcement, alternative to drive reduction, which would have sufficient generality to encompass the action of a wide variety of reinforcers.

One suggestion that appears to offer promise was made by Premack (1959, 1965). In essence, his idea is that a reinforcing activity is one which has a higher preference value for the organism than the one it reinforces. For example, it would be argued from this position that drinking would have a higher preference value than running for a thirsty rat, and we know that drinking water will reinforce the act of running to it. But suppose that running had a higher value than drinking. Would it then reinforce drinking? Premack (1962) made a test of this derivation, using water deprivation to increase the value of drinking in the one case and deprivation of running in an activity wheel in the other. When the animal was reinforced for drinking (in the satiated state) by an opportunity to run (in the deprived state), he learned to drink in that situation, despite the absence of water deprivation. When the conditions were reversed, he learned to run when this activity was followed by drinking. These findings support Premack's prediction, and other evidence he has obtained from children and monkeys as well as from rats also supports it.

Premack's analysis, of course, leads to a relative conception of reinforcement (Hilgard & Bower, 1966, p. 486). This is to say that a given activity will reinforce another, less preferred one but will itself be susceptible to being reinforced by one with greater preference value. Likewise, the value of a given activity may change or vary, as was the case with drinking and running in the example just mentioned. Values of activities can also change with experience and perhaps with growth and maturation. These variations point to difficulties in the application of Premack's model, because suitable means must be at hand to evaluate the relative preferences for activities at a given time in order to decide which one to use as a reinforcer. It may often be difficult to compare activities if the units of performance on them are not commensurate.

Nevertheless, this proposal may meet many of the problems that the drive-reduction interpretation of reinforcement has encountered, and it fits well with what we have said in this and earlier chapters concerning the adaptation level. Some deviation from adaptation level seems to characterize many of the motivational effects of external stimuli (see Berlyne, 1967), and as we have just seen, external stimulus changes have often been found to have reinforcing value. It is possible that changes in stimulation which evoke locomotion, manipulation, and curiosity in general are also those which will reinforce behavior so that it is learned. We need more tests of the motivational-reinforcement relation in these cases than we have had.

A kind of stimulation rather different from external stimulus changes has also been found to be an effective reinforcer, and this kind of reinforcer has been said to disprove the drive-reduction interpretation of reinforcement. This is stimulation of certain areas of the brain by means of a brief electrical shock. Olds and Milner (1954) reported that rats would learn to press a bar when the bar-press resulted in such stimulation, and the behavior of the animals suggested that the stimulation is pleasant, thus supporting the notion that there are "pleasure centers" in the brain. It has also been reported (Delgado, Roberts, & Miller, 1954) that there are areas in the brain, electrical stimulation of which is aversive (see Figure 19).

In these experiments, electrodes were permanently implanted in the brains of rats, and circuitry was arranged so that when the animal pressed a bar he received the shock to his brain. Positive effects of brain stimulation have been reported in a variety of animals (cats, monkeys, dolphins), and in human patients reports of pleasure have accompanied electrical stimulation of several regions of the brain; in one study the patients learned and continued to press a lever the only result of which was electrical stimulation of their brains (Sem-Jacobsen & Torkildsen, 1960).

The distribution of parts of the brain where these rewarding and aversive effects are obtained has been studied extensively in the rat. Many areas of the brain give neither rewarding nor aversive effects; approximately 60 percent of electrode placements yielded neither effect, many of these placements being in the neocortex and the greatest part of the thalamus. Many more placements (35 percent) show rewarding effects than show aversive effects (5 percent), and the aversive placements tend to be located near those which yield positive effects (see Grossman, 1967, p. 569).

Among the structures stimulation of which is rewarding are the rhinen-

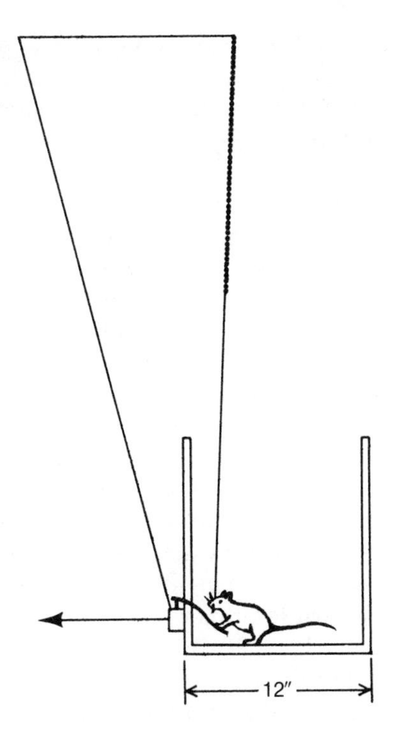

FIGURE 19 Sketch of bar-pressing device by which a rat can administer an electric shock to its own brain. Depression of the bar closes a circuit so that current enters the brain by means of implanted electrodes. Reproduced from Olds, J. Self-stimulation of the brain. *Science*, Vol. 127, Pp. 315–324, Fig. 1, February 14, 1958.

cephalon, the hypothalamus, parts of the thalamus, and the tegmentum. Bar-pressing rates for electrical stimulation vary a good deal among and within these structures, the highest rates occurring for stimulation points in the posterior hypothalamus, the medial tegmentum, the preoptic, and the septal areas (Grossman, 1967, p. 569).

Some areas of the brain, to which the animal administers shock by bar-pressing, are associated with very high rates of bar-pressing. Yet, when the shock apparatus is turned off, the animals cease bar-pressing at once. Olds (1958a) has reported rates as high as 7000 responses an hour, and a rate of 2000 responses an hour in a rat during waking periods over a 48-hour interval.

When the positive effects of intracranial stimulation were first discovered, the phenomenon was seen as being incompatible with a drive-reduction theory of reward, and it was suggested that there are "pleasure centers" in the brain (Olds & Milner, 1954, p. 425). In the early experiments, no "drive" was present, and the rewarding effects arose in the context of an increase in stimulation—that produced by the shock. Alternative interpretations have, however, appeared.

One point is to question the independence of the reward system from motivation systems. The fact is, according to Grossman (1967, p. 575), that

> Hunger, thirst, sexual arousal, and various emotional drives can be elicited or inhibited by electrical stimulation of just those regions that appear to be most directly implicated in the reward and aversion phenomena.

In addition, it is often the case that rates of self-stimulation found for areas of the brain vary with food deprivation and with injection of androgen (sex hormone). Thus Olds (1958b) found that depending on electrode placement either hunger or androgen level was associated with high-response rates, as compared to rates obtained under no hunger or under low androgen levels. Brady and his associates (1957) reported on one animal which could press either one of two levers. When he pressed one (A), he received water, and when he pressed the other (B), the result was shock to the brain. The animal was run after water deprivation. When he was rewarded with water every time that he pressed lever A, he satiated for water rapidly, and his presses of lever B, initially frequent, dropped off. This suggests that the water deprivation was motivating the pressing of lever B. Water was also given on only some presses of lever A (on a variable interval schedule); this routine did not lead to satiation for water, and bar-pressing of lever B did not drop off. Hence, rate of bar-pressing for shock to the brain here depends on the presence of deprivation of water. High rates of self-stimulation also occur from placements in areas, which when they are electrically stimulated by the experimenter reliably elicit eating behavior (Margules & Olds, 1962). Other evidence could be cited, but the general finding is that there is a close, if not perfect, relationship between the occurrence of self-stimulation in an area and that area's role in eliciting, when stimulated, behaviors such as eating, drinking, and sexual arousal. Grossman (1967, p. 591) offers the suggestion that these relationships may mean that

> the reward effect is caused by the excitation of inhibitory (and in some cases excitatory) mechanisms which contribute to the central regulation of *specific* drives. Self-stimulation is thought to provide pseudo-satiation of a prevailing drive (or, in some cases, excitation of specific drives).

Such an interpretation is, at least in part, compatible with a general drive-reduction notion. In other words, electrical self-stimulation may not be, as Olds and Milner originally believed, a basis on which a tension reduction conception of reinforcement can be rejected. On the other hand, the study of self-stimulation offers an interesting way of examining aspects of reward, a concept so central to many of our ideas about behavior.

An interpretation of the rewarding effects of electrical brain stimulation has been made in terms of incentive theory by Trowill, Panksepp, and Gandelman (1969). Their point, which they support by means of various observations reported in the literature and from their own investigations, is that the rewarding effects of electrical brain stimulation do not require a special or unique interpretation, different from that given for the effects of other rewards. However, since incentives are not usually conceived to have their effects via drive reduction, the interpretation of the rewarding effects of electrical brain stimulation in incentive terms does not support a drive-reduction theory of reinforcement. In our earlier discussion, of course, we have seen that there is a good deal of evidence which contradicts that theory.

The question remains whether the process of reinforcement, whatever its mechanism or mechanisms, can in general account for the features of behavior that have led us to consider the motivational concept. Robert Bolles (1967, Chapter 15) has suggested that this is a distinct possibility. In the paragraphs that follow, we shall discuss it.

We have seen already that one does not require a state of deprivation in order for reinforcement to occur, although for many reinforcers, such as food or water, the effectiveness of the reinforcer is much greater with an appropriate state of deprivation than it is without it. One way of judging whether an event is likely to have reinforcement properties is to determine its preference value for the animals or people with whom we are concerned. In the absence of other information, we can make systematic observations as to what an individual does during his free time, i.e., what things he does when he is not under direction, guidance, or compulsion and which, there is every evidence to believe, interest him and give him enjoyment. One can then contrive situations so that the opportunity to do the preferred thing is made contingent on the doing of something else. Thus, for a youngster who is intensely interested in playing his guitar and who does so at every opportunity, one can strengthen his tendency to do other things, like studying, by making the chance to play the guitar contingent on doing the less preferred thing (studying). When there is a reinforcer of high value and when the opportunity to have or to do it can be effectively scheduled, a high degree of control over the occurrence of the less preferred activity can be achieved. (It is often difficult, however, in everyday life to arrange for occurrence of the reinforcer at just the right time and place.)

The question of theoretical interest is whether it adds anything to the kind of description of a reinforcer we have just given to use a motivational term, such as *incentive*. Perhaps if we know what reinforces behavior and the circumstances under which the reinforcer has occurred, we know all that we need to know and the invoking of motivational terms makes no contribution to our understanding.

Bolles, like this writer, has rejected the drive concept as not helpful. However, unlike this writer, he would prefer to omit the concept of incentive so long as a reinforcement concept can do the job. His reasons for rejecting incentive follow.

First (Bolles, 1967, p. 440), he suggests that it is unnecessary to use any motivational concepts like incentive or drive for certain phenomena usually considered to be motivated. He points out that the sexual behavior of the male rat with a receptive female (see Chapter 3, p. 49) is lawful, because we can change it by castrating the animal or by providing him with a nonestrous female or by manipulating other variables. Hence, the behavior can be explained in terms of antecedent or necessary conditions. "But," he says, "the explanation is not motivational in character because none of the antecedent conditions are motivational; they are the conditions in the presence of which the behavior occurs. Hence we are not inclined to consider the behavior motivated" (p. 440). It will be obvious to the reader that this view differs widely from that proposed by Cofer and Appley (1964), who developed SIM as a motivational device to account for the kind of acts just mentioned. Their reason, of course, was that male sexual behavior in the rat does depend on an interaction of the incentive (the female) and the hormonal state. Bolles does not wish, apparently, to call the interaction motivated, but Cofer and Appley, as have many writers, feel that it is useful to refer to certain kinds of antecedent factors and their interactions by a motivational term.

Bolles goes on to say that changes in the animal's behavior—such as a decrease in latency, augmented stereotypy and predictability, persistence, excitement, and the reduction of competing behavior—with repeated sexual encounters in the situation do occur. However, he suggests that these changes arise because "sexual behavior is reinforcing" (p. 440); further evidence that it is reinforcing is that the animal will learn to run an alley to get to the female and other instrumental acts which we may require of it. However, he avers, this shows that "The evidence we use for supporting the claim of motivation is again precisely the same evidence we cite to indicate that the consummatory behavior is reinforcing" (p. 441). Evidently, he believes that motivation and learning (the effect of reinforcement) are "merely two ways of regarding a single set of phenomena;" what he proposes "is that there is just a single set of phenomena to be explained, and that it can best be explained as an effect of reinforcement. This is what is meant by the designation 'reinforcement theory of motivation' (p. 441)." If a reinforcement theory can be developed and substantiated, we would ask of a man's behavior not what motivated it, but rather what conditions of reinforcement underlay its development and underlie its maintenance (p. 451).

Bolles does refer (pp. 442–443) to the problem that behavior seems to be energized (invigorated) by conditions of deprivation, but he believes this problem for a reinforcement theory of motivation can be handled by an incentive mechanism. "The energization of instrumental behavior can then be reduced to an effect of the energization of the mediating or incentive response" (p. 443). Perhaps this is like Cofer and Appley's AIM, although Bolles' discussion is so brief (and Cofer and Appley's is not very full either) as to make a comparison impossible. Bolles refers to this incentive mechanism as one of the associative type, but the present writer is unclear, given the context of this statement, just what is meant by an incentive mechanism of an associative type.

An attempt to eliminate terms and concepts from a discipline when they are no longer useful is praiseworthy and is to be encouraged. In this writer's opinion, however, Bolles' attempt to eliminate motivation concepts (specifically the incentive concept, which, of course, he eliminates by calling it an associative or a habit factor) is premature. There are three reasons.

First, the proposal for a reinforcement theory of motivation is not as yet well worked out. One must, at the present time, suspend judgment as to its potentialities.

Second, Bolles seems to wish to eliminate from the realm of motivation those phenomena for which Cofer and Appley developed the notion of SIM. These phenomena have traditionally been a part of motivation and an important part, as witness, for example, the role of sex in Freud's theory and the role of innate motivational factors in the ethologists' theories. These phenomena cannot be accounted for in stimulus or reinforcement terms alone, and there seems to be no reason to exclude them from motivation just because we can, in some measure, specify their antecedent conditions. The logic of calling them nonmotivated just because something is known concerning their prior circumstances eludes this writer.

Third, the emphasis on reinforcement implies that we know a lot about it and that we know that it is not necessary to speak of motivational variables with reference to it. It is true that we identify reinforcers by means of empirical observation (as in the example of guitar playing mentioned earlier) and that, therefore, for practical purposes perhaps a theory of reinforcement is not necessary.

When we move beyond the purely practical, however, we seem to wish to understand the mechanisms of such an effect as reinforcement. And it is not clear that reinforcers themselves are unrelated to motivational conditions like incentive value. Some reinforcers are clearly effective only when there is a state of deprivation, and they do seem to invigorate as well as to reinforce behavior. We mentioned that events and activities can be reinforcers for other activities when the former have more value than the latter, as indexed by preference, rate of occurrence, persistence, and the like. We are moved to ask, what is this notion of value, what is its source, what is its mechanism? It is not impossible that this value lies in invigoration of behavior, however achieved, and that a full understanding of reinforcers may only be obtained when the mechanisms of this invigoration are understood. Incentive theory, as presented earlier in this chapter, is an attempt to understand invigoration. It is too early in the development of incentive theory to abandon it for the reinforcement mechanism in the explanation of which incentive theory may play an important part (see Bindra, 1969). A further discussion of the differences between incentive and reinforcement will be found in Chapter 9.

SUGGESTED READINGS

Bolles, R. C. *Theory of motivation.* New York: Harper and Row, Publishers, 1967. Chapters 12 and 16.

Cofer, C. N. & Appley, M. H. *Motivation: Theory and research.* New York: John Wiley & Sons, Inc., 1964. Pp. 539–566; 370–386. Chapter 16.

Grossman, S. P. *A textbook of physiological psychology.* New York: John Wiley & Sons, Inc., 1967. Chapter 10.

Helson, H. *Adaptation-level theory.* New York: Harper & Row, Publishers, 1964.

Hilgard, E. R. & Bower, G. H. *Theories of learning.* (3rd ed.) New York: Appleton-Century-Crofts, 1966. Pp. 481–487.

7

Some Motivational Systems in the Human Being

Twenty years ago this chapter would have been entitled "acquired drive" or something very similar, such as "learned drive," "secondary drive," or "learned motives." The current phrase, "motivational system," is intended to cover the same ground as that indicated by the older titles, but its choice reflects the many changes in our thinking about the motivational concept that have occurred in the period since 1950. One reason for rejecting the title, "acquired drive," of course, is the difficulty with the term *drive* itself, but another problem lies in whether the term *drive* was ever an appropriate one for the acquired motivational factor it was supposed to designate. In addition, it seems clear that, in the human being, motivation is a complex factor, such that *system* is a term preferable to others which do not imply much complexity. Learning or experience is undoubtedly responsible for much of human motivation, but how experience operates to produce motivational systems is much less clear today than it seemed to be 20 years ago. For all these reasons, further discussion of which will be provided in the pages of this chapter, the term *motivational system* has been chosen.

A number of systems will be described in this chapter. They have been placed here because they have often been regarded as acquired drives. On the other hand, they might have been placed in Chapter 6, because, as we shall see, the idea of acquired drive was really a form of incentive theory, and as will be brought out in the present chapter, all of the motivational systems treated here have incentivelike characteristics. These systems might have been included in the next chapter, because they have much to do with social motivation. But the balance theories have a rather different historical background from that which characterizes the systems treated in the present chapter. This background will be brought out by our discussion of acquired drives. Then we shall describe a number of motivational systems which have been proposed for and studied in human beings.

ACQUIRED DRIVES

In Chapter 2 the discussion of drive theory included a brief account (p. 26) of fear as an acquired drive and the suggestion that other acquired drives could be conceived along the same or similar lines. We will now discuss the significance and the nature of acquired drives and the difficulties that have arisen concerning this notion.

Drive theory took as its paradigm for motivation the sources of motivation known as primary or biological drives, but there was always awareness that such drives provide an insufficient basis for dealing with the complexities of human motivation. It is obvious that people continue to display motivated behavior even in the absence of states of motivation like hunger, thirst, or sex, and beginning with Woodworth (1918) it has been argued that there must be sources of motivation other than hunger, thirst, and sex. Woodworth, for example, suggested that skills, once learned to some degree, may possess their own motive power which initiates or sustains their use: ". . . the power of acquiring new mechanisms possessed by the human mind is at the same time a power of acquiring new drives. . . ." When a skill or a habit has reached some level of proficiency but without becoming automatic, Woodworth (1918, p. 104) said, it "is itself a drive and capable of motivating activities that lie beyond its immediate scope." The persistent and compulsivelike quality of some activities, such as those activities involved in making a living which endure after the need for money has been met, was used by Woodworth as an example of what he had in mind. Gordon Allport (1937) proposed a very similar idea, speaking of it as the "functional autonomy" which many activities possess. Thus, an activity may have developed under the impetus of some biological drive, but Allport thought that it could become independent of this source (and of any other biological sources) and persist as a motive in its own right. In these formulations, both Woodworth and Allport gave recognition to significant aspects of human motivation but did not offer much in the way of suggestions as to the processes or mechanisms which determine what activities will become functionally autonomous or as to how they achieve this status.

The concept of acquired drive is in some measure a theory advanced to account for functionally autonomous motivated behavior, but in principle it is a proposal that there are *learned* sources of motivation which underlie those activities which are apparently functionally autonomous. The paradigm for acquired drive is Miller's (1948, 1951) conception of fear. To study fear, Miller used a two-compartment apparatus (see Figure 20), one compartment of which was painted white, the other black. The two compartments were separable by a door. The animal (a rat) received electric shock in the white compartment and, with the door open, could

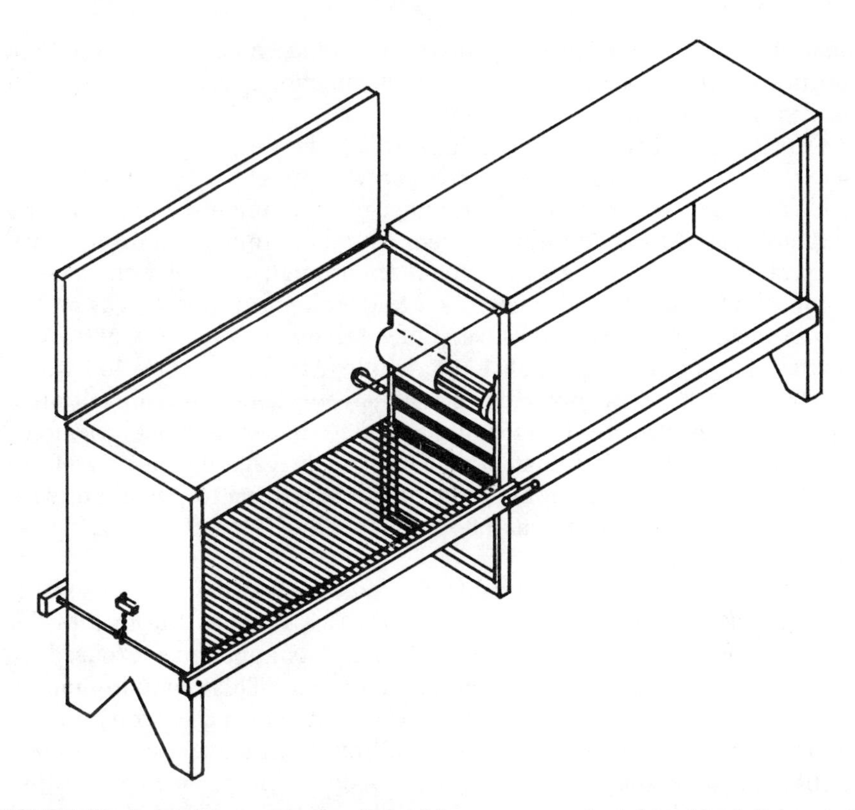

FIGURE 20 Apparatus used in the study of fear as an acquired drive. The left compartment is painted white, the right black. Electric shock can be given through the grid floor of the left compartment. The door between the compartments is painted with horizontal black and white stripes, and it drops out of the way if the experimenter presses a button or if the rat presses the bar or rotates the wheel (above the stripes), depending on conditions. From Miller, N. E. Learnable drives and rewards. In S. S. Stevens (Ed.), *Handbook of experimental psychology*. 1951. P. 437, Fig. 1. By permission of John Wiley & Sons, Inc.

run into the black compartment in which no shock was present. The animals learned to run out of the white compartment into the black one. Then the apparatus was arranged so that the door between the compartments was closed but could be opened if the animal rotated a wheel or pressed a bar. Placed in the white compartment, the animals, over several trials, learned to open the door by rotating the wheel, and when the wheel was no longer functional, they unlearned the response of wheel-turning and learned to press the bar to open the door. Miller proposed that the animal learned to be afraid of the white compartment after he was shocked there, that the fear motivated the behavior which eventuated in wheel-turning or bar-pressing, and that entrance into the black compartment was fear reducing and therefore reinforcing. It must be noted that shock was given only in the initial trials in the apparatus and was not administered during the period when wheel-turning and bar-pressing were learned. A bar-pressing habit, based on fear, was found to persist for hundreds of trials without additional shocks, and the rate of learning is a function of the intensity of the shocks given in the initial trials in the apparatus.

Miller proposed that acquired drives could be developed in the same way when the initial source of motivation was not shock but other drives such as hunger, thirst, or sex. A number of experiments, including one by Myers and Miller (1954), have been conducted in an attempt to verify this proposal. Although an occasional experiment has been successful, the majority of the studies have failed to develop acquired drives on the basis of these appetitive drives (see Cofer & Appley, 1964, pp. 580–582; Brown & Farber, 1968, pp. 106–107; Appley, 1970, pp. 486–487, 505–509). These failures, of course, have seriously weakened the conception of acquired drives, because it is usually assumed that there must be sources of acquired drives other than fear. One can salvage the notion of acquired drive in some form, of course, if he is willing to postulate, with Brown (1961), that fear or anxiety underlies most, if not all, motivated behavior in the human.

There is, however, a considerable question concerning the drive status of Miller's notion of fear. The question arises because the fear Miller demonstrated is situationally induced, i.e., it is apparently aroused by the stimulus complex of the white compartment. This compartment is, of course, external to the animal and, as a source of motivation, is more properly referred to as an incentive condition. In this case it is a negative incentive, which the animal learns to escape from or to avoid, rather than a positive incentive, the kind mainly treated in Chapter 6. Hence, the term *acquired drive* was never really appropriate to Miller's demonstration, and we should say that drive theory was supplemented by the notion of positive and negative incentives rather than by the acquired drives. However, as we have said, only the negative incentive has received adequate experimental support.

We should temper the implication contained in the two preceding paragraphs concerning positive incentives. It has not been possible, with animals, to develop positive incentives in situations modeled on the paradigmatic situation in which Miller demonstrated the negative incentive based on fear. But this does not mean that in other situations positive incentives cannot be or have not been demonstrated. Chapter 6 provides illustrations mostly in the case of animals, and there is a good deal of evidence that people become attracted to situations and to other persons who have been associated with rewards and praise (see Berkowitz, 1969b, pp. 55–59). These effects are not simple and automatic ones, but, on the whole, a person will evaluate positively and prefer individuals who have praised or rewarded him, or he will choose to work with those persons with whom he has previously worked successfully, or he will choose tasks like those on which he has experienced positive outcomes in the past.

MOTIVATIONAL SYSTEMS

There have been a number of attempts to list major human motives of a learned or secondary kind, and several of these motives have received extensive study. One list was proposed by Murray (1938), who spoke of psychogenic (learned) needs; several of the needs he listed are among those which have received a lot of attention in the laboratory, and it is fair to say that Murray has had a large impact on these studies of human motivation. Murray's thinking was much influenced by psychoanalysis and by drive theory generally, and his conception of "need" had much in common with the notion of drive. As we shall see, the human motivational systems we deal with here depend to a large extent for their arousal on situational factors, suggesting the importance of incentive mechanisms in their functioning. Most of the work in this area, however, has been couched in terms of needs or motives, being derived, in large part, from the tradition of thinking about motivation of which drive theory was representative.

Arousal and Measurement Problems

The notion of a motive or a need implies an enduring property or characteristic of persons and further implies that the strength of the motive will vary in a given individual at different times and among different individuals. In thinking seriously about human motives, then, we must have techniques which, on the one hand, allow us to assess the level or the strength of a motive at a given time and, on the other hand, enable us to manipulate, for experimental purposes, the level of the arousal of the motive. To make these points clear, we can refer to hunger as a model. In this case we vary the arousal of hunger by means of depriving the subject of food for some interval of time (or until his body weight has been reduced by some proportion). We measure his hunger by a variety of techniques—amount of food eaten, latency of beginning to eat, the amount of shock he will tolerate in going to an incentive, etc. These are relatively objective procedures and seem, on their face, to be appropriate arousal and measurement techniques for hunger. A major problem in the study of human motivation is to find parallel operations of arousal and assessment.

Sometimes arousal is accomplished experimentally, as we shall see, for example, in the case of the achievement motive later in this chapter. The difficulty here, of course, is whether the technique does in fact arouse the motive in which we are interested and only that motive. Another technique for varying arousal is to select people of whom it can be said that they differ in the motive in question. We do not arouse the motive experimentally but have reason to believe that the people we select vary in the motive we are interested in. If, for example, we are interested in anxiety, we may choose psychiatric patients as individuals with high anxiety and "normal" people as those with low anxiety. There are difficulties here, too, among them that the people we select may differ on traits other than the motive of concern.

Most of the work done has employed essentially verbal means for assessing the motives. For example, questionnaires, rating scales, and storytelling are procedures that are commonly used, as we shall see. Such techniques have to be valid measures of the motives we wish to study, and the judgment of their validity is a difficult one to be certain about. We may, for instance, design a questionnaire which is to measure anxiety. We select the questions because they refer to experiences or symptoms which are commonly thought to occur in anxiety, and we may validate our questions by comparing the responses of (anxious) patients with those of normals. Stories have to be scored in order to yield a measure of a motive, and we may select items from stories to be scored by comparing the stories produced by people in whom we have tried experimentally to arouse the motive with those produced by people in whom no effort to arouse the motive has been made.

Other techniques, such as physiological measures of arousal, have not been used very often. They are, of course, cumbersome to employ, and their interpretation encounters many of the same problems we meet with verbal measures.

From these remarks concerning arousal and measurement problems, it should be clear that the study of human motivation is a difficult task, one whose outcomes are not always clear or satisfying. These considerations should be kept in mind as we survey, in the pages that follow, the motivational systems that have been given serious attention.

Achievement and Fear of Failure

In the late 1940's, David C. McClelland and his associates initiated a series of studies designed to utilize fantasy as revealed in stories as a means of assessing a major human motive, the need for achievement, abbreviated as nAch and defined as concern over competition with a standard of excellence. The first experiments (Atkinson & McClelland, 1948) were concerned, however, with hunger, the reason being that it seemed desirable first to establish that degrees of hunger could be detected in fantasy material. The demonstration of such a relationship, then, made it sensible to go on to develop a way of scoring stories in order to index nAch.

The procedure for measuring motivation was a modified form of the Thematic Apperception Test (TAT), introduced by Morgan and Murray (1935). The subject is asked to write a story to go with each of several pictures. The story is to be organized around four questions: what is happening in the picture and the identity of the people in it; what has taken place in the past to lead up to the situation depicted in the picture;

what is going on (who is thinking what); and what will happen. The use of these questions provides more direction for the writing of the stories than the procedure used by Morgan and Murray.

Given that one has stories, it is necessary to score them for the presence and the degree of achievement motivation. To find story elements that would reflect achievement themes, McClelland et al. (1949) obtained stories from groups of male college students. A common procedure was to have the group take a series of tests and then to write the stories. The groups were treated differently, in conjunction with their performance on the tests which preceded the writing of the stories, in order to create different arousal levels of nAch. One group, the relaxed group, was given the tests under the instructions that the tests were being tried out, so that the tests, not the students, were being evaluated; in another group, the neutral group, the subjects were asked to do their best, as test norms were being developed. In a third group, achievement oriented, the subjects scored their tests after completing them, and the tests were identified as measuring intelligence, leadership, and the like. Considering these three groups, one would expect little arousal of nAch in the first one, somewhat more in the second, and a great deal in the third. (Several other groups, failure, success, and success-failure were also run, but we will not describe them here.) Hence, stories written after the tests were completed were obtained under three degrees of arousal of nAch.

The stories were then examined to determine items that differentiated the achievement-aroused group from the others. A number were found; for example, the aroused group showed more achievement imagery, expressed more need for achievement, indicated more activities designed to attain an achievement goal, and more often indicated affective states when the goal was or was not reached than the other groups. These elements, together with several others, then provide the indicators of the degree of achievement. The score for a story is based on the number of elements indicative of achievement which appear in the story, and the total nAch score is the sum of the values for all the stories written.

The experimental manipulation of arousal of nAch was carried out for the purpose of obtaining valid items. In practice, one would assesss nAch for a group of people without these manipulations, i.e., by obtaining just the stories. There is, however, substantial variation of nAch scores among people under these nonaroused conditions.

It is important to note that the pictures employed are an important source of variation in the results obtained. Not just any pictures will do; the ones typically used show one or more people in an achievement related activity, such as a work scene (e.g., two men at a machine, a boy with a violin) or an athletic contest (e.g., a man trying to shoot a basket in a basketball game). Pictures can be rated for the number of achievement and other cues they contain, and the achievement scores for stories written to them vary with the ratings. Probably, the optimal pictures are those with an intermediate number of achievement cues, if the procedure is to be administered under neutral conditions; pictures with few or no achievement cues will not elicit achievement themes from enough people, whereas pictures with many such cues are likely to elicit achievement themes from almost everyone. Instructional conditions will also have an important effect on the achievement scores obtained (Cofer & Appley, 1964, pp. 734–737).

We have now described the procedures for measuring nAch; one important point which we have not mentioned is how well different judges, scoring the same stories, agree with one another. Studies of inter-judge scores show that they agree reasonably well. Before scoring stories, of course, judges must become familiar with the available scoring manuals (see McClelland et al., 1953) and practice scoring specimen stories. Unfortunately, nAch scores obtained from the same subjects at different times and with no reason for the scores to change do not agree as well as one would like. Despite this fact, there are enough correspondences between nAch scores and other behaviors for us to conclude that the nAch scoring system has some value.

We turn now to the relationship between nAch scores and other behaviors. This relationship is the significant one, because if it is low or lacking there is little point to the entire enterprise. This is to say that one may be able to develop a measure on the basis of different arousal conditions but that such a measure has little interest unless it can be shown to relate to other aspects of peoples' activities. Considerable work has been devoted to the study of such relationships, as well as to the backgrounds of those who obtain high and low scores on the nAch measure. We go now to these topics. But before doing so it should be mentioned that measures of nAch that use questionnaire procedures do not relate well to the fantasy-based measure. In speaking of nAch, then, it is always important to keep in mind what kind of measure of it is under scrutiny. We shall be concerned with fantasy nAch.

There are some relatively direct relationships between nAch and behavior. For example, Lowell (1952) compared the performances of subjects scoring either high or low in nAch on an arithmetic test and a scrambled-words test. The two groups started at about the same level on the scrambled-words test (which required the subjects to make words out of a series of scrambled letters), but the high nAch group showed a substantial improvement in performance over the items, whereas the low nAch subjects showed little improvement. The scores on the arithmetic items of the subjects with high nAch were consistently superior to those of the low nAch group. However, in the main, the research on the behavioral correlates of nAch has shown the relationship to be complex. The first complexity arises from the measure itself, and the second one indicates that performance in the tasks used is a complex function of variables other than nAch. Since it is likely that interacting variables are implicated in all or most situations involving human motives, it will be worthwhile to discuss this second complexity in some detail.

The first complexity was noted in a study by McClelland and Liberman (1949), who asked their subjects to identify words presented for very brief intervals of time and who measured the times for correct recognition of the words. The words presented included words related to achievement, like success and failure. The subjects represented a range of nAch scores. Those with high nAch scores recognized words denoting positive achievement more quickly than subjects with lower scores, but the most interesting finding was that recognition of negative achievement or failure words was slower in the subgroup with intermediate nAch scores than it was for either the high or the low nAch subgroups. This finding suggested that the subjects with intermediate scores fear failure rather than desire success. A study by Atkinson (1953) offered confirmation of this idea. He asked subjects to perform a series of tasks, arranging that half of them would be completed and half not completed.

The tasks were performed under one of three conditions: relaxed, task-oriented, or ego-involved. Then he asked for recall of the tasks. A typical finding in situations in which subjects recall completed and incompleted tasks is that they recall more incomplete than complete tasks (the Zeigarnik effect; see Chapter 8 for further discussion). Under ego-involved conditions (the subjects were told that the tasks measured ability), the subjects with high nAch behaved as expected, remembering more incomplete items. This was not true in the other conditions (relaxed, task-oriented) for these subjects with high nAch. However, those with low nAch scores recalled more completed than incompleted tasks under the ego-involved condition, and more incompleted tasks under the other conditions. These latter findings are compatible with the idea that failure is upsetting to those whose nAch scores are low and that the incomplete tasks represented failure so that those tasks were not remembered. Findings such as these suggest that the nAch scale is not a unidimensional one, but that intermediate and low scores may represent fear of failure, whereas high scores represent a positive attitude toward success and a willingness to undertake a challenge in order to attain it, i.e., a hope of success.

Several efforts have been made to provide measures which would differentiate those with hope of success from those with fear of failure. Projective measures have been designed, and a test anxiety questionnaire (see below) has been used (see Atkinson, 1964; Birney, Burdick & Teevan, 1969). In further discussion of achievement motivation, we shall follow Atkinson (1964) who has used the Test Anxiety Questionnaire (TAQ) to get at the fear of failure. Birney et al. (1969) offer a different interpretation of this facet of achievement motivation.

The findings reported by Atkinson on memory for completed and incompleted tasks, which were summarized above, contained another significant result, this one related to the second complexity alluded to earlier. This was the observation that the pattern of remembering the two classes of tasks differed for those with high and those with low nAch as a function of the ego-involving conditions. Subjects with high nAch scores remembered more incomplete than completed tasks only under ego-involving conditions, conditions which we could say "engage" or "arouse" the achievement motive. When personal evaluation was not involved (relaxed or task-oriented), there was little difference in recall of the two classes of tasks. This suggests that nAch does not come automatically into operation but will do so only when the subject with a high nAch score perceives the situation as an evaluative one.

Another finding related to the second complexity was noted initially by McClelland (1958) in a study of ringtossing in young children in which they were allowed to stand at any distance they chose from the peg. Children with high nAch scores stood neither very near to nor very far from the peg, choosing an intermediate distance from which they had a good chance of success but not certainty of success.

Atkinson (1958) had subjects (college students) perform on tasks and told them how probable it was that they would obtain the monetary incentive ($1.25 or $2.50). They were told that the money would be awarded to one of 20, one of 3, one of 2, or 3 of 4 of the subjects. Performance on the tasks was measured. The subjects with high nAch scores worked hardest at the intermediate probabilities ($1/3$ and $1/2$), rather than at either of the extreme probabilities. The effect was greatest for the reward of $1.25; apparently the $2.50 reward was sufficient to motivate work almost equally at all the probability levels. But for the smaller incentive, the finding suggests that the testing which people with high nAch scores do of themselves against a standard is not done at extreme odds. The very favorable odds ($3/4$) mean that success signifies little with respect to one's abilities, and the very unfavorable odds ($1/20$) may mean the same thing—to win may be seen as a matter more of luck than of ability.

In developing a theoretical integration of the various aspects which contribute to achievement-oriented performance, Atkinson (1964, Chapter 9) has proposed that there are two tendencies, one to attain success and one to avoid failure. In each case, three factors must be considered—the strength of the tendency or motive, the expectancy or the probability of success (or failure), and the incentive value of success (or the negative incentive value of failure). The second and third factors, of course, are essentially situational ones, whereas the first factor is a characteristic of individuals which differs from one person to another.

Atkinson considers that performance in an achievement situation represents the balance of the two tendencies, the value of each of which is the product of the three factors relevant to it. The tendency to success underlies the occurrence of responses instrumental to achievement, whereas the tendency to avoid failure inhibits or suppresses achievement-related responses (see Figure 21).

The combination of the three factors in the case of the tendency to achievement is given by the equation $T_S = M_S \times P_S \times I_S$. T_S is the tendency to approach success, M_s is the motive for success, P_s is the probability

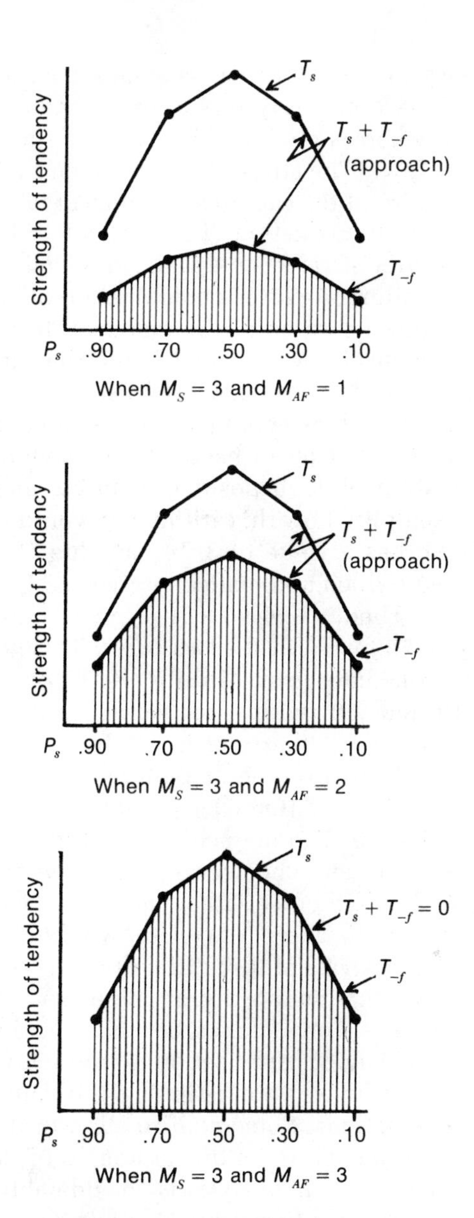

FIGURE 21 Strength of tendency to approach success (T_s), the tendency to avoid failure (T_{-f}), and the resultant tendency ($T_s + T_{-f}$) for levels of M_s and M_{af}. From Atkinson, J. W. *An introduction to motivation*. 1964. P. 247, Fig. 9-1. By permission of Van Nostrand Reinhold Company.

of success, and I_s is the incentive value of success for a particular activity. The three factors combine multiplicatively. Thus, if the motive is strong but one of the other two factors is very weak (e.g., probability), the net effect for achievement behavior will be less than if the other two factors are both of moderate strength. For a subject with high M_s, then, there would be a tendency to strive for success at an intermediate level of task difficulty, because the probability of success at the most difficult level would be very low, whereas the incentive value of success at a very easy level would also be low. (The strength of I_s is given by $1 - P_s$.) The combination of the 3 factors in the case of avoidance of failure is achieved in the same way, i.e., by the equation, $T_{-f} = M_{af} \times P_f \times I_f$, where the subscript f refers to failure, af refers to avoidance of failure, and −f refers also to avoidance of failure. Again the combination of factors is multiplicative, and to find the net value of the tendency to avoid failure, one inserts appropriate values for M_{af}, P_f, and I_f into the equation.

Everyone is presumed to possess, in at least some measure, both M_s and M_{af}, so that in any achievement situation everyone experiences an approach-avoidance conflict (see Chapter 8). Behavior will be the outcome of the summation of T_s, a positive quantity, and T_{-f}, a negative quantity. We can exemplify how this arithmetic would work by an example. Assume that M_s has a value of 3, M_{af} a value of 1, and assume P_s values of .90 and .50 (which automatically gives us I_s values of .10 and .50, respectively). Then, $3 \times .90 \times .10$ gives .27 for T_s and $3 \times .50 \times .50$ gives .75 for T_s, in the two cases; T_s is greater for the performance at an intermediate level of difficulty ($P_s = .50$). Assume also values of P_f of .10 and .50 (with I_f values of −.90 and −.50, respectively). Then, $1 \times .10 \times -.90 = -.09$ for T_f in the one case, and $1 \times .50 \times -.50$ gives −.25 in the other. Combining T_s and T_f for the two cases yields the following: .27 (for T_s) + (− .09, for T_f) = .18 and .75 (for T_s) + (− .25 for T_{f-}) = .50. The net achievement motivation for the two cases is then .18 and .50, and choice, again, is to work on the task with an intermediate level of difficulty. Other sets of values, both for M_s and M_{af}, as well as for P_s, I_s, P_f, and I_f, of course, would mediate predictions of performance at other levels of task difficulty.

This analysis shows the complexity of achievement-related behavior and places much emphasis on factors other than the motive itself in the determination of the behavior. Application of this analysis to actual situations, of course, requires ways of assessing the values of the various components of the equations. Some confirmation of the analysis comes from data in the experimental literature, although it is fair to say that the sophistication of the theoretical analysis is considerably greater than the experimental techniques usually employed to test it.

A number of attempts have been made to assess other motives by the McClelland–Atkinson group by means of projective or fantasy measurement. Among them are power, sex, aggression, fear, and affiliation (Atkinson, 1964, pp. 227–228; Cofer & Appley, 1964, pp. 725–729). Except for affiliation, discussed briefly below, little additional work has been done with them.

There has been interest in the origin of achievement motivation, and Winterbottom (1958) found that emphasis on training for independent attainment characterized the early experiences of boys who make high nAch scores in contrast to those whose nAch scores are low. McClelland (1961, 1965; McClelland et al., 1958) has applied much of the thinking underlying the work on achievement motivation to the comparison of societies and to the development of achievement motivation in "underdeveloped" countries.

The work on achievement motivation represents one of the most sophisticated and well-integrated approaches to the study of human motivation. The resulting complex account with its emphasis on the importance of situational (incentive) contributions to the behavior to be analyzed is a good antidote to simpler theories which put the entire explanatory weight on internal sources of motivation alone.

Affiliation, Dependency, and Approval

The standard of excellence which is involved in achievement-oriented behavior may arise from social conditions, or it may be the basis on which others reward us. However, it is at least conceivable that a standard may not be social in character. On the other hand, relations with other people are clearly a major part of the lives of most human beings, although there is variation among individuals in how extensive and intensive such relations are, and it has seemed to many writers that there must be a motivational basis for this interest in other people. There are several ways in which social behavior has been explained. One sort is treated briefly in the next chapter, and anxiety as the basis for affiliative behavior is considered later in this one. The present interest lies in possible motives which receive expression in direct relations with others, i.e., affiliation, dependency, and approval motives.

Several projective methods for measuring nAffiliation have been described (see Cofer & Appley, 1964, pp. 725–726), but the measure most often studied in relation to other behavior was developed by French (1956b). In this procedure, the subject is presented a series of items each of which indicates behavior said to be characteristic of a man. The subject is required to write an explanation or give the reasons that the man behaves in the way indicated by the item. The subject's statements then can be scored for achievement or for affiliative imagery (for different items). Scorers who have been trained agree well in the scores they assign for these motives.

French (1955) found that performance on a digit-substitution task given under relaxed conditions was related to nAffiliation scores; this finding was interpreted as indicating that the friendly experimenter engaged the affiliation motive in a nonachievement situation. French (1956a) also studied the choice of work partners as a function of achievement and affiliation motivation. Subjects high in nAch but low in nAffiliation choose work partners whom they know to be competent, rather than their friends. Subjects with the reverse pattern of motivation tend to choose friends as work partners. French (1958) also set up work groups which were homogeneous in motivation (see Figure 22). One set of groups was composed of subjects high in nAch and low in nAffiliation and another set of subjects high in nAffiliation and low in nAch. Then the groups worked on a task in which they had to put together, through oral communication, a story from phrases or short sentences. The groups of both types worked under a group orientation, i.e., they had to agree on a single, final solution, or under an individual orientation (agreement not required). There were also two types of feedback. One emphasized performance, the other how well the group members were getting along together (feeling feedback). When performance feedback was emphasized, those with high nAch did better than those with high nAffiliation under both the group and the individual orientations. The subjects with high nAffiliation did better under feeling feedback than for performance feedback and better under group orientation than under individual orientation for both types of feedback. The affiliation group excelled the achievement group under feeling feedback and group orientation combined but not otherwise. These findings give some validity to French's measure of nAffiliation, but to the writer's knowledge her work has not been followed up.

Behavior described as dependent, i.e., behavior which elicits from others aid, reassurance, assistance, attention, physical contact, comfort, etc., has frequently, in the clinical literature and also in discussions of childhood, been ascribed to a motive. The motive has been characterized as an acquired drive (Sears, 1963, p. 29), arising out of the early interactions between a child and its caretakers, but its status as a motive has never been very well established. It is worth mentioning here, because it can serve as an example of a "motive" which can be given explanations alternative to that of being a motive.

Gewirtz (1961,1969a, b) has offered an alternative account. He has reported experiments in which brief social isolation and social stimulation and satiation of and withdrawal of social reinforcers (Gewirtz & Baer, 1958a, b; Gewirtz, 1969b; see Eisenberger, 1970) have had effects upon the effectiveness of social reinforcers used subsequently in another task. His interpretation of these findings is stated, in part, as follows (Gewirtz, 1969a, p. 90): "While satiation and recovery for a social stimulus produced opposite, additive effects like those which characterize satiation and recovery (i.e., deprivation) functions for appetitive stimuli, it would be superfluous to apply in addition the term 'drive' as has traditionally been done . . . the description of the functional relation is sufficient for most requirements." All Gewirtz wishes to conclude from the operation of social stimulation and deprivation, for example, is that they reduce or augment, respectively, the effectiveness of social reinforcers.

Gerwirtz would analyze dependent behaviors (as well as many others) as being developed, strengthened, and maintained by the provision of

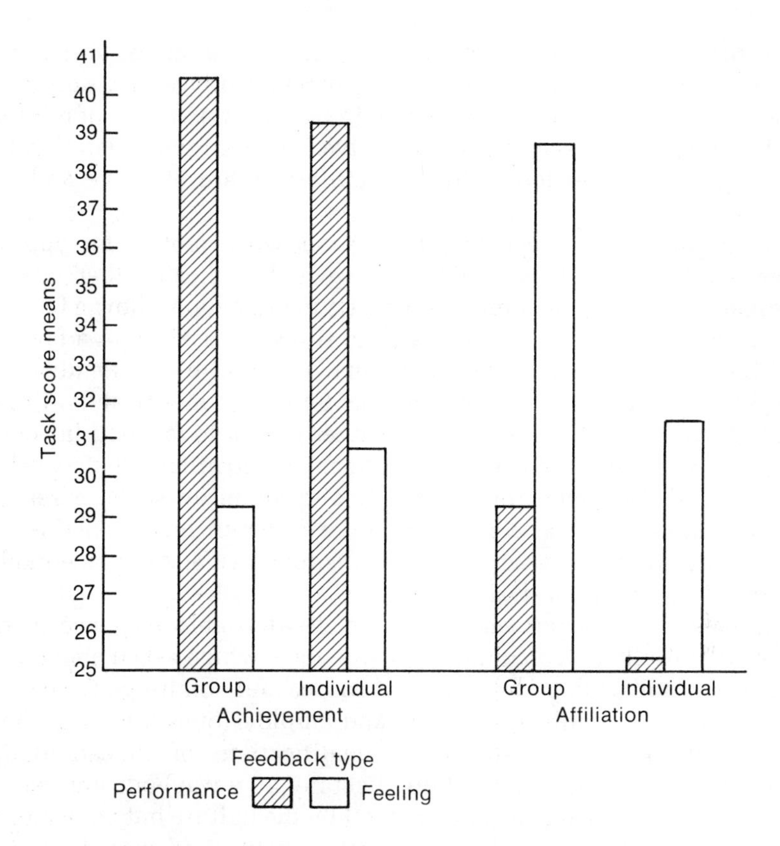

FIGURE 22 Task performance for subjects with high need achievement or with high need affiliation under group or individual orientations and performance or feeling feedback. Drawn from French, E. G. Effects of the interaction of motivation and feedback on task performance. In J. W. Atkinson (Ed.), *Motives in fantasy, action and society.* 1958. P. 404, Table 1. By permission of Van Nostrand Reinhold Company.

reinforcing stimuli by others, especially the chief caretaker (usually the mother). The dependent behaviors occur because they are reinforced, and the effect of social stimulation and isolation, as we have said, is to augment the effectiveness of some of the reinforcers the caretaker administers. The mother becomes a generalized reinforcer, i.e., her effectiveness as a reinforcer arises because she is capable of administering the wide variety of reinforcers which take care of a variety of the child's wants. If dependent behaviors are the kinds she reinforces or if the occurrence of her reinforcements is contingent upon the presence of dependent behaviors, then her child may be characterized as a dependent one. However, dependency consists of a variety of behaviors which may be reinforced; if they are not, then presumably the dependent child will not develop, i.e., there is no need or motive that necessitates its appearance and development.

Gewirtz' analysis of dependency, which he would extend to many other social behaviors sometimes attributed to motives, illustrates a problem with human motives. Many apparent motives may only reflect behavior which has been instrumental in obtaining a variety of reinforcements, rather than arising from a motive. Such an analysis, of course, leaves open the questions why the reinforcers are effective and what they are.

Crowne and Marlowe (1964) have proposed a motive for approval. Their point of departure was research which indicated that in taking personality scales, questionnaires, or tests many people show a tendency to answer questions in such a way as to show themselves in a favorable light, i.e., to give socially desirable answers. While this tendency has been seen as a fault of personality tests by many investigators, Crowne and Marlowe set out to determine whether the set to respond in socially desirable ways may reflect a motivational disposition. Their work includes the development of a new social-desirability scale, a series of demonstrations that people who score at different levels on this scale behave in different ways in other social situations, and a conceptualization of the approval motive.

The personality scales on which socially-desirable response tendencies were initially noted contained many items which asked about symptoms (e.g., I am troubled by attacks of nausea and vomiting). Crowne and Marlowe's scale avoids such items and employs questions (e.g., Before voting I thoroughly investigate the qualifications of all candidates; I sometimes feel resentful when I don't get my own way) one answer (true or false) to which is approved in general by the culture but yet is not true of most people. The scale is satisfactorily reliable, and there is evidence of its validity, as the following summary indicates. People "who display a social-desirability response set on the M–C (Marlowe–Crowne) scale are more conforming, cautious, and persuasible, and their behavior is more normatively anchored, than persons who depict themselves less euphemistically" (Crowne & Marlowe, 1964, p. 189). They show more favorability to a dull task, easier conditionability in verbal conditioning, more social conformity, more cautious goal setting in a risk-taking situation, and more susceptibility to persuasion than people who do not display a social-desirability response set (Crowne & Marlowe, 1964, p. 190). They give popular word associations and are likely to see a task involving perception of "dirty" words as upsetting if it seems to involve evaluation of their behavior. They avoid threats to self-esteem and seek affiliation with others.

People with a high need for approval depend "on the favorable evaluations of others" and avoid self-criticisms. The approval motive itself is "the desire for social support, self-protection, and avoidance of failure. . . ." Its goals "include social recognition and status, protection and dependency, and love and affection" (Crowne & Marlowe, 1964, p. 202).

Of the three motives considered in this section, the approval motive has received more extensive investigation than the affiliation motive, and the research carried out seems to support a motivational tendency for approval better than it does for dependency. Yet, there must be areas of overlap among these motives, as, indeed, some of the quotations from Crowne and Marlowe given above would seem to indicate. And perhaps a Gewirtz type of analysis, if applied to affiliation and to approval, might obviate the requirement for discussion in terms of motives and suggest the importance of certain classes of reinforcers. Unfortunately, to date, little effort has been devoted to the simultaneous analysis of these three motives or to an analysis of affiliation and approval in reinforcement terms.

Aggression

The postulate of a drive or even an instinct of aggression has characterized much thinking about human motivation, especially that stemming from psychoanalysis. This postulate, of course, receives casual support from the many reports, especially in the United States, of aggressive and hostile attacks—murder, assault, rape, for example—that one reads about in the daily press. War, also, has sometimes been taken as evidence for a motivational source of hostility and aggression. Yet, many social scientists and students of animal behavior find little reason to accept an instinct for aggression or even for a drive on the hydraulic model and clearly indicate (cf. Berkowitz, 1969a) that such simple views of aggression, while easy to understand, are wide of the mark when it comes to an attempt to attain a comprehensive understanding of aggression.

Aggression in lower animals is commonplace, but interestingly enough fighting among members of the same species seldom leads to death, except under unusual situations such as captivity or perhaps overcrowding (Harrison Matthews, 1964; Barnett, 1967). Different species of animals may live peaceably with one another in the same general area, except where there is a relation between species of the predator–prey kind. Much of the aggressive (or as it is often called, agonistic) behavior between animals is of the threatening variety, rather than actual combat, and has often been designated as ritualized. Agonistic behavior seems to arise primarily under certain conditions, as in defense of territory or in competition over food or sexual objects, or in predation. Accounts of fights to the death among animals then apparently portray the exception rather than the rule and may often serve a romantic, fictional purpose rather than describing the situation as it is. Speaking of fights to death, Harrison Matthews (1964, p. 22) says, " . . . the more I have sought examples of such intraspecific overt fighting in mammals the less I have succeeded, and I doubt that it normally occurs in nature."

This is not to say that there are no agonistic behavior patterns in animals which are apparently innate in character. Electrical stimulation of brain areas in chickens and cats (see Berkowitz, 1965, p. 320) may elicit aggressive acts or components thereof, but as Flynn (1967) has indicated for cats the manifestation of aggression depends on the appropriateness of objects to which the aggression can be directed (Figure 23). For example, stimulated cats do not attack styrofoam or foam rubber blocks but will attack stuffed or anesthetized rats, the latter somewhat more frequently, on the average, than the former (Flynn, 1967, Figure 3, p. 47). Electrical stimulation of the hypothalamus is effective in eliciting aggression, but the effectiveness of this stimulation can both be facilitated and reduced by simultaneous stimulation of other areas. In addition, stimulation from the periphery is also necessary, the effectiveness of the hypothalamic stimulation in producing aggression being much reduced when the cats are blindfolded or when they are both blindfolded and have had severed the two sensory branches of the trigeminal nerve which are important to biting (Flynn, 1967). While it is clear that brain structures (see Kaada, 1967), in some animals at least, mediate the occurrence of aggressive acts, external stimulation is also necessary.

In the human, aggression can be habitual, because aggressive behavior is often effective in obtaining a variety of reinforcements; hence, it can be learned as a general pattern and need not be specifically motivated. However, this formulation does not speak to the question whether aggression may arise from a drive or perhaps from an emotion.

We shall follow the account proposed by Berkowitz (1962, 1965) in discussing motivational aspects of aggression. He seems to regard aggressive behavior as being predicated on anger and on "the presence of some cue functioning as a releaser. . . ." (1965, p. 313). One source of anger is frustration, and Berkowitz adopts a modified form of the frustration–aggression hypothesis, stated initially, in a fairly formal fashion, by Dollard et al. (1939). This hypothesis proposed that frustration is occasioned by interference with the occurrence of a goal response at some point in a sequence of acts which would normally be completed by the goal response which the individual is motivated to make. The aggressive behavior itself has, as its goal, injuring someone or something. However, since there is habitual aggression, all aggressive behavior does not presuppose frustration, and there are many other responses, aside from aggression, that may be made to frustration.

Berkowitz argues that the anger creates a readiness for aggressive behavior but that the occurrence of aggression is dependent on the presence of ". . . suitable cues, stimuli associated with the present or previous anger instigators" (Berkowitz, 1965, p. 308) and on the absence of effective inhibitors of the expression of aggression. It is clear that Berkowitz rejects the notion of "energy" underlying an aggressive drive or any kind of hydraulic conception of aggression. It follows from this that we should not expect the expression of aggression to reduce aggressiveness, i.e., to have a "cathartic" effect. The expression of aggression or the witnessing of episodes of aggression as in a movie, boxing match, or TV

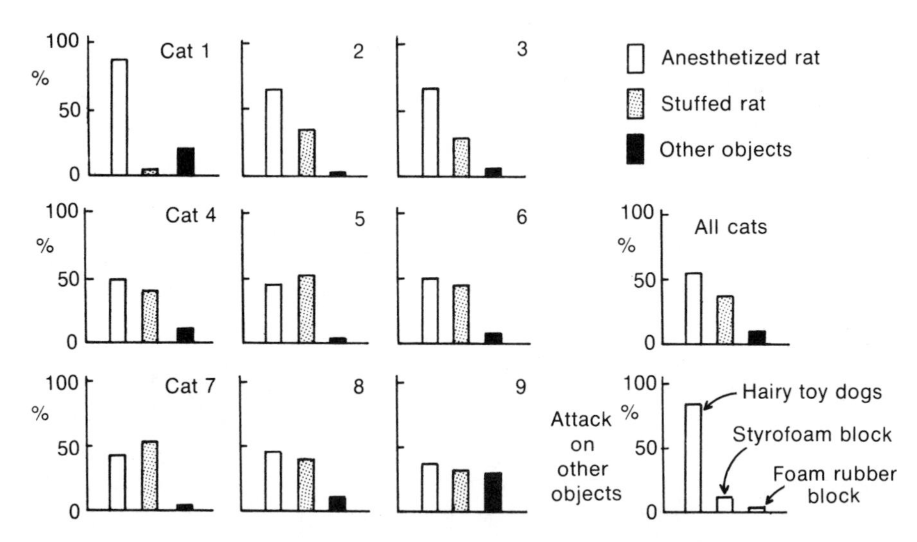

FIGURE 23 Data showing frequency of attack by 9 cats on three objects. From Flynn, J. P. The neural basis of aggression in cats. In D. C. Glass (Ed.), *Neurophysiology and emotion*. 1967. P. 47, Fig. 3. By permission of Rockefeller University Press.

show is likely to augment the expression of aggression, rather than reduce it (see Berkowitz, 1970; Holt, 1970).

It will be helpful to our understanding of this account of aggression to describe some experiments which exemplify rather well the interaction of cues and the emotional state (anger) in producing aggressive behavior (see Berkowitz, 1965, pp. 313–318). These experiments (see Figure 24) employ the device of having the subject view a film of a prizefight, after having been angered by the experimenter's accomplice. (Control conditions are included, both for the content of the film and the behavior of the accomplice toward the subject.)

In one experiment the accomplice was introduced as a college boxer in one condition, whereas in another he was presented as a speech major. Following the movie, the subject was given the chance to administer electric shocks to the accomplice, who was in another room. This opportunity was disguised as a way of evaluating the accomplice's performance on another task. More shocks were administered by the angered subjects who had seen the prizefight film and who thought the accomplice was a boxer than by the angered subjects who thought the accomplice was a speech major or who were not angry, whatever the role of the accomplice or the kind of film. If administering electric shocks is an aggressive behavior, then the results show that anger had been aroused, the film had activated habits of aggressiveness, and greater aggression was shown to the cue (the boxer) which is strongly associated with aggression than to the other cue (the speech major).

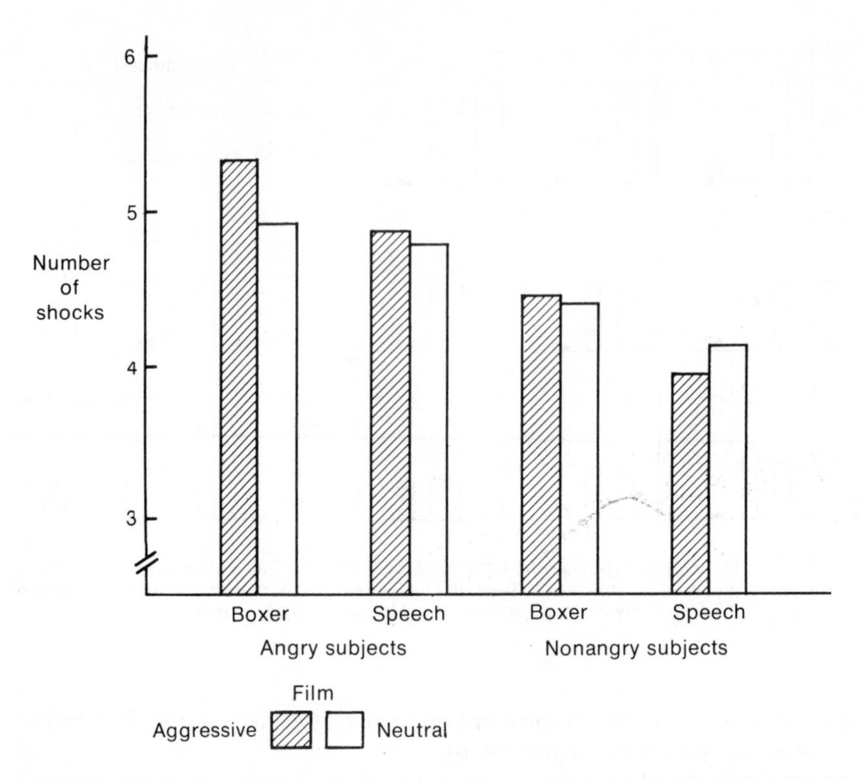

FIGURE 24 Number of shocks administered to the "boxer" and the "speech major" by angry and nonangry subjects after seeing either an aggressive or a neutral film. Drawn from Berkowitz, L. The concept of aggressive drive: Some additional considerations. In *Advances in experimental social psychology.* Vol 2, P. 315, Table 1. Copyright Academic Press, Inc.

In another experiment, the main procedural difference was to associate the accomplice with aggression by introducing him with a name which overlapped with that of the character in the film who received a bad beating. This role was played by Kirk Douglas and so the accomplice was named as Kirk Anderson (or as Bob Anderson in the control condition). The subjects whom Kirk Anderson had insulted and criticized, thus angering them, gave the accomplice more shocks than they gave to Bob Anderson. This was also true for the subjects who had seen the boxing film as compared to those who had seen a "neutral" film of an exciting track race. Another experiment confirmed these results, with the association between the accomplice and aggression being arranged through overlap between his name and that of the character in the film, i.e., the role Kirk Douglas played carried the name Midge Kelly and the person who fought him was named Dunne. So, for different subjects, the accomplice was introduced as Bob Kelly, Bob Dunne, or Bob Riley.

This evidence suggests the importance of the cue, the name of the accomplice, as well as the role of anger and of witnessed aggression (the film) in instigating aggression. Berkowitz presents these experiments as models, more or less, for the occurrence of aggression. But what of "chronic aggression" or the aggressive and brutal acts committed so frequently in the United States, according to our daily newspapers?

First, Berkowitz (1967, p. 258) argues, if there is an intention to carry out an aggressive act but there is no opportunity to commit such an act, "aggression builds up in the individual," i.e., the goal response must be made for the instigation to subside. There is a parallel here with the Zeigarnik effect (see Chapter 8). In addition, in some people, given arousal, there is perhaps a wider range of cues than there is in others which can trigger aggression. As Berkowitz puts it, ". . . if an emotionally aroused person, while walking down the street, encounters someone who for one reason or another triggers in his mind an association with frustration, he responds aggressively" (1967, p. 259). We must also remember, of course, that many aggressive behaviors serve ends other than the expression of aggression itself, such as status, prestige, or obtaining money to be used for a variety of purposes. Aggression is a complex affair, and simple analyses of it will yield little understanding.

Fear and Anxiety

Anxiety and fear enter into motivation in two ways. In one, they are regarded as drives or motives whose effects may be seen in a variety of behaviors. In this form, anxiety and fear are usually measured by means of questionnaires. In the other, they are seen as providing the underlying force or energy which leads to behavior often suggested as expressive of another motive. In this section we shall see an exemplification of this use in the attempt to show that affiliative behavior, rather than expressing a motive for affiliation, actually is a way of coping with fear or anxiety.

Fear is usually defined as a reaction to a present, real danger, whereas anxiety arises in anticipation of a danger or threat, real or unreal. The questionnaires usually tap anxiety, but the manipulations employed in attempting to study affiliative behavior are perhaps properly regarded as arousing fear.

Questionnaire Anxiety Two questionnaires have served as the techniques mainly employed in the measurement of anxiety. One of them, the Manifest Anxiety Scale (MAS), was developed by Taylor (1953). It consists of a set of questions originally judged by clinical psychologists as indicative of chronic anxiety and further refined in later studies. Two specimen items, both indicative of anxiety if answered "true" are: "I have nightmares every few nights;" "I am easily embarrassed."

This scale was developed (Taylor, 1956; Spence, 1958) as a means of measuring a human motive (anxiety or emotionality) so that its contributions to performance can be assessed. Briefly, the argument was that habits require for their execution energization from a drive source. Anxiety was conceived as such a drive force, and, therefore, people with high anxiety should have their habits energized more, in a given situation, than people with low anxiety. Tests of this proposition involved comparison of learning scores of people with high or low anxiety scores on the MAS. The learning situations varied from relatively simple ones like eyelid conditioning to more complex ones such as paired-associate, serial verbal, and maze learning. Where the dominant habits possessed or developed by subjects were directly related to successful performance on the learning task, the subjects with high anxiety were expected to perform better than those with low anxiety, but the reverse finding was expected for tasks in which there were habits which compete with the one or ones necessary to successful performance. A great deal of research was stimulated by this formulation. It is safe to say that persons with high anxiety do develop eyelid conditioning more rapidly than persons with low anxiety (Spence, 1958), but the results outside this conditioning situation do not clearly support expectations.

The other questionnaire is called the Test Anxiety Questionnaire (TAQ) and was developed by Mandler and Sarason (1952). These writers conceive anxiety as a stimulus which has responses associated with it. To the extent that these responses are compatible or incompatible with the responses required in a test situation, the test anxiety will not affect or will affect adversely performance in that situation.

The questions in the TAQ relate to the subject's responses before and during examinations, such as ". . . uneasiness, accelerated heartbeat, perspiration, emotional interference, and 'worry'. . ." (Mandler & Sarason, 1952, p. 167) and attitudes toward tests. The test was studied by comparing persons who had made high or low scores on the TAQ in a situation in which the subject was told that his intelligence was being measured and that he had failed or succeeded on the first tests (or was told nothing) and then was tested on an additional test of the same kind. The major finding of interest here is that evaluation (success or failure) resulted in less adequate performance in the highly anxious subjects whereas performance of the low anxiety subjects improved (see Figure 25). This suggests that responses which interfere with performance were made by the high anxiety subjects, whereas the low anxiety subjects were activated to perform well by evaluation. The interpretation of these results in terms of anxiety is not as certain as one would like, as relations with the tendency to success and the tendency to avoid failure (see above) may have been present in the two classes of subjects. As we have seen, Atkinson (1964) has used the TAQ in his efforts to evaluate the fear of failure in achievement-related situations.

The work with anxiety scales gives us a clear indication that these procedures tap a significant individual difference, but it is not entirely clear whether these differences relate only to anxiety or represent a combination of factors, such as nAffiliation and fear of failure.

Affiliation Brown (1961) has argued that it is unnecessary to speak of motives whose goals are such effects as praise, prestige, affection, emi-

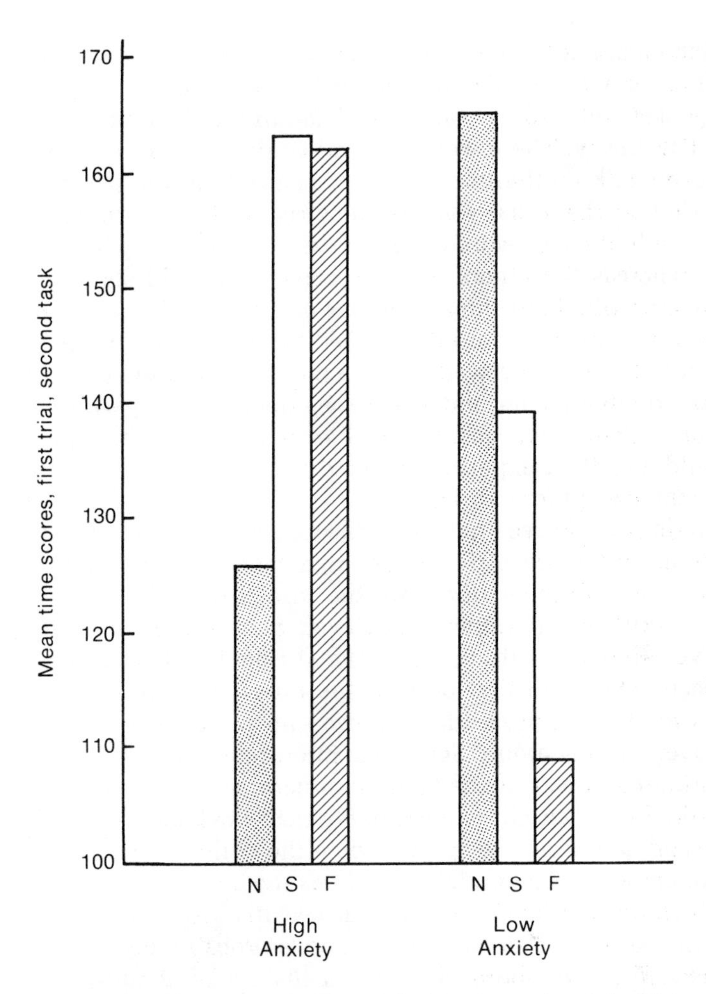

FIGURE 25 Mean Time Scores for the first trial of the second task for high- and low-anxious subjects following an evaluation of first-task performances as Neutral (N), Successful (S), or Failing (F). Low values of time scores indicate good performance. Drawn from Mandler, G. and Sarason, S. B. A study of anxiety and learning. *Journal of Abnormal and Social Psychology.* Vol. 47, P. 170, Table 2B. By permission of the American Psychological Association.

nence, or money but that the behaviors which suggest that there are motives of these kinds may actually serve to prevent or to reduce anxiety. Schachter (1959) has reported experiments which have suggested that affiliative behavior, to some degree at least, may be a way of coping with fear. While Schachter's work was not specifically engendered by Brown's argument, its results and their interpretation provide support for the argument.

Schachter used manipulations designed to arouse fear (but he refers to it as anxiety), the manipulation being the threat of receiving electric shock. In a typical experiment, female college students volunteered to participate. A small group (strangers to one another) was asked to report to the laboratory at the same time and were met by a man who identified himself as Dr. Gregor Zilstein. He wore a white coat with a stethoscope in his pocket and said he was a physician in the Department of Neurology and Psychiatry. There was electrical equipment in the room, and Zilstein gave a talk on the importance of research on the effects of electric shock. He told them that some of the girls, in the experiment for which they had volunteered, would receive painful and strong but not harmful shocks, whereas the others would receive very mild shocks. After this talk, the girls filled out questionnaires or rating scales designed to measure their anxiety and were then asked to wait a little while for the experiment to begin. They were given a choice of waiting alone in a room with comfortable chairs and magazines or of waiting with others in a classroom. (They were also allowed to discontinue their participation but would lose their experimental credit if they did so.) This ended the experiment, except for debriefing.

The ratings indicated that the subjects were made fearful by the manipulation, and more girls in the high fear (severe shock) condition chose to wait with others than was the case of those in the low fear condition. In further experiments, however, Schachter discovered that the affiliative behavior (waiting with others) under fear occurred primarily in subjects who were first born or the only children in their families, whereas the later-born children showed no preference for waiting with others over waiting alone. Schachter interpreted this finding as indicating continuing effects of the familial situation in his subjects. The first-born child, he suggested, is more likely than the later born to receive solicitude and care from the mother when the child evidences expressions of fear or anxiety. (The mother is perhaps too busy with the larger family which includes the later born to be as sensitive to such reactions in the later born. Further, from experience, she is probably less concerned herself.) Hence, the first-born child has a history of attention from social interaction, which the later born does not. Consequently, the induction of fear at the college age leads the first-born subjects to find security in the presence of others to a greater extent than do the later born. A number of other experiments have provided data which replicate Schachter's initial findings, but there do not seem to be any direct tests of the theoretical formulation just summarized.

We have spoken of fear in conjunction with the Schachter experiments, because as far as the subjects were concerned the threat of shock was a real one. Sarnoff and Zimbardo (1961) have shown that anxiety does not necessarily induce affiliative behavior if the activities which presumably are to induce the anxiety are accompanied by the possibility of embarrassment. Sarnoff and Zimbardo aroused anxiety by telling their subjects they would be required to indulge in oral activities (e.g., sucking their thumbs or a baby bottle). These activities would arouse anxiety, they thought, because they are related to the oral drive postulated in psychoanalysis. It is not possible to decide whether, in this experiment, anxiety was aroused, but the subjects chose to wait alone rather than with others under the threat of having to engage in oral behavior.

In view of the work we have just summarized, fear, and perhaps anxiety, can apparently motivate affiliative behavior. On the basis of present evidence, it is not possible to say how much affiliative behavior is motivated in this way and how much of it may arise from nAffiliation as discussed earlier in this chapter. In any case, we should stand warned that just because we observe a coherent behavior pattern there is no necessity to find an underlying motive specific to the goal to which the pattern seems to be directed. Some other motive may underlie the behavior.

GENERAL CONSIDERATIONS

The motive systems we have surveyed in this chapter are representative of many that have been mentioned in the literature, and our account has suggested many of the problems that are associated with the postulation of one motive or another. It is still not possible, in this writer's view, to conclude that we have a satisfactory account or understanding of any of these motive systems. In any event, it should be clear by now that these motive systems are complex, involving both a disposition to perceive and behave in a certain typical way and an important role for cue or incentivelike factors. It is difficult to conceive energy sources for these systems on the drive or need model.

Our acccount in this chapter has implied that there are a number of motive systems which are relatively independent of one another. This conception has been challenged (Allport, 1937; Maslow, 1954, Chapter 5). Maslow, for example, has argued that there is a hierarchy of motives (or needs, as he calls them) and that the functioning of the motives high in the hierarchy is possible only or primarily when the satisfaction of the lower needs is attained or when there is no concern over the satisfaction of the lower needs. At the bottom of the hierarchy are the physiological needs, such as hunger and thirst. Above them are the safety needs, i.e., the search for security and avoidance of anxiety. Next come the belongingness needs, i.e., the desire for affectionate relations, and then the esteem needs, those involved in respectful evaluation of oneself. When some satisfaction of all of these needs has been achieved, those at the top of the hierarchy can emerge—generally the need for self-actualization. This need cannot be specified very well, because it is, in a sense, unique, being "the desire to become more and more what one is, to become everything that one is capable of becoming" (Maslow, 1954, p. 92).

There is some evidence (see Cofer & Appley, 1964, pp. 684–685) that behavior can be dominated by severe hunger, cold, heat, thirst, and fear to the exclusion of other concerns. But aside from this, little can be said in fact to support the hierarchy. The motive of self-actualization, Maslow has said, does dominate the behavior of some people, examples being Thomas Jefferson, Albert Einstein, Eleanor Roosevelt, and Spinoza, and presumably there are others not so famous or so intellectual. But self-actualization remains a poorly specified, poorly understood concept, which, despite its appeal, has met none of the criteria for a well specified motivational concept.

SUGGESTED READINGS

Atkinson, J. W. (Ed.) *Motives in fantasy, action and society.* New York: D. Von Nostrand Co., Inc., 1958.

Atkinson, J. W. *An introduction to motivation.* New York: D. Von Nostrand Co., Inc., 1964. Chapter 9.

Berkowitz, L. *Aggression: A social psychological analysis.* New York: McGraw-Hill Book Company, 1962.

Cofer, C. N. & Appley, M. H. *Motivation: Theory and research.* New York: John Wiley & Sons, Inc., 1964. Pp. 566–587; Chapters 13 and 14.

Crowne, D. P. & Marlowe, D. *The approval motive: Studies in evaluative dependence.* New York: John Wiley & Sons, Inc., 1964.

Levitt, E. E. *The psychology of anxiety.* New York: The Bobbs-Merrill Co., Inc., 1967.

McClelland, D. C., Atkinson, J. W., Clark, R. A., & Lowell, E. L. *The achievement motive.* New York: Appleton-Century-Crofts, 1953.

Spielberger, C. D. (Ed.) *Anxiety and behavior.* New York: Academic Press, Inc., 1966.

8

Conflict and Balance or Consistency Theories

In this chapter, we consider the motivational effects of cases of conflict among response tendencies and of inconsistencies between or among our cognitions. The study of conflict is one of long-standing and has its origins in considerations of abnormal and maladaptive behavior, as in neurosis and psychosis. Interest in consistency, or inconsistency, is a much later development, and it came to the fore initially in social psychology. The literatures of conflict and inconsistency do not have much overlap, and they are often treated separately. Because, however, they have in common effects arising from some kind of incompatibility, we have put them together in this chapter.

CONFLICT

Conflict is said to arise when there exist simultaneously two or more response tendencies which are incompatible with one another. The source of the conflict may, of course, lie in incompatible goals, i.e., the presence of two incentives the attainment of one of which precludes the attainment of the other. Or, it may be that a goal is attainable, but to reach it one runs the risk of punishment, so that the positive value of reaching the goal is in conflict with the negative value (perhaps fear) of doing so. In the first case the response of approaching the one goal is incompatible with that of approaching the other one, and in the second case approach is incompatible with avoidance. We shall have more to say about the paradigms of conflict in a moment.

The effect of unresolved conflict is that neither incentive is attained or that one cannot go forward to the attainment of an incentive because of the fear doing so brings. This is to say that conflict produces tension, which may be unpleasant, and its effect on behavior is to produce vacillation and hesitancy with concomitant fatigue. We often escape from our conflicts, rather than resolving them.

Types of Conflict

Students of conflict (Lewin, 1931; Miller, 1944) have identified four basic paradigms of conflict situations. They are displayed in schematic form in Figure 26.

The first one is called approach–approach conflict and is the case in which one must choose between two equally attractive and desirable alternatives. If this paradigm occurs, it apparently does not give much trouble, except where the analysis is really that of a double approach–avoidance (see below) conflict, because simple approach–approach conflicts are usually solved by making a choice.

The second kind of conflict, avoidance–avoidance, faces us with the choice of equally undesirable alternatives, and most of the time these conflicts are solved by escaping the situation or by "leaving the field," as Lewin put it. However, if escape is not possible, then vacillation and blocking of responses may go on with resultant tension and discomfort.

Approach–avoidance conflicts, the third kind, are exemplified by a desire to attain the goal together with a fear of doing so. Lewin's example was that of a small child, who was afraid of the water but who wished to get a ball which was in the waves at the beach. He would approach the ball and stop when he came near the water; a wave washing in on the beach would send him scurrying out of the way. His vacillatory behavior would include approaches to the ball and withdrawal away from the water, as well as runs along the beach, lateral to the water. Presumably, the conflict would go on indefinitely, except for the intercession of someone else, who would retrieve the ball for the child.

The last type of conflict is double approach–avoidance. This may arise when the approach to one goal involves the loss of the other, so that approach to either one carries with it an avoidance tendency because of the loss of the other one. Or, it may arise as in the example given in the Figure, in which the act of climbing the tree has intrinsic approach and avoidance features, and the social situation will support approach but will ridicule avoidance.

Theory of Approach–Avoidance Conflict

Miller (1944) has shown that a number of the phenomena of approach–avoidance conflict can be derived from a model which he has proposed. Using a spatial situation, in which the desired but feared goal is at one end of a runway, he speaks of the following phenomena: the animal may run toward the goal but stop some distance from it. He may retreat, then approach a little way, and so on, vacillating back and forth. This kind of behavior can be derived from five assumptions. These are

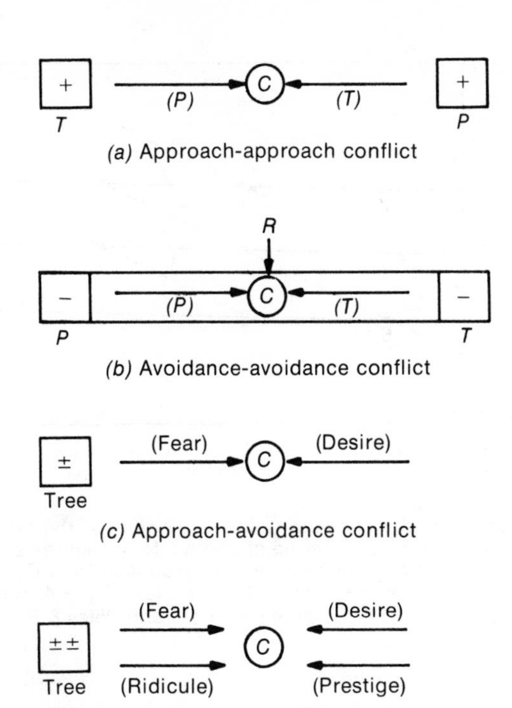

FIGURE 26 Four types of conflict. The + and − signs represent positive and negative attractiveness of goal objects and the arrows direction of forces acting upon the person (C). On the top part of the figure, the choice is between playing with a new toy (T) or going to see a parade (P). In the second, the task (T) is undesirable, but the alternative is Punishment (P). In the third, climbing a tree is opposed to fear of being hurt, and in the fourth, the prestige from tree-climbing is opposed to ridicule for failure in that act. Reproduced from Cofer, C. N. and Appley, M. H. *Motivation: Theory and research*. 1964. P. 434, Fig. 9-3. By permission of John Wiley & Sons, Inc.

(1) gradients of approach and (2) gradients of avoidance tendencies. This means that the strengths of the tendencies are greatest at or near the goal, less so further away. (3) The avoidance gradient is steeper than the approach gradient. This means that the strength of the avoidance tendency decreases with distance from the goal more rapidly than does the approach tendency. (4) Approach and avoidance tendencies vary in strength with the intensity of the underlying motivation. (5) The stronger of two incompatible response tendencies will occur.

Figure 27 has been constructed on the basis of these assumptions, and the points at which conflict is shown to occur are those where given the strengths of approach and avoidance the gradients intersect. These points will be near to or distant from the goal, as the relative strengths of the two tendencies vary. It should be obvious that the assumption of the greater steepness of the avoidance gradient than that of the approach gradient is necessary for the gradients to intersect. If the gradients were parallel to one another, either avoidance or approach would be com-

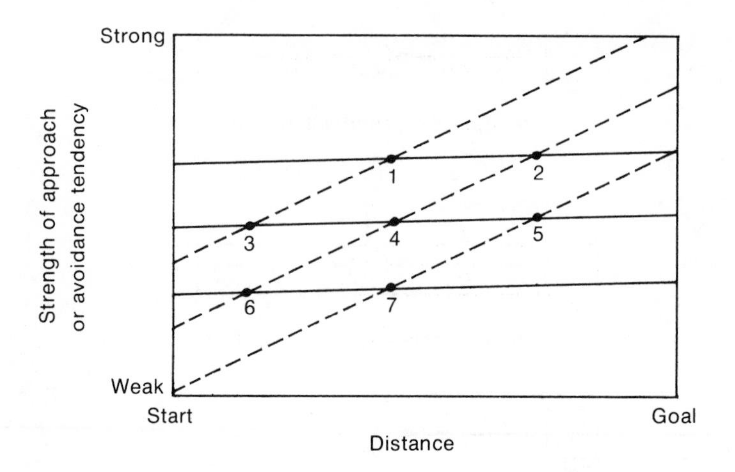

FIGURE 27 Schematic diagram showing points of conflict at the intersections of approach and avoidance gradients of differing strengths. Note that the slope of the avoidance gradient is steeper than that for approach. Reproduced from Cofer, C. N. and Appley, M. H. *Motivation: Theory and research*. 1964. P. 437, Fig. 9-4. Based on diagrams by Miller (1951c) and Brown (1957). By permission of John Wiley & Sons, Inc.

plete, depending on which one was stronger, and there would perhaps be no conflict.

Empirical tests of these five assumptions have been made, and they have received verification. Dollard and Miller (1950) have made a number of applications of the conflict theory to psychopathology and psychotherapy, and the applications have seemed plausible to many clinicians. In the present space, however, we cannot discuss them here.

So far as motivation is concerned, conflict, when it cannot be resolved, is, as we have said, an unpleasant tension state, and the behavior associated with it is that of vacillation and blocking. We should anticipate that behaviors which escape conflict, thus reducing the tension, will be learned and that the individual thereafter will often attempt to avoid conflict situations to the extent that he can. Whether such avoidance is desirable is a matter which can only be judged in terms of what goals cannot be achieved because of the conflict and whether the fear which enters into a conflict of the approach–avoidance type is unrealistic. If, as is often the case in neurosis, the fear is unrealistic, then efforts to reduce the fear by treatment will be worthwhile in order to reduce the conflict. The alternative, that of increasing the approach tendency, may often be undesirable because with the fear still present approaches closer to the goal will, as Figure 27 shows, bring one to high points on the avoidance gradient, with consequent augmented discomfort. Therapeutic efforts in the case of conflict, then, tend to be concentrated on reducing avoidance tendencies.

BALANCE OR CONSISTENCY THEORIES

Background

It is a curious feature of the history of psychology that one of the most dynamic of its viewpoints, Gestalt psychology, is seldom given any consideration in treatments of motivation. An exception to this statement arises in the case of Kurt Lewin, but as we shall see below his motivational concepts are rather different from those we have considered elsewhere in this book.

The reasons that Gestalt psychology is not thought of as a motivational psychology are not far to seek. We can consider two of them. One is the stress put on phenomenology ("naïve introspection") by the Gestalt psychologists. The dominance of the field of motivation by the Freudian emphasis on unconscious motives, which are by definition refractory to introspection, and by work with animals, which cannot introspect, is incompatible, or at least inconsistent, with a strong emphasis on phenomenological observation. The second reason is that the Gestalt psychologists seldom spoke of drives, incentives, or reinforcements (and their modern representatives seldom refer to such concepts, either). The dynamics treated by the Gestaltists were seen as arising from relations within a field, and changes in behavior and experience were derived from "field forces," rather than from drives (see Heider, 1960). As we will see later in considering cognitive dissonance, which has been likened to a drive, the source of the dissonance lies in the relations between elements of a structure or a field, not from deprivation operations or from the value of incentives.

The first Gestalt psychologists were much interested in visual perception, and their dynamic laws were constructed initially for dealing with the problems of visual organization and of changes in it. A distorted figure, for example, contains forces arising from its imbalance or asymmetry which lead it to be perceived and to be remembered as more balanced or symmetrical than it actually is. These forces provide the dynamic factor in the perception, but they arise from the figure and from the field of which it is a part, rather than from external drives or incentives.

Lewin was one Gestalt psychologist who treated motivation (see Deutsch, 1968). However, he seldom spoke of biological drives or of enduring acquired motives. Rather, he emphasized tensions in the field arising from intentions or psychological needs, the tensions in one region of the field giving rise to forces to resolve the tension, i.e., to restore a state of equilibrium. We can gain some of the character of Lewin's motivational thinking by summarizing several of the experiments carried out by his students.

In one, a subject was given a number of tasks to perform but was prevented, on a pretext, from completing half of them. Afterward, he was asked to recall the names of the tasks, and it was found that recall was better for the names of the interrupted tasks than for the completed tasks. The interpretation of this observation, known as the Zeigarnik* effect, after the experimenter who demonstrated it, was that accepting a task to perform creates a tension; when the task is completed this tension abates, but interruption permits the tension to continue. The continuation of the tension is the reason, in Lewin's terms, for the better recall for the unfinished than for the completed tasks. A further demonstration of the effect of interruption was shown in a study by another experimenter. Ovsiankina's* subjects thought that their work on tasks had been interrupted by chance. Later, when they were free to do as they pleased (in the laboratory), they resumed working on the tasks, thus reducing the tension left over following the interruption. Substitute activities, if they were similar enough to those interrupted, however, could prevent the resumption of the original tasks (Lissner)*, and continued repetition of the same task led to satiation for it (Karsten)*. These investigations illustrate, without going into Lewin's system in great detail, the kinds of motivational factors he dealt with.

It must be stressed that manipulations like interruption must be perceived by the subject as leaving the task unfinished; if he thought that he had accomplished what he was supposed to do, he would not perceive that the task had been interrupted. This is to say that Lewin conceived behavior as occurring within a psychological environment, rather than in a strictly physical environment, although the two would be closely related. We can illustrate the importance of the subject's evaluation of the situation by discussing the technique for the study of goal setting known as the level of aspiration situation.

To simplify the exposition, consider the game of throwing darts at a target, which contains a bull's-eye and concentric rings around it. The subject's performance can be scored, say, as five if he hits the bull's-eye, as four if his dart enters the next concentric ring, and so on to zero if the dart hits outside the rings altogether. In the level of aspiration situation, the subject would throw the dart, observe the result, and predict what his score would be on the next trial. This predicted score is the level of aspiration.

Although in some sense, the subject probably hopes on any trial to hit the bull's-eye, most subjects do not state this hope or expectation as their level of aspiration. Why don't they? Lewin et al. (1944) suggested that while a bull's-eye may well be the most desired outcome of a throw, i.e., have a high positive valence, the subject knows that his chances of achieving it are poor, that is, the subjective probability of success is low. So in setting his goal (stating his level of aspiration), the subject takes into account the positive value of a given score (and the negative value

---

*See Cofer and Appley, (1964,) pp. 782–783.

of not achieving it) and the subjective probability that he will achieve it. The result, a compromise, will be a level of aspiration short of the bull's-eye. There are a number of manipulations in this situation that can be used to modify the values, positive and negative, of a given level of performance, and to alter subjective probabilities. In general, these manipulations are successful in influencing the stated level of aspiration, so long as the subject's subjective evaluations of the situation correspond to the experimental manipulations.

Lewin's field-theoretical approach to motivation has had widespread influence in two ways. One is the stress on subjective evaluations made by the subject. The other is the emphasis on the interrelations of parts of the field. Balance theories, which we take up next, are not all derived from Lewin's work, but some of them do represent an extension of Lewin's influence. Deutsch (1968, p. 445) points out that Festinger's theory of cognitive dissonance "elaborates Lewin's view that the situation prior to decision differs from the post decision situation." We discuss Festinger's theory in a moment.

Cognitive Dissonance

According to Zajonc (1968, p. 338), *the* social-psychological problem of the 1960's was cognitive conflict and change. He identifies three major viewpoints: Heider's balance theory (1946, 1958), Osgood and Tannenbaum's congruity principle (1955), and Festinger's theory of cognitive dissonance (1957). These theories are referred to as balance or consistency theories, because balance or consistency among cognitions seems to be the end or goal state postulated by the theories. The actual basis of change in cognitions, of the forces that play roles in cognitive dynamics, is imbalance of or inconsistency among cognitions. When the cognitions are "out of joint," so to speak, changes take place to restore the equilibrium.

Most writers (e.g., Singer, 1966, pp. 52–54) on consistency theories indicate that neither balance nor congruity theories say much of anything about the motivational bases of the theories. In dissonance theory, however, there is an explicit motivational basis for the theory: cognitive dissonance is a drive, much like hunger (Festinger, 1958, p. 70); therefore, we shall limit the discussion of balance theories to the treatment of the theory of cognitive dissonance.

The notion that discrepancy might lead to activities of a balancing kind, central to dissonance theory, had its precursors in Festinger's work. For example, in 1950 he suggested that in a group, discrepant attitudes, beliefs, or opinions among the group members might be inimical to the achievement of some group goal, and such discrepancies might lead, he proposed, to communication among group members. Uniformity among the group members would be increased if some of them changed their opinions, etc., as a result of the interchange.

Later, seeming to shift to the standpoint of the individual rather than the group, Festinger (1954a, b) postulated a "drive for self-evaluation," that is, a desire "to know that one's opinions are correct and to know precisely what one is and is not capable of doing" (1954b, p. 217). This drive, Festinger said, would often require that the individual enter into social behavior to resolve it, as only by comparing himself with others can he reach an evaluation on such nonobjective matters as opinions, abilities, attitudes, and beliefs. This theory of social comparison would not be required when one can compare his ideas and knowledge with the evidence of his senses. For example, if one believes that the sun always arises at the same point in the sky, this belief can be checked by observing where it rises, over a several month period, against a fixed point on the earth. But to know whether one's opinion as to the honesty of a public official is accurate is much more difficult to verify. However by talking to other people, one can gain some sense of what the official's reputation for honesty is and evaluate his own opinion against the prevailing consensus. Of course, one might not accept the opinions of everyone and evaluate his opinion against those only of his friends or of people presumed to be "in the know" with respect to public figures.

The theory of social comparison led to some research (see the symposium edited by Latané, 1966), but as Singer (1966) has observed, the major offshoots of the theory were its influences on Schachter's work on emotions (see Chapter 4) and on affiliation (see Chapter 7). Perhaps the reason the theory was not as influential as it might have been is that it was followed so soon (1957) by the theory of cognitive dissonance. Singer points out (1966, p. 104) that the same studies used to support the theory of social comparison were used in evidence for dissonance theory.

At any rate, dissonance theory appeared (Festinger, 1957) and has stimulated a great deal of investigation, more, Zajonc (1968, p. 359) says, than any other theory in social psychology. What is this theory?

To answer this question, it is first necessary to speak of cognitions. These are pieces of information, bits of knowledge. There is no good definition of cognitions, and the foregoing statement will have to suffice. However, what cognitions are can be seen with greater clarity in the context of experiments and examples, as given below.

Cognitions may be related to one another or they may not be related, and further they may be important or unimportant to us. For dissonance to arise, elements must be related to one another and be important. Given these conditions, dissonance will arise when the cognitions are inconsistent or incompatible with one another, i.e., when what one cognition implies is not what is implied by another. Of course, cognitions may be compatible with one another, in which case there is no dissonance but rather consonance.

The state of dissonance is a noxious state, one we try to resolve or reduce or to avoid if possible. There are various ways to reduce dissonance. For example, we may change some existing cognitions so that they are not any longer inconsistent with the remaining, related ones. We can add new cognitions, which favor one side of the conflict, so that the proportion of the dissonant elements will be reduced. Thus, we may seek new information in order to reduce dissonance (see Zajonc, 1968, pp. 360–361).

Let us take an example, which will help to define the conditions of dissonance and methods for its resolution. Suppose that a high-school senior has made applications to five colleges for admission the following fall and has been accepted by all of them. He must make a decision as to which one he will attend, and he makes the decision in favor of College C and notifies this college that he will come and the others that he will not come to them. He is then in a postdecisional state. We may presume that the decision was an important and a central one to him. Will he experience dissonance?

Our prospective student has, of course, examined the advantages and disadvantages of each college. Presumably, he has chosen the one with the most advantages and the fewest disadvantages so far as he is concerned. But the rejected colleges all have attractive features, whereas the one he has chosen will, no doubt, have about it some things that are not so desirable. So there is dissonance following the decision: the cognitions involve the advantages of the rejected institutions and the disadvantages of the one chosen, as well as the fact that he has made a choice. He can't be sure that the choice was a wise one, and he will be plagued by the advantages he has overruled and the disadvantages he will have to endure. This is dissonance; how may he go about resolving or lessening it?

One way is to seek more information about the college he selected, perhaps from alumni who are favorable to it. He may read selectively newspaper accounts of events on the campus of his chosen institution, finding support for his decision in any favorable story he can read about it. He may talk to other seniors who have made the same choice and perhaps avoid others or avoid talking to them about college when he knows that they have considered his choice but have decided to go elsewhere. The new information about his college and the support he receives from alumni and from those who also will be going there will help to reduce the dissonance. Any unfavorable information or rumor he can come up with concerning the rejected alternatives will also lessen his dissonance over the decision he has reached.

It will be instructive to consider several experiments which have been performed in conjunction with dissonance theory. Brehm and Cohen (1962, pp. 302–309) were able to list a number of conditions which affect the arousal of dissonance, all supported by one or more studies, and before turning to illustrative experiments we summarize their list. Dissonance increases the more attractive the rejected alternative seems to be to the individual when he must choose among attractive alternatives;

dissonance also increases the more negative characteristics there are that the alternative he chooses possesses. Greater dissonance occurs when there are many rejected alternatives, rather than a few, and when attractive alternatives do not overlap too much cognitively, though being related. The more recent the decision the more dissonance there is, and the importance of the cognitions is associated positively with augmented dissonance. When the individual engages in behavior that is discrepant with his attitudes, opinions, and beliefs, as he often does in experimental studies designed to test dissonance theory, the less inducement or reward there is for doing the discrepant acts, the more the dissonance, and the more commitment he has made to perform the discrepant acts the more dissonance he suffers. Several other features of the conditions of the discrepant behavior also contribute to the amount of dissonance: the less the individual is coerced into doing it, the less he sees the behavior as compatible with his self-esteem, the more of the behavior in which he must engage, and the more negative information he has concerning the discrepant circumstances to which he has committed himself.

Dissonance reduction may be accomplished in many ways. The ones most commonly seen in the experimental literature are (Brehm & Cohen, 1962), as listed by Cofer and Appley (1964, p. 792):

> changes in opinions in relation to a number of issues; changes in evaluations of people, groups, objects, foods, etc.; selective exposure to information; selective recall; perceptual distortion; and such behavioral changes as ordering things to eat, amount of water drunk, job productivity, modifications in performance so as to produce failure, and conforming to a group norm.

The dissonance formulation has been extended, as may be seen from this list, beyond the postdecisional situation.

Illustrative Experiments

Brehm (1956) had his subjects rate each of 8 products (worth around $20 apiece), and the subjects knew that afterward they would receive one of them. After the rating was completed, the subjects were asked to choose between two of the alternatives, neither one either very highly or very poorly rated. However, for the high dissonance subjects the objects had received highly similar ratings, whereas for the low dissonance subjects the ratings of the two objects were discrepant. Brehm measured the attractiveness of the alternatives after these choices were made. In both high and low dissonance subjects changes were observed but were greater for the former than the latter subjects; the chosen alternative had become more attractive, the rejected alternative less so. A control group showed no changes in attractiveness. These results conform well to expectation from dissonance theory.

Aronson and Mills (1959) obtained volunteers (college girls) to participate in a group which was to discuss the psychology of sex. When a subject arrived for the group meeting, she was told that she would have to undergo a screening procedure for admission to the group. Half the girls were given a mild "screening" procedure involving reading some sex-related words that were not obscene. The other half were subjected to an "embarrassing" procedure. They had to read aloud in the presence of a male experimenter obscene words and some vivid descriptions of sexual activity. The subjects thought their reactions to the screening procedure were being evaluated clinically and might or might not admit them to the group.

After the screening, a pretext was used to have the girls listen to the discussion over an audio system. What they actually heard was a tape of a dull discussion on the sex behavior of animals. Ratings of the discussion were obtained. The girls subjected to the embarrassing screening gave more favorable ratings to the discussion and to the participants in it than did the girls given the mild screening. Presumably, dissonance arose between the cognition that they had been badly embarrassed and the cognition of the dullness of the discussion, and the resolution was to regard the discussion as more interesting than it actually was.

Several studies have evaluated the role of dissonance in modifying bodily motive states (see Zimbardo, 1968). Brehm (1962) obtained subjects who agreed to drink no liquids from the time they went to bed to the next afternoon when they reported to the laboratory. On arrival, the subjects rated their thirst and performed several tasks. Then they were induced to go without water for another 24 hours, half being offered five dollars (low dissonance) and half being offered one dollar (high dissonance) for doing so. After agreement to continue their participation, the subjects performed some more tasks and then rerated their thirst. The ratings made by the high dissonance subjects showed a decline in thirst, but those made by the low dissonance subjects did not. There was a difference, as well, in the amount of water drunk by the two groups, the high dissonance subjects drinking less, though the difference was not large. Presumably, again the commitment to go on without water for only $1.00 was dissonant with their degree of thirst for the high dissonance subjects. Hence, they gave evidence of being less thirsty at the second rating than the low dissonance subjects. A similar experiment on hunger (Brehm & Cohen, 1962, Chapter 8) by Brehm and Crocker yielded similar results, the high dissonance subjects rating their hunger as less and ordering fewer food items than the low dissonance subjects.

The pain of electric shock also is evaluated as less severe by subjects given little justification for voluntarily enduring a second series of painful shocks (Zimbardo et al., 1966). In addition, Cohen and Zimbardo (in

Brehm & Cohen, 1962, Chapter 8) found that subjects who agreed to return to perform a very difficult task on which they were told they would do poorly did not opt (as did more of the subjects told they would perform at an average level) for either a lesser difficulty level of the task or for an alternative task. The dissonance between the element of having committed themselves to the difficult task despite the predicted poor performance, which is an element of failure, evidently was reduced by reducing the avoidance of failure.

As a last example of dissonance experiments, we cite work with animals by Lawrence and Festinger (1962). Their concern was with resistance to extinction of a learned response, and the argument was that there should be greater resistance to extinction if the animal had been made to perform for an insufficient reward than if he had had an adequate reward.

Hilgard and Bower (1966, p. 491) have summarized this research as follows: first determine the relative choice of two rewards in a preference situation and suppose that reward A is preferred to reward B. "Then the hypothesis predicts that, in a nonchoice situation (e.g., a runway), animals trained under condition B will extinguish more slowly than those trained under condition A." Hilgard and Bower observe that the prediction is verified under a number of conditions, i.e., where condition B means relative delay of reward, a relatively smaller reward, more nonrewards, some punishment as well as reward, more effort than does condition A. A dissonance interpretation fits these facts, as the reader by now should be able to see, and is consistent with new experiments designed and carried out by Lawrence and Festinger. Hilgard and Bower (p. 493) point out that if the dissonance theory interpretation continues to be valid the conceptual scheme for learning in rats will have to include "some peculiar elements, such as accepting rats that compare cognitions, that feel dissonance and that attempt to justify what they do to reduce dissonance."

Evaluation

Dissonance theory seems to have a certain plausibility, and many of the experiments it has stimulated have successfully confirmed derivations from the theory that would not be likely to have occurred to common sense or to other psychological theories. Yet, there are a number of problems with the theory and with the research that is advanced in its support.

Dissonance is supposed to be an aversive motivational condition, yet no one has measured it directly. And there are no operations, such as deprivation, which can induce it outside a specific situation. Many of the experimental situations contrived to establish dissonance, as Zajonc (1968, pp. 390–391) says, "involve the resources of a minor theatrical production." One is tempted to add that the social psychologists who have conducted these experiments might have profited from work in method acting before embarking on their laboratory research.

The complexity of the experiments designed to test the theory has two unfortunate consequences. One is that it is difficult to replicate any of them exactly. The other is that it is possible that other variables, in addition to or instead of dissonance, may be involved in producing the results. In any case, it seems unlikely (Berkowitz, 1968) that all the operations used to induce dissonance have all aroused the "same dissonance." Dissonance is often viewed as a unitary drive state, a conception that, as we have seen, has been largely given up among students of motivational psychology.

One could speculate, also, about why inconsistency should give rise to dissonance. There may be many reasons, although none is specified in the theory. Perhaps our experience has rewarded us, in the past, for consistency and punished us for inconsistency. Perhaps some kind of anxiety arises from this background in the face of inconsistency, or perhaps self-esteem or self-concept is upset by the realization of inconsistency. Little attention has been paid to the consequences of behavior inconsistent with one's attitudes (Pepitone, 1966, 1968) in dissonance theory. For example, if one is going to communicate to another person that an experience he has had was interesting and enjoyable, when in fact it was dull (and this maneuver has been employed in a number of experiments), it makes a difference in one's reaction whether the communication is to be face to face or indirect. The thought of facing that person to whom one has lied not only at the time of the communication but later on in campus and classroom activities may be the reason for the dissonance, not the inconsistent cognitions (Pepitone, 1966). One might fear a negative evaluation from the other person, for example, that one is dishonest after the other person has received a false report from one.

Situational consequences and the possible presence of other motives may provide alternative accounts for some, at least, of the results of investigations concerning dissonance. It is also possible that nonmotivational factors (Singer, 1968) may be involved. It is known (Miller, 1956) that the capacity of the human to process information is limited and that one way to overcome this limitation is to organize our cognitive processes so as to encode inputs into cognitive structures, such as schemata, which already exist. It is at least possible that some of the changes which we work upon cognitive inconsistency may arise because if a cognition cannot be encoded into an existing schema it is not processed adequately for retention or for integration with existing structures.

As a last point, it may be noted that the goal of consistency is at least superficially incompatible with the kinds of motives for variety of stimulation (Maddi, 1968) that we discussed in Chapter 5. Consistency may lead to boredom, and we saw earlier that deviations from the adaptation level (perhaps akin to boredom) provoke curiosity and exploratory behavior. It may well be, of course, that there are separate tendencies, one for consistency and one for variety or complexity, and that each will be prominent under very different conditions. The research which dissonance theory has spawned is so different from that done under the banner of curiosity that no meaningful comparison or integration seems to be possible at the present time (McGuire, 1968).

SUGGESTED READINGS

Abelson, R. P., Aronson, E., McGuire, W. J., Newcomb, T. M., Rosenberg, M. J., & Tannenbaum, P. H. (Eds.) *Theories of cognitive consistency: A sourcebook.* Chicago: Rand McNally & Co., 1968.

Brehm, J. W. & Cohen, A. R. *Explorations in cognitive dissonance.* New York: John Wiley & Sons, Inc., 1962.

Cofer, C. N. & Appley, M. H. *Motivation: Theory and research.* New York: John Wiley & Sons, Inc., 1964. Pp. 428–441; Chapter 15.

Feldman, S. (Ed.) *Cognitive consistency: Motivational antecedents and behavior consequents.* New York: Academic Press, Inc., 1966.

Lindzey, G. & Aronson, E. (Eds.) *The handbook of social psychology.* (2nd ed.) Reading, Massachusetts: Addison-Wesley Publishing Company, 1968, 1969. 5 vols. Chapters 5 and 6 (vol. 1); Chapter 20 (vol. 3).

9

Conclusions

We have reviewed the rise of motivational concepts in this century to a position of major prominence in the analysis of behavior, and we have summarized the major ideas that have been proposed as fundamental to motivation–instincts, drives, incentives, reinforcement, emotion, and arousal. Several themes have appeared throughout our discussions, and it is the task of this final chapter to bring them together and to determine the status of the motivation concept and the theoretical ideas which relate to it.

Motivation seems to have been a major vehicle by which determinism reached a firm status in the analysis of behavior. It seemed necessary to cope with the intentional and striving aspects of conduct, a matter to which associationism, a similarly deterministic precept, did not appear to be adequate. Motivation became, in the popular vocabulary, equated with the reasons for behavior, the explanatory principle above all others.

Much of motivation's appeal came from the functionalist's account of conduct, whether psychoanalytic or otherwise. It made biological sense to see behavior as instrumental to the organism's needs and as spurred automatically by forces over which the individual had little or no control. Motivation was, in a sense, the antithesis of rational accounts of conduct which had held sway for so long. A picture of the organism as a pawn in the grip of energies arising from within and seeking release from their tensions, though perhaps somewhat overdrawn, does not miss far the mark of portraying the fundamental conception of organisms and their behavior implied by a thoroughgoing motivational account.

The period since about 1950 has seen a retreat from this position. Internal "forces" are no longer considered to push behavior out of the organism, so to speak, or to operate without the agency of external stimulation. Organisms seem to seek, at least on some occasions, increases in stimulation, and their perceptions and evaluations of situations which are cognitive (if not entirely rational) in nature make significant differences in the ways in which motivational variables function with regard to what they do. Factors other than motivational ones—abilities and habit patterns, for example—exercise significant control over what behavior will occur in situations. Monolithic motivational interpretations of behavior are far too simple, however complex and seemingly compelling, to give an adequate understanding of why behavior occurs when and where it takes place.

The retreat has brought its problems. Among them is what function to give motivational concepts or, indeed, the question whether they are necessary at all. And, given that they are necessary in some measure and have a function, what theoretical account shall be proposed for their operation?

For many years, there have been three functions attributed to motivation. One is response selection, often designated as the directional component of behavior, i.e., the determination of which response or response sequence will occur in a situation. For example, hunger is said to account for the fact that eating occurs, rather than drinking or mating, when food, water, and a mate are present. A second is to suggest that motivation energizes responses or invigorates behavior more or less indiscriminately and to leave to habits and the stimuli which control them the function of directing behavior. The third is to hold that motivation provides the condition for reinforcement of a response which produces a suitable goal object.

Bindra (1969) has offered a reconceptualization of these matters, in the context of animal motivation. His view emphasizes the important role of incentives, a role stressed by other writers as well (Cofer & Appley, 1964; Bolles, 1967) and will be summarized here as the most recent attempt, known to the author, to resolve the problems of the function of motivation, whether reinforcement can replace motivation, and what a theoretical account of motivation might be.

Bindra argues that reinforcement and motivation are identical (p. 2) and that the major effect of a reinforcing event is not to reinforce a response but rather "the creation of a motivational state that influences a wide variety of subsequent behavior of an animal" (p. 7). Let us see first how Bindra reaches this conclusion about reinforcement.

First, he argues that reinforcement can influence the probability that a response will occur even though the response in question does not occur in conjunction with the reinforcement. Thus, there can be learning without responding, as Solomon and Turner (1962) have shown in curarized animals, and reinforcement of one response (e.g., walking) can apparently influence the occurrence of another response (swimming) which has not itself been reinforced (MacFarlane, 1930). A possible interpretation of these findings is that the reinforcement engenders a motivational effect which influences nonreinforced responses as well as reinforced ones, and the notion that reinforcement only reinforces responses can be rejected. Second, he indicates that responses denoting motivational excitement are not those which are reinforced in the presence of an incentive. Thus, for example, food, an incentive, arouses sniffing, biting, and swallowing in a rat, whereas the responses of excitement are exploration and searching (p. 4). The experiment by Bindra and Palfai (1967), described earlier in this book (pp. 75–76), supports this distinction. Hence, the strengthening of responses by reinforcement is not the mechanism underlying motivational excitement. Third, there is evidence (pp. 5–7) that reinforcing events (or manipulations of incentives) have motivational effects. These three points, then, are used to support the generalization that reinforcing events create a motivational state.

As to motivation, Bindra (pp. 9–11) rejects drive and suggests that motivation is "generated by a combination of physiological and incentive stimulation," and he suggests the term "central motive state" (see Chapter 2) as a name for the neural processes underlying the interaction of the physiological and incentive stimulation (pp. 11–12). The physiological or organismic state "may be a general state (e.g., being awake, sleepy, or sick) or a more specific physiological condition of the type traditionally called a drive . . ." (p. 12). Incentives are those stimuli which we call incentives, reinforcers, or emotional stimuli. The central motive state, once set into operation, persists for some period of time.

The central motive state is the basis for "exploratory, instrumental, and incentive-linked" responses (p. 12). It can be used for emotions as well as for those phenomena usually termed motivational. Stimuli that have been associated with a primary incentive can, in interaction with a suitable physiological condition, act as primary incentives do to arouse the central motive state. Secondary motivation, then, functions through incentive processes, not by means of acquired drives, a conclusion we reached in an earlier chapter.

Bindra attributes both the selection of a particular response and the fact of its occurrence to the motivational processes he has outlined, i.e., both selection and energization of responses arise from these mechanisms. He accepts the principle that animals, probably innately, will approach positive incentive and withdraw from negative incentive stimuli. If the animal has eaten in a particular environment, various cues there will have become associated with the central motive state and thus be able to arouse it as secondary incentives in the presence of a suitable physiological condition. These incentives, together with the central motive state, would elicit approach responses which will lead the animal, on a later occasion, to the food. Stimulation arising from the food, of course, would elicit eating. Augmentation in strength of the central motive state as well as of the tendency of the incentive stimuli to elicit it would occur with repeated trials and thus produce the changes in behavior normally seen in an animal running, say, a maze to small bits of food—decreased latency of starting to run, increased speed of running, and increased probability of running. Response selection really arises because of the specific stimuli in the situation, but because they are incentives, they will contribute, in interaction with the physiological state, to the central motive state and, thus, in the sense of increased speed, probability of occurrence, and decreased latency, to the invigoration of the behavior in question.

Bindra's analysis was applied primarily to the case of behavior toward a positive incentive, like food, but could presumably be extended to the case of withdrawal from a negative incentive. The analysis has also remained close to the classical appetitive drive states (hunger and thirst). It appears to the author that Bindra's formulation is very similar to that proposed by Cofer and Appley (1964, Chapter 16; see Chapter 6 in this book), except that his proposal is somewhat more detailed than theirs and introduces the notion of the central motive state where they referred only to arousal. Bindra's emphasis on the interaction of incentive stimuli and a physiological state was explicit in Cofer and Appley's discussion of SIM but perhaps only implicit in their discussion of AIM. Presumably, Bindra's analysis could be extended beyond hunger and thirst, as was Cofer and Appley's, to include such conditions as sex, curiosity, maternal activities, and the like.

It remains to say something more concerning human motivation. Can we find in anxiety, aggression, achievement, approval, for example, something like a central motive state and incentive stimuli? Is cognitive dissonance the equivalent of a central motive state?

Our discussion of these various human motive systems clearly depicted, where the evidence permitted it—as in achievement, affiliation, aggression, and, to some extent, in anxiety—an interactive process. That is, we said, for example, that nAch had to be "engaged" by a situation that seemed to the subject to possess evaluative possibilities and that anger was not sufficient for the occurrence of aggression in the absence of "releasing" stimuli. So Bindra's emphasis on cues finds support in our discussion of human motive systems. What is perhaps missing is an equivalent to the physiological state. Although the existence of such a state is plausible and has been reported in the cases of anxiety and aggression (and other emotions), it is not so clearly suggested in the case of achievement and affiliation, and, to the writer's knowledge, no firm evidence of a physiological state accompanying these systems has been reported. This is not to say, of course, that physiological arousal will not be found to accompany motive systems like these. However, the arousal is likely to be of a general, unspecific kind, subject to interpretation as being one or the other motive in the light of the situational circumstances, as in Schachter's work on emotion. Human motivation, if what has just been said is true, may well consist of undifferentiated arousal, interpreted in the light of situational instigations and the behavioral outcomes which allay it.

The argument just presented implies that we should speak of human motives only when the arousal side of the interaction can be demonstrated to be present or can be plausibly inferred. The writer thinks that this kind of limitation on the use of the word motivation is desirable and might well have beneficial effects. It would limit the promiscuous use of the word *motive* in discussions of human behavior, with the aura of explanatory adequacy which the use of this term seems to carry, whatever its virtues. Many behavioral problems are "solved" or dismissed by the assertion that they are motivational problems. Little is accomplished by invocation of the word *motivation*, as the survey of human motivational systems presented in Chapter 7 should suggest. What is needed is a close examination of the conditions under which a behavior pattern of interest was developed and is sustained, and it will probably turn out, in many instances, that it is not very helpful to emphasize motivational concepts in the process of making the analysis.

This completes our survey. We have seen the emergence of an area, the variety of concepts which have developed, and the vicissitudes which thinking about motivation has undergone during more than half a century. The reader may have anticipated more certain answers and more clearcut concepts than have been provided. The present status of the field of motivation does not, unfortunately, provide them.

Bibliography

Allport, G. W. *Personality: A psychological interpretation*. New York: Holt, Rinehart & Winston, Inc., 1937.

Amsel, A. Frustrative nonreward in partial reinforcement and discrimination learning: Some recent history and a theoretical extension. *Psychol. Rev.*, 1962, **69,** 306–328.

Amsel, A. & Roussel, J. Motivational properties of frustration: I. Effect on a running response of the addition of frustration to the motivational complex. *J. exp. Psychol.*, 1952, **43,** 363–368.

Andersson, B. The effect of injections of hypertonic NaCL-solutions into different parts of the hypothalamus in goats. *Acta physiol. Scand.*, 1953, **28,** 188–201.

Andersson, B. & McCann, S. M. A further study of polydipsia evoked by hypothalamic stimulation in the goat. *Acta physiol. Scand.*, 1955a, **33,** 333–346.

Andersson, B. & McCann, S. M. Drinking, antidiuresis and milk ejection from electrical stimulation within the hypothalamus of the goat. *Acta physiol. Scand.*, 1955b, **35,** 191–201.

Appley, M. H. Derived motives. *Annual rev. Psychol.*, 1970, **21,** 485–518.

Ardrey, R. *The territorial imperative: A personal inquiry into the animal origins of property and nations*. New York: Atheneum Publishers, 1966.

Aronson, E. & Mills, J. The effect of severity of initiation on liking for a group. *J. abnorm. soc. Psychol.*, 1959, **59,** 177–181.

Atkinson, J. W. The achievement motive and recall of interrupted and completed tasks. *J. exp. Psychol.*, 1953, **46,** 381–390.

Atkinson, J. W. Towards experimental analysis of motives, expectations, and incentives. In J. W. Atkinson (Ed.), *Motives in fantasy, action, and society*. New York: D. Van Nostrand Co., Inc., 1958. Pp. 288–305.

Atkinson, J. W. *An introduction to motivation*. Princeton, N. J.: D. Van Nostrand Co., Inc., 1964.

Atkinson, J. W. & McClelland, D. C. The projective expression of needs: II. The effect of different intensities of the hunger drive on thematic apperception. *J. exp. Psychol.*, 1948, **38,** 643–658.

Ayres, C. E. Instinct and capacity: I. The instinct of belief-in-instincts. *J. Philos.*, 1921, **18,** 561–566.

Baker, R. A. Aperiodic feeding in the albino rat. *J. comp. physiol. Psychol.*, 1953, **46,** 422–426.

Baker, R. A. The effects of repeated deprivation experience in feeding behavior. *J. comp. physiol. Psychol.*, 1955, **48,** 37–42.

Baldwin, J. M. (Ed.) *Dictionary of philosophy and psychology.* New York: The Macmillan Company, 1911. 3 vols.

Bard, P. On emotional experience after decortication with some remarks on theoretical views. *Psychol. Rev.*, 1934, **41,** 309–329; 424–449.

Barnes, G. W. & Kish, G. B. Reinforcing properties of the termination of intense auditory stimulation. *J. comp. physiol. Psychol.*, 1957, **50,** 40–43.

Barnes, G. W. & Kish, G. B. Reinforcing properties of the onset of auditory stimulation. *J. exp. Psychol.*, 1961,**62,** 164–170.

Barnett, S. A. Attack and defense in animal societies. In C. D. Clemente. & D. B. Lindsley (Eds.), *Aggression and defense: Neural mechanisms and social patterns* (Brain Function, Vol. V). Los Angeles: University of California Press, 1967. Pp. 35–56.

Beach, F. A. Analysis of the stimuli adequate to elicit mating behavior in the sexually inexperienced male rat. *J. comp. Psychol.*, 1942, **33,** 163–207.

Beach, F. A. The snark was a boojum. *Amer. Psychologist*, 1950, **5,** 115–124.

Beach, F. A. Instinctive behavior: Reproductive activities. In S. S. Stevens (Ed.), *Handbook of experimental psychology.* New York: John Wiley & Sons, Inc., 1951. Pp. 387–434.

Beach, F. A. The descent of instinct. *Psychol. Rev*,. 1955, **62,** 401–410.

Beach, F. A. Characteristics of masculine sex drive. In M. R. Jones (Ed.), *Nebraska symposium on motivation, 1956.* Lincoln: University of Nebraska Press, 1956. Pp. 1–32.

Bélanger, D. & Feldman, S. M. Effects of water deprivation upon heart rate and instrumental activity in the rat. *J. comp. physiol. Psychol.*, 1962, **55,** 220–225.

Berkowitz, L. *Aggression: A social psychological analysis.* New York: McGraw-Hill Book Company, 1962.

Berkowitz, L. The concept of aggressive drive: Some additional considerations. *Advances exp. soc. Psychol.*, 1965, **2,** 301–329. New York: Academic Press, Inc.

Berkowitz, L. Experiments on automatism and intent in human aggression. In C. D. Clemente & D. B. Lindsley (Eds.), *Aggression and defense: Neural mechanisms and social patterns.* Los Angeles: University of California Press, 1967. Pp. 243–266.

Berkowitz, L. The motivational status of cognitive consistency theorizing. In R. P. Abelson et al. (Eds.), *Theories of cognitive consistency: A sourcebook.* Chicago: Rand McNally & Co., 1968. Pp. 301–310.

Berkowitz, L. Simple views of aggression: An essay review. *American Scientist*, 1969a, **57,** 372–383.

Berkowitz, L. Social motivation. In G. Lindzey & E. Aronson (Eds.), *The handbook of social psychology*. (2nd ed.) vol. 3. Reading, Mass.: Addison-Wesley, 1969b. Pp. 50–135.

Berkowitz, L. Experimental investigations of hostility catharsis. *J. consult. clin. Psychol.*, 1970, **35,** 1–7.

Berlyne, D. E. Conflict and information-theory variables as determinants of human perceptual curiosity. *J. exp. Psychol.*, 1957, **53,** 399–404.

Berlyne, D. E. The influence of the albedo and complexity of stimulation on visual fixation in the human infant. *Brit. J. Psychol.*, 1958a, **49,** 315–318.

Berlyne, D. E. The influence of complexity and novelty in visual figures on orienting responses. *J. exp. Psychol.*, 1958b, **55,** 289–296.

Berlyne, D. E. Arousal and reinforcement. In D. Levine (Ed.), *Nebraska symposium on motivation, 1967*. Lincoln, Neb.: University of Nebraska Press, 1967. Pp. 1–110.

Berlyne, D. E. & Slater, J. Perceptual curiosity, exploratory behavior, and maze learning. *J. comp. physiol. Psychol.*, 1957, **50,** 228–232.

Bernard, L. L. *Instinct: A study in social psychology*. New York: Holt, Rinehart & Winston, Inc., 1924.

Bexton, W. H., Heron, W., & Scott, T. H. Effects of decreased variation in the sensory environment. *Canad. J. Psychol.*, 1954, **8,** 70–76.

Bindra, D. The interrelated mechanisms of reinforcement and motivation, and the nature of their influence on response. In W. J. Arnold & D. Levine (Eds.), *Nebraska symposium on motivation, 1969*. Lincoln, Neb.: University of Nebraska Press, 1969. Pp. 1–33.

Bindra, D. & Palfai, T. Nature of positive and negative incentive-motivational effects on general activity. *J. comp. physiol. Psychol.*, 1967, **63,** 288–297.

Birney, R. C., Burdick, H., & Teevan, R. C. *Fear of failure*. New York: Van Nostrand-Reinhold, 1969.

Bolles, R. C. Grooming behavior in the rat. *J. comp. physiol. Psychol.*, 1960, **53,** 306–310.

Bolles, R. C. *Theory of motivation*. New York: Harper & Row, Publishers, 1967.

Bolles, R. C. Species-specific defense reactions and avoidance learning. *Psychol. Rev.*, 1970, **77,** 32–48.

Boring, E. G. *Sensation and perception in the history of experimental psychology*. New York: Appleton-Century-Crofts, 1942.

Brady, J. V., Boren, J. J., Conrad, D. G., & Sidman, M. The effect of food and water deprivation upon intra-cranial self-stimulation. *J. comp. physiol. Psychol.* 1957, **50,** 134–137.

Brehm, J. W. Post-decision changes in the desirability of alternatives. *J. abn. soc. Psychol.*, 1956, **52,** 384–389.

Brehm, J. W. Motivational effects of cognitive dissonance. In M. R. Jones (Ed.), *Nebraska symposium on motivation, 1962*. Lincoln, Neb.: University of Nebraska Press, 1962. Pp. 51–77.

Brehm, J. & Cohen, A. R. *Explorations in cognitive dissonance.* New York: John Wiley & Sons, Inc., 1962.

Breland, K. & Breland, J. The misbehavior of organisms. *American Psychologist*, 1961, **16,** 681–684.

Brobeck, J. R. Neural control of hunger, appetite and satiety. *Yale J. biol. med.*, 1957, **29,** 565–574.

Brown, J. S. *The motivation of behavior*. New York: McGraw-Hill Book Company, 1961.

Brown, J. S. & Farber, I. E. Secondary motivational systems. *Ann. rev. Psychol.*, 1968, **19,** 99–134.

Butler, R. A. Discrimination learning by Rhesus monkeys to visual-exploration motivation. *J. comp. physiol. Psychol.*, 1953, **46,** 95–98.

Butler, R. A. Discrimination learning by Rhesus monkeys to auditory incentives. *J. comp. physiol. Psychol.*, 1957, **50,** 239–241.

Campbell, B. A. & Misanin, J. R. Basic drives. In P. H. Mussen & M. R. Rosenzweig (Eds.), *Ann. rev. of Psychol.*, 1969, **20,** 57–84.

Campbell, B. A. & Sheffield, F. D. Relation of random activity to food deprivation. *J. comp. physiol. Psychol.*, 1953, **46,** 320–322.

Cannon, W. B. The physiological basis of thirst. *Proc roy. soc. London. B, 1918,* **90,** 283–301.

Cannon, W. B. The James-Lange theory of emotions: A critical examination and an alternative. *Amer. J. Psychol.*, 1927, **39,** 106–124.

Cannon, W. B. *Bodily changes in pain, hunger, fear, and rage.* (2nd ed.) New York: Appleton-Century-Crofts, 1929.

Cannon, W. B. *The wisdom of the body.* (2nd ed.) New York: W. W. Norton & Company, Inc., 1939.

Cannon, W. B. & Washburn, A. L. An explanation of hunger. *Amer. J. Physiol.*, 1912, **29,** 441–454.

Carlson, A. J. *The control of hunger in health and disease.* Chicago: University of Chicago Press, 1916.

Cofer, C. N. & Appley, M. H. *Motivation: Theory and research.* New York: John Wiley & Sons, Inc., 1964.

Crespi, L. P. Quantitative variation of incentive and performance in the white rat. *Amer. J. Psychol.*, 1942, **55,** 467–517.

Crowne, D. P. & Marlowe, D. *The approval motive: Studies in evaluative dependence.* New York: John Wiley & Sons, Inc., 1964.

Dana, C. L. The anatomic seat of the emotions: A discussion of the James-Lange theory. *Arch. Neurol. Psychiat.* (Chicago), 1921, **6,** 634-669.

Dashiell, J. F. *Fundamentals of objective psychology.* Boston: Houghton-Mifflin Company, 1928.

Davis, D. M. Self-selection of diet by newly weaned infants. *Amer. J. Dis. Child.*, 1928, **36,** 651–679.

Davis, R. C., Garafalo, L., & Kveim, K. Conditions associated with gastrointestinal activity. *J. comp. physiol. Psychol.*, 1959, **52,** 466–475.

Davitz, J. R. *The language of emotion.* New York: Academic Press, Inc., 1969.

Delgado, J. M. R. & Anand, B. K. Increased food intake induced by electrical stimulation of the lateral hypothalamus. *Amer. J. Physiol.*, 1953, **172,** 162–168.

Delgado, J. M. R., Roberts, W. W., & Miller, N. E. Learning motivated by electrical stimulation of the brain. *Amer. J. Physiol.*, 1954, **179,** 587–593.

Deutsch, M. Field theory in social psychology. In G. Lindzey & E. Aronson (Eds.), *The handbook of social psychology.* (2nd ed.) Reading, Mass.: Addison-Wesley, Publishing Co., Inc., 1968. Pp. 412–487.

Dollard, J., Doob, L. W., Miller, N. E., Mowrer, O. H., & Sears, R. R. *Frustration and aggression.* New Haven: Yale University Press, 1939.

Dollard, J. & Miller, N. E. *Personality and psychotherapy: An analysis in terms of learning, thinking and culture.* New York: McGraw-Hill Book Company, 1950.

Ducharme, R. & Bélanger, D. Influence d'une stimulation électrique sur le niveau d'activation et la performance. *Canad. J. Psychol.*, 1961, **15,** 61–68.

Duffy, E. An explanation of "emotional" phenomena without the use of the concept "emotion." *J. gen. Psychol.*, 1941, **25,** 283–293.

Duffy, E. Leeper's "motivational theory of emotion . . ." *Psychol. Rev.*, 1948, **55,** 324–328.

Duffy, E. *Activation and behavior.* New York: John Wiley & Sons, Inc., 1962.

Dufresne, C. Influence de la privation de nourriture sur le rythme cardiaque et l'activité instrumentale. Unpublished Master's thesis, Université de Montreal, 1961.

Dunlap, K. *Elements of scientific psychology.* St. Louis: The C. V. Mosby Co., 1922.

Eisenberger, R. Is there a deprivation-satiation function for social approval? *Psychol. Bull.*, 1970, **74,** 255–275.

Elliott, M. H. The effect of change of reward on the maze performance of rats. *Univ. Calif. Publ. Psychol.*, 1928, **4,** 19–30.

Fantz, R. L. Pattern vision in young infants. *Psychol. Rec.*, 1958, **8,** 43–48.

Festinger, L. Informal social communication. *Psychol. Rev.*, 1950, **57,** 271–282.

Festinger, L. A theory of social comparison processes. *Hum. relations*, 1954a, **7,** 117–140.

Festinger, L. Motivations leading to social behavior. In M. R. Jones (Ed.), *Nebraska symposium on motivation, 1954.* Lincoln, Neb.: University of Nebraska Press, 1954b. Pp. 191–219.

Festinger, L. *A theory of cognitive dissonance.* Evanston, Ill.: Row, Peterson, 1957.

Festinger, L. The motivating effect of cognitive dissonance. In G. Lindzey (Ed.), *Assessment of human motives.* New York: Holt, Rinehart, & Winston, Inc., 1958. Pp. 65–86.

Flynn, J. P. The neural basis of aggression in cats. In D. C. Glass (Ed.), *Neurophysiology and emotion*. New York: The Rockefeller University Press, 1967. Pp. 40–60.

Ford, C. S. & Beach, F. A. *Patterns of sexual behavior*. New York: Harper & Row, Publishers, 1951.

Freeman, G. L. The relationship between performance level and bodily activity level. *J. exp. Psychol.*, 1940, **26,** 602–608.

French, E. G. Some characteristics of achievement motivation. *J. exp. Psychol.*, 1955, **50,** 232–236.

French, E. G. Motivation as a variable in work-partner selection. *J. abn. soc. Psychol.*, 1956a, **53,** 96–99.

French, E. G. *Development of a measure of complex motivation*. Lackland Air Force Base, Texas: Res. Rep. AFPTRC-TN-56-48, Air Force Personnel and Training Research Center, 1956b.

French, E. G. Effects of the interaction of motivation and feedback on task performance. In J. W. Atkinson (Ed.), *Motives in fantasy, action, and society*. New York: D. Van Nostrand, Co., Inc., 1958. Pp. 400–408.

Fuster, J. M. Effects of stimulation of brain stem on tachistoscopic perception. *Science*, 1958, **127,** 150.

Gewirtz, J. L. A learning analysis of the effects of normal stimulation, privation, and deprivation on the acquisition of social motivation and attachment. In B. M. Foss (Ed.), *Determinants of infant behavior*. London: Methuen, 1961. Pp. 213–290.

Gewirtz, J. L. Mechanisms of social learning: Some roles of stimulation and behavior in early development. In D. A. Goslin (Ed.), *Handbook of socialization theory and research*. Chicago: Rand-McNally, & Co., 1969a. Pp. 57–212.

Gewirtz, J. L. Potency of a social reinforcer as a function of satiation and recovery. *Developmental Psychology*, 1969b, **1,** 2–13.

Gewirtz, J. L. & Baer, D. M. The effect of brief social deprivation on behaviors for a social reinforcer. *J. abn. soc. Psychol.*, 1958a, **56,** 49–56.

Gewirtz, J. L. & Baer, D. M. Deprivation and satiation of social reinforcers as drive conditions. *J. abn. soc. Psychol.*, 1958b, **57,** 165–172.

Ghent, L. The relation of experience to the development of hunger. *Canad. J. Psychol.*, 1951, **5,** 77–81.

Ghent, L. Some effects of deprivation on eating and drinking behavior. *J. comp. physiol. Psychol.*, 1957, **50,** 172–176.

Glanzer, M. The role of stimulus satiation in spontaneous alternation. *J. exp. Psychol.*, 1953, **45,** 387–393.

Grossman, M. I. & Stein, I. F., Jr. Vagotomy and the hunger-producing action of insulin in man. *J. appl. Physiol.*, 1948, **1,** 263–269.

Grossman, S. P. Eating or drinking elicited by direct adrenergic or cholinergic stimulation of hypothalamus. *Science*, 1960, **132,** 301–302.

Grossman, S. P. *A textbook of physiological psychology.* New York: John Wiley & Sons, Inc., 1967.

Haber, R. N. Discrepancy from adaptation level as a source of affect. *J. exp. Psychol.*, 1958, **56,** 370–375.

Harlow, H. F. Learning and satiation of response in intrinsically motivated complex puzzle performance by monkeys. *J. comp. physiol. Psychol.*, 1950, **43,** 289–294.

Harlow, H. F. The nature of love. *Amer. Psychologist*, 1958, **13,** 673–685.

Harlow, H. F. The heterosexual affectional system in monkeys. *Amer. Psychologist*, 1962, **17,** 1–9.

Harlow, H. F., Blazek, N. C., & McClearn, G. E. Manipulatory motivation in the infant Rhesus monkey. *J. comp. physiol. Psychol.*, 1956, **49,** 444–448.

Harlow, H. F., Harlow, M. K., & Meyer, D. R. Learning motivated by a manipulation drive. *J. exp. Psychol.*, 1950, **40,** 228–234.

Harriman, A. E. The effect of a preoperative preference for sugar over salt upon compensatory salt selection by adrenalectomized rats. *J. Nutrit.*, 1955, **57,** 271–276.

Harrison Matthews, L. Overt fighting in mammals. In J. D. Carthy & F. J. Ebling (Eds.), *The natural history of aggression.* New York: Academic Press, Inc., 1964. Pp. 23–32.

Hebb, D. O. Drives and the C. N. S. (conceptual nervous system). *Psychol. Rev.*, 1955, **62,** 243–254.

Heider, F. Attitudes and cognitive organization. *J. Psychol.*, 1946, **21,** 107–112.

Heider, F. *The psychology of interpersonal relations.* New York: John Wiley & Sons, Inc., 1958.

Heider, F. The Gestalt theory of motivation. In M. R. Jones (Ed.), *Nebraska symposium on motivation, 1960.* Lincoln, Neb.: University of Nebraska Press, 1960. Pp. 145–172.

Helson, H. *Adaptation-level theory.* New York: Harper & Row, Publishers, 1964.

Hilgard, E. R. & Bower, G. H. *Theories of learning.* (3rd ed.) New York: Appleton-Century-Crofts, 1966.

Hill, W. F. The effect of long confinement on voluntary wheel-running by rats. *J. comp. physiol. Psychol.*, 1958, **51,** 770–773.

Hinde, R. A. *Animal behavior: A synthesis of ethology and comparative psychology.* (2nd ed.) New York: McGraw-Hill Book Company, 1970.

Holt, R. R. On the interpersonal and intrapersonal consequences of expressing or not expressing anger. *J. consult. clin. Psychol.*, 1970, **35,** 8–12.

Hull, C. L. *Principles of behavior.* New York: Appleton-Century, 1943.

Hull, C. L. *A behavior system: An introduction to behavior theory concerning the individual organism.* New Haven: Yale University Press, 1952.

Hunt, J. McV. Intrinsic motivation and its role in psychological development. In D. Levine (Ed.), *Nebraska symposium on motivation, 1965*. Lincoln, Neb.: University of Nebraska Press, 1965. Pp. 189–282.

Hutt, C. Exploration and play in children. In P. A. Jewell & C. Loizos (Eds.), *Play, exploration and territory in mammals*. Symposium of the Zoological Society of London, No. 18, New York: Academic Press, Inc., 1966. Pp. 61–81.

James, W. What is an emotion? *Mind*, 1884, **9,** 188–205.

Kaada, B. Brain mechanisms related to aggressive behavior. In C. D. Clemente & P. B. Lindsley (Eds.), *Aggression and defense: Neural mechanisms and social patterns*. Los Angeles: University of California Press, 1967. Pp. 95–133.

Kety, S. S. Psychoendocrine systems and emotion: Biological aspects. In D. C. Glass (Ed.), *Neurophysiology and emotion*. New York: The Rockefeller University Press, 1967a. Pp. 103–108.

Kety, S. S. The central physiological and pharamacological effects of the biogenic amines and their correlations with behavior. In G. C. Quarton, T. Melnechuk, & F. O. Schmitt (Eds.), *The neurosciences*. New York: Rockefeller University Press, 1967b. Pp. 444–451.

Kish, G. B. Learning when the onset of illumination is used as reinforcing stimulus. *J. comp. physiol. Psychol.*, 1955, **48,** 261–264.

Lacey, J. I. Individual differences in somatic response patterns. *J. comp. physiol. Psychol.*, 1950, **43,** 338–350.

Lacey, J. I. Somatic response patterning and stress: Some revisions of activation theory. In M. H. Appley & R. Trumbull (Eds.), *Psychological stress: Issues in research*. New York: Appleton-Century-Crofts, 1967.

Latané, B. (Ed.) Studies in social comparison. *J. exp. soc. Psychol.*, 1966, **2,** Supplement 1, pp. 115.

Lawrence, D. H. & Festinger, L. *Deterrents and reinforcement*. Stanford, Calif.: Stanford University Press, 1962.

Lewin, K. Environmental forces in child behavior and development. In C. Murchison (Ed.), *A handbook of child psychology*. Worcester, Mass.: Clark University Press, 1931. Pp. 94–127.

Lewin, K., Dembo, T., Festinger, L., & Sears, P. S. Level of aspiration. In J. McV. Hunt (Ed.), *Personality and the behavior disorders*. Vol. 1. New York: The Ronald Press Company, 1944. Pp. 333–378.

Lindsley, D. B. Emotion. In S. S. Stevens (Ed.), *Handbook of experimental psychology*. New York: John Wiley, & Sons, Inc., 1951. Pp. 473–516.

Lindsley, D. B., Bowden, J., & Magoun, H. W. Effect upon the EEG of acute injury to the brain stem activating system. *EEG clin. Neurophysiol.*, 1949, **1,** 475–486.

Lorenz, K. *On aggression*. New York: Harcourt, Brace, & World, Inc., 1966.

Lowell, E. L. The effect of need for achievement on learning and speed of performance. *J. Psychol.*, 1952, **33,** 31–40.

MacFarlane, D. W. The role of Kinaesthesis in maze learning. *Univ. Calif. Publ. Psychol.*, 1930, **4,** 277–305.

Maddi, S. R. The pursuit of consistency and variety. In R. P. Abelson et al. (Eds.), *Theories of cognitive consistency: A sourcebook.* Chicago: Rand McNally & Co., 1968. Pp. 267–274.

Malmo, R. B. Activation: A neuropsychological dimension. *Psychol. Rev.*, 1959, **66,** 367–386.

Malmo, R. B. & Bélanger, D. Related physiological and behavioral changes: What are their determinants? In S. S. Kety et al. (Eds.), *Sleep and altered states of consciousness.* Baltimore: The Williams & Wilkins Co., 1967. Pp. 288–318.

Mandler, G. Emotion. In R. Brown, E. Galanter, E. H. Hess, & G. Mandler, *New directions in psychology.* New York: Holt, Rinehart & Winston, Inc., 1962. Pp. 267–343.

Mandler, G. & Sarason, S. B. A study of anxiety and learning. *J. abn. soc. Psychol.*, 1952, **47,** 166–173.

Margules, D. L. & Olds, J. Identical "feeding" and "rewarding" systems in the lateral hypothalamus of rats. *Science*, 1962, **135,** 374–375.

Maslow, A. H. *Motivation and personality.* New York: Harper & Row, Publishers, 1954.

Mason, W. A. Early social deprivation in the nonhuman primates: Implications for human behavior. In D. C. Glass (Ed.), *Environmental influences.* New York: Rockefeller University Press and Russell Sage Foundation, 1968. Pp. 70–101.

Mason, W. A. & Harlow, H. F. Initial responses of infant Rhesus monkeys to solid foods. *Psychol. Reps.*, 1959, **5,** 193–199.

Mayer, J. Glucostatic mechanisms of regulation of food intake. *New England J. med.*, 1953, **249,** 13–16.

Mayer, J. Regulation of energy intake and the body weight: The glucostatic theory and the lipostatic hypothesis. *Annals N. Y. Acad. Sci.*, 1955, **63,** Art. 1, 15–43.

McClelland, D.C. Risk-taking in children with high and low need for achievement. In J. W. Atkinson (Ed.), *Motives in fantasy, action, and society.* Princeton, N.J.: D. Van Nostrand Co., Inc., 1958. Pp. 306–321.

McClelland, D. C. *The achieving society.* Princeton, N.J.: D. Van Nostrand Co., Inc., 1961.

McClelland, D. C. Toward a theory of motive acquisition. *Amer. psychologist*, 1965, **20,** 321–333.

McClelland, D. C., Atkinson, J. W., Clark, R. A., & Lowell, E. L. *The achievement motive.* New York: Appleton-Century-Crofts, 1953.

McClelland, D. C., Baldwin, A. L., Bronfenbrenner, J., & Strodtbeck, F. L. *Talent and society.* Princeton, N.J.: D. Van Nostrand Co., Inc., 1958.

McClelland, D. C., Clark, R. A., Roby, T. B., & Atkinson, J. W. The projective expression of needs: IV. The effect of the need for achievement on thematic apperception. *J. exp. Psychol.*, 1949, **39,** 242–255.

McClelland, D. C. & Liberman, A. M. The effect of need for achievement on recognition of need-related words. *J. Personal.*, 1949, **18,** 236–251.

McDougall, W. *An introduction to social psychology.* (30th ed., 1950). London: Methuen, 1908.

McGuire, W. J. Résumé and response from consistency theory viewpoint. In R. P. Abelson et al. (Eds.), *Theories of cognitive consistency: A sourcebook.* Chicago: Rand McNally & Co., 1968. Pp. 275–297.

McNiven, M. A. "Social-releaser mechanisms" in birds—a controlled replication of Tinbergen's study. *Psychol. Rec.*, 1960, **10,** 259–265.

Melzack, R. Brain mechanisms and emotion. In D. C. Glass (Ed.), *Neurophysiology and emotion.* New York: Rockefeller University Press, 1967. Pp. 60–69.

Melzack, R. & Wall, P. D. Pain mechanisms: A new theory. *Science*, 1965, **150,** 971–979.

Miller, G. A. The magical number seven plus or minus two: Some limits on our capacity for processing information. *Psychol. Rev.*, 1956, **63,** 81–97.

Miller, N. E. Experimental studies of conflict. In J. McV. Hunt (Ed.), *Personality and the behavior disorders.* Vol. 1. New York: The Ronald Press Company, 1944. Pp. 431–465.

Miller, N. E. Studies of fear as an acquirable drive: I. Fear as motivation and fear-reduction as reinforcement in the learning of new responses. *J. exp. Psychol.*, 1948, **38,** 89–101.

Miller, N. E. Learnable drives and rewards. In S. S. Stevens (Ed.), *Handbook of experimental psychology.* New York: John Wiley & Sons, Inc., 1951. Pp. 435–472.

Montgomery, K. C. The relation between exploratory behavior and spontaneous alternation in the white rat. *J. comp. physiol. Psychol.*, 1951, **44,** 582–589.

Montgomery, K. C. Exploratory behavior as a function of "similarity" of stimulus situations. *J. comp. physiol. Psychol.*, 1953, **46,** 129–133.

Montogomery, K. C. The role of the exploratory drive in learning. *J. comp. physiol. Psychol.*, 1954, **47,** 60–64.

Morgan, C. T. *Physiological Psychology.* New York: McGraw-Hill Book Company, 1943.

Morgan, C. D. & Murray, H. A. Method for investigating fantasies—The thematic apperception test. *Arch. Neurol. Psychiat.*, 1935, **34,** 289–306.

Morris, D. *The naked ape: A zoologist's study of the human animal.* New York: McGraw-Hill Book Company, 1968.

Moruzzi, G. & Magoun, H. W. Brain stem reticular formation and activation of the EEG. *EEG and clin. Neurophysiol.*, 1949, **1,** 455–473.

Murray, H. A. *Explorations in personality.* New York: Oxford University Press, 1938.

Myers, A. K. & Miller, N. E. Failure to find a learned drive based on hunger: Evidence for learning motivated by "exploration." *J. comp. physiol. Psychol.*, 1954, **47,** 428–436.

Olds, J. Self-stimulation of the brain. *Science*, 1958a, **127,** 315–324.

Olds, J. Effects of hunger and male sex hormones on self-stimulation of the brain. *J. comp. physiol. Psychol.*, 1958b, **51,** 320–324.

Olds, J. & Milner, P. Positive reinforcement produced by electrical stimulation of septal area and other regions of rat brain. *J. comp. physiol. Psychol.*, 1954, **47,** 419–427.

Osgood, C. E. & Tannenbaum, P. H. The principle of congruity in the prediction of attitude change. *Psychol. Rev.*, 1955, **62,** 42–55.

Paintal, A. S. A study of gastric stretch receptors: Their role in the peripheral mechanism of satiation of hunger and thirst. *J. Physiol.*, 1954, **126,** 255–270.

Pepitone, A. Some conceptual and empirical problems of consistency models. In S. Feldman (Ed.), *Cognitive consistency: Motivational antecedents and behavioral consequents.* New York: Academic Press, Inc., 1966. Pp. 258–297.

Pepitone, A. The problem of motivation in consistency models. In R. P. Abelson et al. (Eds.), *Theories of cognitive consistency: A sourcebook.* Chicago: Rand McNally & Co., 1968. Pp. 319–326.

Peters, R. S. (Ed.) *Brett's history of psychology.* New York: The Macmillan Company, 1953.

Peters, R. S. *The concept of motivation.* New York: Humanities Press, Inc., 1958.

Premack, D. Toward empirical behavior laws: I. Positive reinforcement. *Psychol. Rev.*, 1959, **66,** 219–233.

Premack, D. Reversibility of the reinforcement relation. *Science*, 1962, **136,** 255–257.

Premack, D. Reinforcement theory. In M. R. Jones (Ed.), *Nebraska symposium on motivation, 1965.* Lincoln, Neb.: University of Nebraska Press, 1965. Pp. 123–180.

Quigley, J. P. The role of the digestive tract in regulating the ingestion of food. *Annals N.Y. Acad. Sci.*, 1955, **63,** Art. 1, 6–14.

Richter, C. P. Animal behavior and internal drives. *Quart. rev. Biol.*, 1927, **2,** 307–343.

Richter, C. P. Total self-regulatory functions in animals and human beings. *Harvey Lectures*, 1942–1943, **38,** 63–103.

Roberts, C. L., Marx, M. H., & Collier, G. Light onset and light offset as reinforcers for the albino rat. *J. comp. physiol. Psychol.*, 1958, **51,** 575–579.

Rosin, P. & Rodgers, W. Novel-diet preferences in vitamin-deficient rats and rats recovered from vitamin deficiency. *J. comp. physiol. Psychol.*, 1967, **63,** 421–428.

Rowell, C. H. F. Displacement grooming in the chaffinch. *Animal Behavior*, 1961, **9,** 38–63.

Sarnoff, I. & Zimbardo, P. G. Anxiety, fear and social affiliation. *J. abn. soc. Psychol.*, 1961, **62,** 356–363.

Schachter, S. *The psychology of affiliation: Experimental studies of the sources of gregariousness.* Stanford, Calif.: Stanford University Press, 1959.

Schachter, S. The interaction of cognitive and physiological determinants of emotional state. In L. Berkowitz (Ed.), *Advances in experimental social psychology.* Vol. 1. New York: Academic Press, Inc., 1964. Pp. 49–80.

Schachter, S. & Singer, J. E. Cognitive, social and physiological determinants of emotional state. *Psychol. Rev.*, 1962, **69,** 379–399.

Schildkraut, J. J. & Kety, S. S. Biogenic amines and emotion. *Science*, 1967, **156,** 21–30.

Schlosberg, H. Three dimensions of emotion. *Psychol. Rev.*, 1954, **61,** 81–88.

Schultz, D. P. *Sensory restriction: Effects on behavior.* New York: Academic Press, Inc., 1965.

Sears, R. R. Dependency motivation. In M. R. Jones (Ed.), *Nebraska symposium on motivation, 1963.* Lincoln, Neb.: University of Nebraska Press, 1963. Pp. 25–64.

Seligman, M. E. P. On the generality of the laws of learning. *Psychol. Rev.*, 1970, **77,** 406–418.

Sem-Jacobsen, C. W. & Torkildsen, A. In E. R. Ramsey & D. S. O'Doherty (Eds.), *Electrical studies on the unanesthetized brain.* New York: P. Hoeber, 1960.

Sheffield, F. D. & Campbell, B. A. The role of experience in the "spontaneous" activity of hungry rats. *J. comp. physiol. Psychol.*, 1954, **47,** 97–100.

Sheffield, F. D. & Roby, T. B. Reward value of a non-nutritive sweet taste. *J. comp. physiol. Psychol.*, 1950, **43,** 471–481.

Sheffield, F. D., Wulff, J. J., & Backer, R. Reward value of copulation without sex drive reduction. *J. comp. physiol. Psychol.*, 1951, **44,** 3–8.

Simmons, R. The relative effectiveness of certain incentives in animal learning. *Comp. psychol.* Monog., 2, No. 7, 1924.

Singer, J. E. Motivation for consistency. In S. Feldman (Ed.), *Cognitive consistency: Motivational antecedents and behavioral consequents.* New York: Academic Press, Inc., 1966. Pp. 48–73.

Singer, J. E. The bothersomeness of inconsistency. In R. P. Abelson et al. (Eds.), *Theories of cognitive consistency: A sourcebook.* Chicago: Rand McNally & Co., 1968. Pp. 393–399.

Skinner, B. F. *The behavior of organisms: An experimental approach.* New York: Appleton-Century, 1938.

Solomon, R. L. & Turner, L. H. Discriminative classical conditioning in dogs paralyzed by Curare can later control discriminative avoidance responses in the normal state. *Psychol. Rev.*, 1962, **69,** 202–219.

Spence, K. W. A theory of emotionally based drive (D) and its relation to performance in simple learning situations. *Amer. Psych.*, 1958, **13,** 131–141.

Stellar, E. & Hill, J. H. The rat's rate of drinking as a function of water deprivation. *J. comp. physiol. Psychol.*, 1952, **45,** 96–102.

Stennett, R. G. The relationship of performance level to level of arousal. *J. exp. Psychol.*, 1957, **54,** 54–61.

Storr, A. *Human aggression*. New York: Atheneum Publishers, 1968.

Taylor, J. A. A personality scale of manifest anxiety. *J. abn. soc. Psychol.*, 1953, **48,** 285–290.

Taylor, J. A. Drive theory and manifest anxiety. *Psychol. Bull.*, 1956, **53,** 303–320.

Thorndike, E. L. *Animal intelligence: Experimental studies*. New York: The Macmillan Company, 1911.

Tinbergen, N. *The study of instinct*. Oxford: Clarendon Press, 1951.

Trowill, J. A., Panksepp, J., & Gandelman, R. An incentive model of rewarding brain stimulation. *Psychol. Rev.*, 1969, **76,** 264–281.

Verinis, J. S., Brandsma, J. M., & Cofer, C. N. Discrepancy from expectation in relation to affect and motivation: Tests of McClelland's hypothesis. *J. pers. soc. Psychol.*, 1968, **9,** 47–58.

Verney, E. B. The antidiuretic hormone and the factors which determine its release. *Proc. Royal Soc.* (London), B, 1947, **135,** 25–106.

Wang, G. H. The relation between "spontaneous" activity and oestrus cycle in the white rat. *Comp. psychol. Monog.*, 2, No. 6, 1923.

Warden, C. J. *Animal motivation: Experimental studies on the albino rat.* New York: Columbia University Press, 1931.

Warren, J. M. Learning: Vertebrates. In D. A. Dewsbury (Ed.), *Comparative psychology: A modern survey.* New York: McGraw-Hill Book Company, 1971, in press.

Watson, J. B. *Behaviorism*. New York: W. W. Norton & Company, Inc., 1924.

Watson, J. B. & Morgan, J. J. B. Emotional reactions and psychological experimentation. *Amer. J. Psychol.*, 1917, **28,** 163–174.

Watson, J. B. & Rayner, R. Conditioned emotional reactions. *J. exp. Psychol.*, 1920, **3,** 1–14.

Welker, W. I. Variability of play and exploratory behavior in chimpanzees. *J. comp. physiol. Psychol.*, 1956, **49,** 181–185.

Welker, W. I. An analysis of exploratory and play behavior in animals. In D. W. Fiske & S. R. Maddi (Eds.), *Functions of varied experience.* Homewood, Ill.: Dorsey Press, 1961. Pp. 175–226.

Wilm, E. C. *The theories of instinct: A study in the history of psychology.* New Haven: Yale University Press, 1925.

Winterbottom, M. R. The relation of need for achievement to learning experiences in independence and mastery. In J. W. Atkinson (Ed.), *Motives in fantasy, action, and society.* New York: D. Van Nostrand Co., Inc., 1958. Pp. 453–478.

Woodworth, R. S. *Dynamic psychology.* New York: Columbia University Press, 1918.

Wynne, L. & Solomon, R. L. Traumatic avoidance learning: Acquisition and extinction in dogs deprived of normal peripheral autonomic function. *Genėt. psychol. Monog.*, 1955, **52,** 241–284.

Young, P. T. Food-seeking drive, affective process and learning. *Psychol. Rev.*, 1959, **56,** 98–121.

Young, P. T. & Chaplin, J. P. Studies of food preference, appetite and dietary habit: III. Palatability and appetite in relation to bodily need. *Comp. psychol. Monog.*, 1945, **18,** No. 3, 1–45.

Zajonc, R. B. Cognitive theories in social psychology. In G. Lindzey & E. Aronson (Eds.), *The Handbook of social psychology.* (2nd ed.) Reading, Mass.. Addison-Wesley Publishing Co., Inc., 1968. Pp. 320–411.

Zeaman, D. Response latency as a function of the amount of reinforcement. *J. exp. Psychol.*, 1949, **39,** 466–483.

Zeigler, H. P. Displacement activity and motivational theory: A case history in the study of ethology. *Psychol. Bull.*, 1964, **61,** 362–376.

Zilboorg, G. & Henry, G. W. *A history of medical psychology.* New York: W. W. Norton & Company, Inc., 1941.

Zimbardo, P. G. Cognitive dissonance and the control of human motivation. In R. P. Abelson et al. (Eds.), *Theories of cognitive consistency: A sourcebook.* Chicago: Rand McNally & Co., 1968. Pp. 439–447.

Zimbardo, P. G., Cohen, A. R., Weisenberg, M., Dworkin, K., & Firestone, I. Control of pain motivation by cognitive dissonance. *Science,* 1966, **151,** 217–219.

Zubek, J. P. (Ed.) *Sensory deprivation: Fifteen years of research.* New York: Appleton-Century-Crofts, 1969.

Name Index

Subject Index